William J. Patterson

Freebird Publishers
www.FreebirdPublishers.com

Freebird Publishers
Box 541, North Dighton, MA 02764
Info@FreebirdPublishers.com
www.FreebirdPublishers.com

Chapter 7 Bankruptcy:
Seven Steps to Financial Freedom
By William J. Patterson

All Freebird Publishers titles, imprints and distributed lines are available at special quantity discounts for bulk purchases for sales promotions, premiums, fundraising educational or institutional use.

ISBN 978-0-9980361-8-2

Printed in the United States of America

DEDICATION

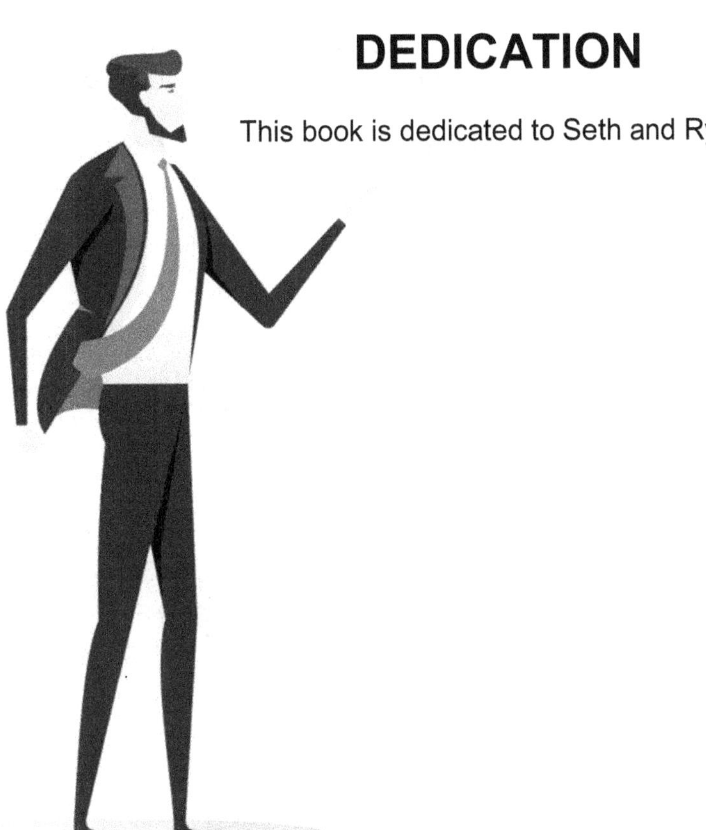

This book is dedicated to Seth and Ryan.

DISCLAIMER

Much of bankruptcy procedure is technical and very straight forward. More often than not, there is only one way to complete a required form and only one set of rules that apply to that form.

Much of the information derived herein is based on publications in the public domain. This book provides basic information to incarcerated debtors and the general public on different aspects of federal bankruptcy laws. It also provides individuals who may be considering bankruptcy with a basic explanation of the different chapters under which a bankruptcy case may be filed and answers some of the most commonly asked questions about the bankruptcy process. This book is not a substitute for the advice of competent legal counsel or a financial expert and does not constitute legal or financial advice. Such advice may be obtained from a competent attorney, accountant, or financial adviser.

While I have done my best to present accurate information as of the date of publication, this book should not be cited or relied upon as a legal authority. It should not be used as a substitute for reference to the United States Bankruptcy Code (title 11, United States Code) and the Federal Rules of Bankruptcy Procedure, both of which may be reviewed at local law libraries, or to local rules of practice adopted by each bankruptcy court. Again, this publication should not substitute for the advice of competent legal counsel.

The following public documents were heavily relied upon in researching this project: *Bankruptcy Basics*, by the Bankruptcy Judges Division, Administrative Office of the United States Courts; and *Instructions – Bankruptcy Forms for Individuals*, by the U.S. Bankruptcy Court.

TABLE OF CONTENTS

INTRODUCTION

In the fall of 2012, I was indicted by a Federal Grand Jury. I was 41 years of age and had lived a crime free-life to that point. I had a professional career and considered myself a successful member of society. Little did I know just how upside down my life was about to become. Complete devastation, the consequences of my careless actions, reached into every aspect of my life.

After I was arrested, I was held without bond. I wasn't sure how long it would be before I saw freedom again. I was in complete panic mode in every regard. I was single, and my family lived hours away. I had no one to take immediate care of my vehicle, home, and personal property. Financially, things deteriorated quickly.

During my time in county jail, I was given notice to appear regarding a personal loan (second mortgage) on my home. Unable to appear, the bank was granted a default judgment against me. I lost hope in saving my house or resolving any financial matters. The foreclosure of my home proceeded a short time later. Nearly a year after my arrest, I was sentenced to 108 months. Facing the loss of my family and career at the time, control of my finances was the absolute least of my concerns.

During my years of incarceration, I have read a lot of material pertaining to credit repair. One tactic often suggested is settling debt for much less than the amount owed. This works if one has money to offer. Another option is to just ignore the debts, hoping they will be written or charged off. Those debts will usually be removed after 7 years. However, a judgment from the court against an individual personally, as in my case, has no expiration in regards to garnishment, even though it may be removed from their credit report after a set amount of years.

As I began to get closer to my release, I started thinking more often about the mess that was waiting for me. I began to think about saving money while in the halfway house and preparing for the future. A new life and fresh start were needed. Many of my debts had been charged off; but I wanted to avoid any future liens, garnishments, or freezing of funds in my bank accounts. It became clear that the only way to eliminate nearly all of my debt was filing Chapter 7 bankruptcy. I could then put all my focus where needed, which was reestablishing myself as a productive and responsible member of society.

The more I considered the big picture, that of a new life and fresh start, the clearer it became to me that Chapter 7 bankruptcy was my best avenue. I would be relieved of most of my debts and allowed a new lease on life after my release.

I swore to myself in my early adult life that I would never file bankruptcy, no matter the circumstances. Boy, did I eat those words. I have come to realize that bankruptcy, especially Chapter 7, was created for people just like me. I am very appreciative that there is a mechanism in place to help me achieve a new financial start.

When I decided to go forward with filing bankruptcy, I knew the process would be tedious and have a steep learning curve. But I was up for the challenge. Of course I wanted the process to go as smoothly as possible, so I made every attempt to be prepared and have everything ready before submitting the paperwork.

My bankruptcy filing was not without its challenges. It is my goal to help you through all of the steps, to point out obstacles along the way and resources both inside and out of prison, and finally, to provide you with inspiration and encouragement that you too can do this on your own. To that end, I have provided copies of needed forms and schedules in this book. With preparation, patience, and perseverance, you can accomplish anything – including the successful discharge of your own Chapter 7 bankruptcy. If you follow these 7 basic steps to completing a Chapter 7 bankruptcy, you too can enjoy the freedoms that a fresh start will provide.

Best wishes,

William John Patterson

CHAPTER 1
THE BASICS OF BANKRUPTCY

OVERVIEW

If you purchased this book, you are most likely incarcerated and have decided that Chapter 7 bankruptcy, otherwise known as "Liquidation," is the right choice for you. This book should serve as a resource guide that will assist you in that process from start to finish. I will share my personal experience and the specific challenges I encountered along the way, as well as the remedies I employed.

The decision to declare bankruptcy is a big one and should not be taken lightly. Careful thought and consideration are a must. It is extremely difficult to succeed in a Chapter 11, 12, or 13 case without an attorney, thus this book will focus on Chapter 7 only. If you are like I was and unable to afford an attorney, you might qualify for free legal services if they are provided in your area. Feel free to contact your state or local bar association for help in obtaining free legal services; however, being incarcerated may pose a significant barrier to receiving any outside help ... or even a response to your requests.

Ultimately you will be responsible for properly completing the forms. As with any document submitted to the court, you should review all your forms carefully and read the instructions for each. If you miss a deadline, forget to file the proper forms, or file them incorrectly, you can be denied a discharge or may have to file at a later date. So prepare yourself, and do it right the first time.

Because bankruptcy can have serious and long-term financial and legal consequences, including loss of property, you should consult with an attorney and carefully consider all your options before you file. Only an attorney can give you legal advice about what can happen as a result of filing for bankruptcy and what your options are. If you do file for bankruptcy, an attorney can help you fill out the forms properly and protect you, your family, your home, and your possessions.

Although the law allows you to represent yourself in bankruptcy court, you should understand that many people find it difficult to represent themselves successfully. The rules are technical, and a mistake or inaction may harm you. If you file without an attorney, you are still responsible for knowing and following all legal requirements. You should NOT file for bankruptcy if you are not eligible to file, or if you do not intend to file the necessary documents.

Bankruptcy fraud is a serious crime; you could be fined and imprisoned if you commit fraud in your bankruptcy case. Making a false statement, concealing property, or obtaining money or property by fraud in connection with a bankruptcy case can result in both fines and imprisonment (18 U.S.C. §§152, 1341, 1519, and 3571).

Now that we have that out of the way, take a huge deep breath and relax. I must admit that in the beginning I felt almost overwhelmed with the task itself. I would ask myself, "How in the world am I going to accomplish this?" What I learned, through trial and error, was to approach the process slowly and methodically. I cannot emphasize the following enough: You must have all the required material and documents ready so once you start the process it is a smooth transition to completion. If the court asks for something once you file, you will most likely be given only 14 days to provide the requested documents. A timeline like that is extremely stressful while incarcerated. With the proper preparation before filing, you can hope to avoid any unnecessary stressors, delays, or a potential dismissal.

The procedural aspects of the bankruptcy process are governed by the Federal Rules of Bankruptcy Procedure and the local rules of each bankruptcy court. (Chapter 7 forms are provided in Chapter 10.) The bankruptcy Code – codified as Title 11 of the United States Code – the Procedural Rules, and the local rules all set the legal procedures in dealing with your financial debts.

Each judicial district in the United States has its own bankruptcy court. Each district will most likely have its own bankruptcy clerk. The bankruptcy judge will preside over your case. The judge will also decide any matter connected with your case, such as your eligibility to file or whether you should receive a discharge of your debts. Under Chapter 7, most of your administrative work will be carried out by a trustee that is appointed by the court to oversee your case.

Typically, as a Chapter 7 debtor, you will not appear in court; however, you must appear at the meeting of creditors, which is usually held at the U.S. Trustee Office. Code 341 of the Bankruptcy Code requires you to attend this meeting so that creditors can question you about debts and property you own. Obviously, if incarcerated, your personal appearance will have to be waived. You will attend this meeting via phone or by interrogatory examination, both under oath by the trustee and any creditors who wish to examine you. (We will cover this in greater detail in Chapter 9.) This meeting is merely a formality in order to answer pertinent questions. It is unlikely any creditors will attend or file objections.

A goal of the federal bankruptcy laws enacted by Congress is to give you a "fresh start." This goal is accomplished through bankruptcy discharge, which releases you from personal liability for specific debts and prohibits creditors from ever taking action against you to collect those debts.

Chapter 7 of the Bankruptcy Code, entitled "Liquidation," contemplates an orderly, court-supervised procedure by which a trustee takes over the assets of the debtor's estate, reduces them to cash, and makes distributions to creditors. These distributions are subject to the debtor's right to retain certain exempt property and the rights of secured creditors. Normally there is little or no nonexempt property in Chapter 7 cases, thus there may not be an actual liquidation of debtor's assets. These are called "no-asset cases."

The majority of cases filed by prisoners will be "no-asset cases." A creditor holding an unsecured claim will get a distribution from the bankruptcy estate only if the case is an asset case and the creditor files a proof of claim with the bankruptcy court. In most Chapter 7 cases, if the debtor is an individual, he or she receives a discharge that releases him or her from personal liability for certain dischargeable debts. The debtor normally receives a discharge just a few months after the petition is filed. Amendments to the Bankruptcy Code enacted by the Bankruptcy Abuse Prevention and Consumer Protection Act of 2005, require the application of a "means test" to determine whether individual consumer debtors qualify for relief under Chapter 7. If such a debtor's income is in excess of certain thresholds, the debtor may not be eligible for Chapter 7 relief. This will most likely not be an issue if you are incarcerated.

DISCHARGE OF DEBT

A bankruptcy discharge releases you from personal liability for certain specified types of debts. In other words, you are no longer legally required to pay any debts that are discharged. The discharge is a permanent order prohibiting your creditors from taking any form of collection action on discharged debts, now or later, including legal action and communications with you, such as telephone calls, letters, and personal contacts.

Although you are not personally liable for discharged debts, if a creditor has a valid lien (*i.e.,* a charge upon specific property to secure payment of a debt, such as a home or vehicle) and the payments are made unenforceable in the bankruptcy case, the lien will remain even after the case. Therefore, a secured creditor may enforce the lien to recover that property.

The timing of the discharge varies depending on the chapter under which the case is filed. In a Chapter 7 (liquidation) case, the court usually grants the discharge promptly if there are no objections from creditors within 60 days of the first date set for their meeting or motions to dismiss the case for substantial abuse. Typically, the discharge occurs about four months after the date you file your petition with the clerk of the bankruptcy court. The court may deny you a discharge in Chapter 7, if you fail to complete "an instructional course concerning financial management."(We will discuss more details on this in Chapter 9.) The Bankruptcy Code provides limited exceptions to the "financial management" requirement if the U.S. Trustee or bankruptcy administrator determines there are inadequate educational programs available, or if the debtor is incapacitated or on active military duty in a combat zone. Being in prison is not an exception, also discussed in greater detail in Chapter 9.

Unless there is litigation involving objections to the discharge, the debtor will usually automatically receive a discharge. The Federal Rules of Bankruptcy Procedure provide for the clerk of the bankruptcy court to mail a copy of the order of discharge to all creditors, the U.S. trustee, the trustee in the case, and the trustee's attorney, if any. You and your attorney (if one is retained) also receive copies of the discharge order. The notice, which is simply a copy of the final order of discharge, is not specific as to those debts determined by the court to be nondischargeable (*i.e.,* not covered by this discharge). The notice informs creditors generally that the debts owed to them have been discharged and that they should not attempt any further collection. They are cautioned in the notice that continuing collection efforts could subject them to punishment for contempt. Any inadvertent failure on the part of the clerk to send you or any creditor a copy of the discharge order promptly, within the time required by the rules, does not affect the validity of the order granting the discharge.

DISCHARGEABLE DEBTS OR NOT

Not all debts are discharged. The debts discharged vary under each chapter of the Bankruptcy Code. Section 523(a) of the Code specifically exempts various categories of debts from the discharge granted to individual debtors. Therefore, the debtor must still repay these debts after bankruptcy. Congress has determined that these types of debts are not dischargeable for public policy reasons (based either on the nature of the debt or the fact that the debts were incurred due to improper behavior of the debtor, such as the debtor's drunken driving).

Generally speaking, the exceptions to discharge apply automatically if the language prescribed by section 523(a) applies. These are the most common types of nondischargeable debts: certain types of tax claims, debts not set forth by the debtor on the lists and schedules the debtor must file with the court, debts for spousal or child support or alimony, debts for willful and malicious injuries to person or property, debts to governmental units for fines penalties, forfeitures and criminal restitution , debts for most government-funded or guaranteed educational loans or benefit overpayments, debts for personal injury caused by the debtor's operation of a motor vehicle while intoxicated, debts owed to certain tax-advantaged retirement plans, and debts for certain condominium or cooperative housing fees.

The types of debts described in section 523(a)(2),(4), and (6) (obligations affected by fraud or maliciousness) are not automatically excepted from discharge. Creditors must ask the court to determine that these debts are exempted from discharge. In the absence of an affirmative request by the creditor and the granting of the request by the court, the types of debts set out in sections 523(a)(2), (4), and (6) will be discharged.

A slightly broader discharge of debts is available to a debtor in a Chapter 13 case than in a Chapter 7 case. Debts dischargeable in a Chapter 13, but not in Chapter 7, include debts for willful and malicious injury to property, debts incurred to pay nondischargeable tax obligations, and debts arising from property settlements in divorce or separation proceedings. Although a Chapter 13 debtor generally receives a discharge only after completing all payments required by the court-approve (*i.e.,* "confirmed") repayment plan, there are some limited circumstances under which the debtor may request the court to grant a "hardship discharge," even though the debtor has failed to complete the planned payments. Such a discharge is available only to a debtor whose failure to complete the planned payments is due to circumstances beyond the debtor's control. The scope of a Chapter 13 "hardship discharge" is similar to that of Chapter 7 case, with regards to the types of debts that are exempted from the discharge. A hardship discharge also is available in Chapter 12, if the failure to complete the planned payments is due to "circumstances for which the debtor should not justly be held accountable." Keep in mind that Chapter 13 is for those with a regular source of income, and it enables a debtor to keep certain assets, such as a home. This will most likely not apply to prisoners, as most have no regular source of income.

CREDITORS OBJECTION TO DISCHARGE

In Chapter 7 cases, the debtor does not have an absolute right to a discharge. An objection to your discharge may be filed by a creditor, by the trustee in the case, or by the U.S. trustee. Creditors receive a notice shortly after the case is filed that sets forth much important information, including the deadline for objecting to the discharge. To object to your discharge, a creditor must file a complaint in the bankruptcy court before the deadline set out in the notice. Filing a complaint starts a lawsuit referred to in bankruptcy as an "adversary proceeding."

REVOCATION OF DISCHARGE

The court may revoke a discharge under certain circumstances. For example, a trustee, creditor, or the U.S. trustee, may request that the court revoke your discharge in a Chapter 7 case based on allegations that you: obtained the discharge fraudulently, failed to disclose the fact that you acquired or became entitled to acquire property that would constitute property of the bankruptcy estate, committed one of several acts of impropriety described in section 727(a)(6) of the Bankruptcy Code, failed to explain any misstatements discovered in an audit of the case, or failed to provide documents or information requested in an audit of the case. Typically, a request to revoke your discharge must be filed within one year of the discharge or, in some cases, before the date that the case is closed. The court will decide whether such allegations are true and if so, whether to revoke the discharge.

CAN YOU PAY A DISCHARGED DEBT?

A debtor who has received a discharge may voluntarily repay any discharged debt. You may repay a discharged debt even though it can no longer be legally enforced. Sometimes a debtor agrees to repay a debt because it is owed to a family member or because it represents an obligation to an individual for whom the debtor's reputation is important, such as a family doctor.

YOUR RIGHTS: COLLECTION ATTEMPTS AFTER A DISCHARGE

If a creditor attempts collection efforts on a discharged debt, you can file a motion with the court reporting the action and asking that the case be reopened to address the matter. The bankruptcy court will often do so to ensure that the discharge is not violated. The discharge constitutes a permanent statutory injunction prohibiting creditors from taking any action, including the filing of a lawsuit, designed to collect a discharged debt. A creditor can be sanctioned by the court for violating the discharge injunction. The normal sanction for violating the discharge injunction is civil contempt, which is often punishable by a fine.

PROHIBITION AGAINST DISCRIMINATORY TREATMENT

The following information most likely will not apply to prisoners but is included for informational purposes. The law provides express prohibitions against discriminatory treatment of you by both governmental units and private employers. A governmental unit or private employer may not discriminate against you solely because you were a debtor, were insolvent before or during the case, or have not paid a debt that was discharged in the case. The law prohibits the following forms of governmental discrimination: terminating an employee; discriminating with respect to hiring; or denying, revoking, suspending or declining to renew a license, franchise or similar privilege. A private employer may not discriminate with respect to employment if the discrimination is based solely upon the bankruptcy filing.

OBTAINING A COPY OF YOUR DISCHARGE ORDER

If you lose or misplace the discharge order, another copy can be obtained by contacting the clerk of the bankruptcy court that entered the order. The clerk will charge a fee for searching the court records and there will be additional fees for making and certifying copies. If the case has been closed and archived, there will also be a retrieval fee, and obtaining the copy will take longer.

The discharge order may be available electronically. The PACER system provides the public with electronic access to selected case information through a personal computer located in many clerks' offices. Although, as an inmate, your internet access may be limited, a family member or friend can access PACER on your behalf. Users must set up an account to acquire access to PACER and must pay a per-page fee to download and copy documents filed electronically.

CHAPTER 2
LEGAL LAW LIBRARY RESOURCES

OVERVIEW

As you will see throughout this book, my filing Chapter 7 bankruptcy was not without its challenges. It's my goal to help save you time, aggravation, and expense throughout your process. If you are without the following resources this book should suffice in helping you successfully navigate and complete your Chapter 7 filing. Much of my knowledge came from trial and error. When I first entered the prison legal law library someone handed me a hardcover law book containing U.S. Code Title 11. After reading it for a while, I realized that there must be a more efficient and simple way to ascertain this information. Fortunately within the Federal Bureau of Prisons, we have access to an electronic legal law library. This can be a gold mine of information if properly navigated. Although the system contains much of what is needed, it is not always user friendly. I will share some examples of how it was both beneficial and inadequate, including, but not limited to, avoiding excessive printing costs.

LOCAL FEDERAL DISTRICT COURT RULES

Within the Trulincs legal law library system there are a number of publication sources that are relevant to the process of filing bankruptcy. One important source is a folder entitled "Local Federal District Court Rules:" In this folder you will be able to locate the state and district of which you intend to file. These local rules are important because they are specific to the district in which you are filing. Information located inside this folder includes the court, address, and telephone number of the bankruptcy clerk. Other items of importance include installment payments, filing costs, and instructions regarding your matrix list and so forth. It clearly states that the person filing is solely responsible for compliance with the rules therein. Therefore, you must take your time when completing your forms and always double check your work.

FEDERAL COURT RULES

Another important source of information is a folder entitled "Federal Court Rules." Once inside this folder you may scroll down till you locate the "Federal Rules of Bankruptcy Procedure and Official Bankruptcy Forms." Federal Rules of Bankruptcy Procedure govern procedure in cases under Title 11 of the United States Code. This folder contains a wealth of information needed, along with the required forms. The “forms” section of this folder was one of the areas I mentioned earlier as being inadequate and costly. When printing forms from this section the image is only half the size of a standard form making it nearly impossible to fill in the blanks with your information, not to mention, the additional cost for printing. Sample forms are provided in Chapter 10 However you or a family member can download the required forms online at wwwuscourts.gov.

BENDERS FEDERAL PRACTICE FORMS

Located within this folder is a subfolder entitled “Official Bankruptcy Forms.” At the time of my filing, my access to outside resources was limited at best. In order for me to file, I had to first obtain and then complete the necessary forms. Forms printed from this folder were only slightly larger print than those printed from the Federal Court Rules section. As you will notice in the example forms throughout this book, my typing space was very limited when using forms printed from this section. Again, there was the added cost of printing each form. For these reasons I do not recommend that you use this method but rather have an outside contact mail you the required forms. However if you find yourself needing a form not provided, you will have the knowledge where to quickly locate a specific form. This folder also contains a document entitled “Instructions Bankruptcy Forms for Individuals,” this information is thoroughly covered throughout the book to save you time and in case you don’t have access to the document.

UNITED STATES CODE SERVICE

This folder contains all the United States Code. Bankruptcy is located under Title 11. Chapter 7 bankruptcy falls within Title 11. There is enough information located here to keep you busy reading for a long time; however it is not necessary unless you need it for further reference.

I have provided the information in this chapter in hopes to save you time and money. It took me many hours to search through and differentiate between all these folders. I am certain this book will provide you with all you need to succeed, but if you do find yourself in need of other resources or have other questions you will know right where to search. If you encounter problems logging in, locating any of these previously mentioned folders or navigating your electronic law library, I recommend you seek the assistance of one of your inmate law clerks.

CHAPTER 3

STEP I: OBTAINING YOUR CREDIT REPORT

FREE ANNUAL CREDIT REPORT

As we will discuss in a later chapter, you will be required to list all creditors holding secured or unsecured claims against you. These may include, but are not limited to, consumer debts, judgment liens, garnishments, mortgages, etc. It is very important that you obtain copies of your credit reports prior to filing so that you can be thorough in listing all creditors, account numbers, and amounts owed. Please note that not all of your debt may be stated in your credit report.

HOW TO OBTAIN A COPY OF YOUR CREDIT REPORT

As of December 1, 2005, The Fair Credit Reporting Act allows all consumers over the age of 18 to receive one free copy per year of their credit report on file with all three nationwide credit reporting agencies. This free copy enables the consumer to review his/her report annually and to assure that no fraud has been committed against them. You can request your free annual credit report by if you have form as provided in this chapter, or on the internet at www.annualcreditreport.com, or by calling (877) 322-8228. Mail the Annual Credit request form to: Annual Credit Report Request Service, P.O. Box 105281 Atlanta, Ga. 30348

If mailing from a correctional institution, you must include some type of "Certification of Identity." A B.O.P. sample form is included in this chapter. It's fairly common for inmates to receive a response stating something to the effect of, "Credit reports aren't allowed to be sent to a correctional institution." If you encounter this response after requesting your credit report, you should respond via letter to each credit bureau that refused to honor your request. A sample response letter to the credit bureaus is also included in this chapter.

The simplest approach, if available to you, is to complete the Annual Credit Report Request Form, and have a relative or friend mail it on your behalf. Once they receive the credit reports back, they can in turn mail them to you. I found this to be the most efficient and expeditious way for me. I did not include a "Certification of Identification" and all 3 of my reports were received. Reports should arrive approximately 15 days after the request is received by the credit bureaus. Remember, you are only allowed one request per year, so I recommend you shade in the circles on the form requesting all 3 credit bureau reports.

CREDIT BUREAUS
Under the Fair Credit Reporting Act, as a consumer you have the right to contact each credit reporting agency individually at the following addresses:

EXPERIAN
National Consumer Assistance Center
P.O. Box 2002
Allen, TX 75013
(888) 397-3742

TRANSUNION
Consumer Relations
P.O. Box 2000
Chester, PA 19016
(800) 916-2000

EQUIFAX
Office of Consumer Affairs
P.O. Box 740250
Atlanta, GA 30374
(800) 685-1111

ADDITIONAL CREDIT INFORMATION
After reviewing your credit report, you may have additional questions. I've included a page in this chapter that addresses some commonly asked questions and some facts you should know. For example, a Chapter 7 bankruptcy will remain on your credit report for up to 10 years from the date filed. In addition, I have included a page on your consumer rights under the Fair Credit Reporting Act (FCRA), and an example of your rights to place a "security" freeze on your credit.

FREEZING YOUR CREDIT
After my discharge was granted, and due to the fact I was still incarcerated, I felt the safest measure going forward to prevent any future fraudulent activity on my credit would be to place a freeze with all 3 credit bureaus. As of the summer of 2018, Equifax waived my fee because of a recent large data breach of consumers' information. The cost to freeze my credit at the other two bureaus was $7.50 each. Your credit reports will provide instructions and all costs associated with placing a freeze. Be advised that once your credit is frozen there is a small fee, in some states, to lift the freeze.

PRISON ADDRESS ON YOUR CREDIT REPORT
Inmates often spread information that can be unreliable. Up to the filing of my bankruptcy, I avoided placing my prison address on anything linking to my credit report; however, after filing, I realized that I could not avoid my prison address from appearing on my report. I reviewed my credit reports after my discharge and confirmed that due to the bankruptcy filing, the prison address was added to all 3 of them. One report described the P.O. Box as just that, an additional mailing address. However, the other reports labeled the address as "high risk," being a government Correctional Institution. I suppose the downside may be that one's

address history is there to stay, but I guess it is a small sacrifice to make in order to achieve the liberating benefits that come from a successful bankruptcy process.

FEDERAL INCOME TAX RETURNS

You may be required to submit copies of your income tax returns. If you've ever filed, you may request copies for the last two years from the address below:

Internal Revenue Service
United States Department of Treasury
Philadelphia, Pa. 19255-1498

EQUIFAX experian TransUnion.

Annual Credit Report Request Form

You have the right to get a free copy of your credit file disclosure, commonly called a credit report, once every 12 months, from each of the nationwide consumer credit reporting companies - Equifax, Experian and TransUnion.

For instant access to your free credit report, visit www.annualcreditreport.com.

For more information on obtaining your free credit report, visit www.annualcreditreport.com or call 877-322-8228.

Use this form if you prefer to write to request your credit report from any, or all, of the nationwide consumer credit reporting companies. The following information is required to process your request. **Omission of any information may delay your request.**

Once complete, fold (do not staple or tape), place into a #10 envelope, affix required postage and mail to:

Annual Credit Report Request Service P.O. Box 105281 Atlanta, GA 30348-5281.

Please use a Black or Blue Pen and write your responses in PRINTED CAPITAL LETTERS without touching the sides of the boxes like the examples listed below:

A B C D E F G H I J K L M N O P Q R S T U V W X Y Z 0 1 2 3 4 5 6 7 8 9

Social Security Number: ___ - __ - ____

Date of Birth: Month / Day / Year

Fold Here ——— Fold Here

First Name — M.I.

Last Name — JR, SR, III, etc.

Current Mailing Address:

House Number — Street Name

Apartment Number / Private Mailbox — For Puerto Rico Only: Print Urbanization Name

City — State — ZipCode

Previous Mailing Address (complete only if at current mailing address for less than two years):

House Number — Street Name

Fold Here ——— Fold Here

Apartment Number / Private Mailbox — For Puerto Rico Only: Print Urbanization Name

City — State — ZipCode

Shade Circle Like This → ●

Not Like This → ⊗ ✓

I want a credit report from (shade each that you would like to receive):

○ Equifax
○ Experian
○ TransUnion

○ Shade here if, for security reasons, you want your credit report to include no more than the last four digits of your Social Security Number.

31238

If additional information is needed to process your request, the consumer credit reporting company will contact you by mail.

Your request will be processed within 15 days of receipt and then mailed to you.

G-1

CERTIFICATION OF IDENTITY WITH PHOTO

(U.S. Department of Justice, Federal Bureau of Prisons Identification Card)

Full Name:______________________________ Reg. #______________
(As it would appear on your credit report)

Current Address:____
(Institutional Mailing Address) Street Address City State Zip

Previous Address:____
Street Address City State Zip

Date of Birth:__________________ Place of Birth:__________________
Month/Day/Year City/State

Social Security #:______________ Mother's Maiden Name:______________

Before Me, The undersigned authority, on this day personally appeared

______________________________, who being by me duly sworn, on oath said:

My name is ______________________________________. I verify the following to be true and correct. This is my Commissary Card. It is my identification while I am incarcerated at *F.C.I. Seagoville.* There is a true photocopy of it at the bottom of this document.

____
Signature

SUBSCRIBED AND SWORN TO BERFORE ME on this_____ day of______, 20___

____

NOTARY PUBLIC, STATE OF TEXAS

Revised 6/17/2015

EXAMPLE LETTER - RESPONSE TO CREDIT BUREAUS

Date

Your Name & Inmate #
Your Institution
Your Address
City, State, Zip

Equifax
P.O. Box 740250
Atlanta,Ga. 30374

RE: Your Refusal Of One Complete Free Copy Of My Credit Report

Dear Equifax,

Please send me one complete free credit report per the Fair Credit Reporting Act (FCRA) in compliance with section 612(a) of the FCRA, 15 U.S.C. 1681j(a). I am entitled to a free complete annual credit report. If you do not send this credit report within 30 days, I will file complaints with the BBB, State Attorney General's Office, and the Federal Trade Commission. I very much appreciate your prompt assistance in this matter.

Respectfully,
Sign Your Name Here

Commonly Asked Questions About Credit Files

Q. ***How can I correct a mistake in my credit file ?***

A. Complete the Research Request form and give details of the information you believe is incorrect. We will then check with the credit grantor, collection agency or public record source to see if any error has been reported. Information that cannot be verified will be removed from your file. If you and a credit grantor disagree on any information, you will need to resolve the dispute directly with the credit grantor who is the source of the information in question.

Q. ***If I do have credit problems, is there someplace where I can get advice and assistance ?***

A. Yes, there are a number of organizations that offer assistance. For example, the Consumer Credit Counseling Service (CCCS) is a non-profit organization that offers free or low-cost financial counseling to help people solve their financial problems. CCCS can help you analyze your situation and work with you to develop solutions. There are more than 600 CCCS offices throughout the country. Call 1 (800) 388-2227 for the telephone number of the office nearest you.

Facts You Should Know

- The length of time an account or record remains in your credit file is shown below:

  Collection Agency Accounts: Remain for up to 7 years from the Date of 1st Delinquency.

  Credit or Other Reported Accounts: Accounts paid as agreed remain for up to 10 years from the Date Reported. Accounts not paid as agreed (i.e. delinquent, charge off, accounts placed for collection) remain for up to 7 years from the Date of 1st Delinquency.

  Public Records: Remain for up to 7 years from the date filed, except:
  Bankruptcy - Chapter 7 and 11 remain for up to 10 years from the date filed.
  Bankruptcy - Chapter 13 dismissed or no disposition rendered remain for up to 10 years from the date filed.
  Unpaid tax liens remain for up to 10 years from the date filed.
  Paid tax liens remain for up to 7 years from the date released or up to 10 years from the date filed, whichever is earlier.

  New York State Residents Only: Satisfied judgments remain for up to 5 years from the date filed; paid collections remain for up to 5 years from the Date of 1st Delinquency.

  Payment history and Historical Account Information for an account on your credit file, if any, is found at the bottom of an account under the title "Account History with Status Codes" or "Historical Account Information" respectively.

  This payment history reflects the month, year and late payment status, and is generally supplied by credit grantors or other furnishers of information to Equifax with whom you have a relationship. This history is included on both open accounts and accounts that have already been closed.

  The historical account information reflects a broader view of your credit behavior over a 24 month period. This history is also included on both open accounts and closed accounts.

  Payment in full does not remove your payment history or historical account information. If you have always paid an account as agreed, the account should not have payment history status information. Specific payment history typically remains on your credit file for up to 7 years from the date shown for it.

- Name, address, and Social Security Number information may be provided to businesses that have a legitimate need to locate or identify a consumer.

Additional Notice to Consumer:

You may request a description of the procedure used to determine the accuracy and completeness of the information, including the business name and address of the furnisher of information contacted, and if reasonably available the telephone number.

If the reinvestigation does not resolve your dispute, you have the right to add a statement to your credit file disputing the accuracy or completeness of the information; the statement should be brief and may be limited to not more than one hundred words (two hundred words for Maine residents) explaining the nature of your dispute.

If the reinvestigation results in the deletion of disputed information, or you submit a statement in accordance with the preceding paragraph, you have the right to request that we send your revised credit file to any company specifically designated by you that received your credit report in the past six months (twelve months for California, Colorado, Maryland, New Jersey and New York residents) for any purpose or in the past two years for employment purposes.

Summary of Rights

GENERAL SUMMARY OF CONSUMER RIGHTS UNDER THE FCRA

Para informacion en espanol, visite www.consumerfinance.gov/learnmore o escribe a la Consumer Financial Protection Bureau, 1700 G Street N.W., Washington, DC 20552.

A Summary of Your Rights Under the Fair Credit Reporting Act

The federal Fair Credit Reporting Act (FCRA) promotes the accuracy, fairness, and privacy of information in the files of consumer reporting agencies. There are many types of consumer reporting agencies, including credit bureaus and specialty agencies (such as agencies that sell information about check writing histories, medical records, and rental history records). Here is a summary of your major rights under the FCRA. **For more information, including information about additional rights, go to www.consumerfinance.gov/learnmore or write to: Consumer Financial Protection Bureau, 1700 G Street N.W., Washington, DC 20552.**

- **You must be told if information in your file has been used against you.** Anyone who uses a credit report or another type of consumer report to deny your application for credit, insurance, or employment -- or to take another adverse action against you-must tell you, and must give you the name, address, and phone number of the agency that provided the information.
- **You have the right to know what is in your file.** You may request and obtain all the information about you in the files of a consumer reporting agency (your "file disclosure"). You will be required to provide proper identification, which may include your Social Security Number. In many cases, the disclosure will be free. You are entitled to a free file disclosure if:
    - a person has taken adverse action against you because of information in your credit report;
    - you are the victim of identity theft and place a fraud alert in your file;
    - your file contains inaccurate information as a result of fraud;
    - you are on public assistance;
    - you are unemployed but expect to apply for employment within 60 days.

  In addition, all consumers are entitled to one free disclosure every 12 months upon request from each nationwide credit bureau and from nationwide specialty consumer reporting agencies. See www.consumerfinance.gov/learnmore for more additional information.
- **You have the right to ask for a credit score.** Credit scores are numerical summaries of your credit-worthiness based on information from credit bureaus. You may request a credit score from consumer reporting agencies that create scores or distribute scores used in residential real property loans, but you will have to pay for it. In some mortgage transactions, you will receive credit score information for free from the mortgage lender.
- **You have the right to dispute incomplete or inaccurate information**. If you identify information in your file that is incomplete or inaccurate, and report it to the consumer reporting agency, the agency must investigate unless your dispute is frivolous. See www.consumerfinance.gov/learnmore for an explanation of dispute procedures.
- **Consumer reporting agencies must correct or delete inaccurate, incomplete, or unverifiable information.** Inaccurate, incomplete, or unverifiable information must be removed or corrected, usually within 30 days. However, a consumer reporting agency may continue to report information it has verified as accurate.
- **Consumer reporting agencies may not report outdated negative information.** In most cases, a consumer reporting agency may not report negative information that is more than seven years old, or bankruptcies that are more than 10 years old.
- **Access to your file is limited.** A consumer reporting agency may provide information about you only to people with a valid need usually to consider an application with a creditor, insurer, employer, landlord, or other business. The FCRA specifies those with a valid need for access.
- **You must give your consent for reports to be provided to employers.** A consumer reporting agency may not give out information about you to your employer, or a potential employer, without your written consent given to the employer. Written consent generally is not required in the trucking industry. For more information, go to www.consumerfinance.gov/learnmore.
- **You may limit "prescreened" offers of credit and insurance you get based on information in your credit report.** Unsolicited "prescreened" offers for credit and insurance must include a toll-free phone number you can call if you choose to remove your name and address from the lists these offers are based on. You may opt-out with the nationwide credit bureaus at 1-888-567-8688 (888-5OPTOUT).
- **You may seek damages from violators.** If a consumer reporting agency, or, in some cases, a user of consumer reports or a furnisher of information to a consumer reporting agency violates the FCRA, you may be able to sue in state or federal court.
- **Identity theft victims and active duty military personnel have additional rights.** For more information, visit www.consumerfinance.gov/learnmore.

States may enforce the FCRA, and many states have their own consumer reporting laws. In some cases, you may have more rights under state law. For more information, contact your state or local consumer protection agency or your state Attorney General. For information about your federal rights, contact:	
TYPE OF BUSINESS:	**CONTACT:**
1.a. Banks, savings associations, and credit unions with total assets of over $10 billion and their affiliates	Bureau of Consumer Financial Protection 1700 G Street NW Washington, DC 20552
b. Such affiliates that are not banks, savings associations, or credit unions also should list, in addition to the CFPB:	Federal Trade Commission Consumer Response Center - FCRA Washington, DC 20580 1-877-382-4357
2. To the extent not included in item 1 above: a. National banks, federal savings associations, and federal branches and federal agencies of foreign banks	Office of the Comptroller of the Currency Customer Assistance Group 1301 McKinney Street, Suite 3450 Houston, TX 77010-9050
b. State member banks, branches and agencies of foreign banks (other than federal branches, federal agencies, and insured state branches of foreign banks), commercial lending companies owned or controlled by foreign banks, and organizations operating under section 25 or 25A of the Federal Reserve Act	Federal Reserve Consumer Help (FRCH) PO Box 1200 Minneapolis, MN 55480 1-888-851-1920
c. Nonmember Insured Banks, Insured State Branches of Foreign Banks, and Insured state savings associations	FDIC Consumer Response Center 1100 Walnut Street, Box #11 Kansas City, MO 64106
d. Federal Credit Unions	National Credit Union Administration Office of Consumer Protection (OCP) Division of Consumer Compliance and Outreach (DCCO) 1775 Duke Street Alexandria, VA 22314
3. Air carriers	Asst. General Counsel for Aviation Enforcement & Proceedings Aviation Consumer Protection Division Department of Transportation 1200 New Jersey Avenue, S.E. Washington, DC 20590 1-202-366-1306
4. Creditors Subject to Surface Transportation Board	Office of Proceedings, Surface Transportation Board Department of Transportation 395 E Street, S.W. Washington, DC 20423
5. Creditors subject to Packers and Stockyards Act, 1921	Nearest Packers and Stockyards Administration area supervisor
6. Small Business Investment Companies	Associate Deputy Administrator for Capital Access United States Small Business Administration 409 Third Street, SW, 8th Floor Washington, DC 20416
7. Brokers and Dealers	Securities and Exchange Commission 100 F Street NE Washington, DC 20549
8. Federal Land Banks, Federal Land Bank Associations, Federal Intermediate Credit Banks, and Production Credit Associations	Farm Credit Administration 1501 Farm Credit Drive McLean, VA 22102-5090
9. Retailers, Finance Companies, and All Other Creditors Not Listed Above	FTC Regional Office for region in which the creditor operates or Federal Trade Commission: Consumer Response Center-FCRA Washington, DC 20580 1-877-382-4357

TENNESSEE BILL OF RIGHTS

NOTICE OF RIGHTS:Tennessee Consumers Have the Right to Obtain a Security Freeze

You have the right to place a "security freeze" on your credit report, which will prohibit a consumer reporting agency from releasing information in your credit report without your express authorization. A security freeze must be requested in writing by certified mail or by electronic means as provided by a consumer reporting agency.

The security freeze is designed to prevent credit, loans, and services from being approved in your name without your consent. If you are actively seeking a new credit, loan, utility, or telephone account, you should understand that the procedures involved in lifting a security freeze may slow your applications for credit.

When you place a security freeze on your credit report, you will be provided a personal identification number or password to use if you choose to remove the security freeze on your credit report or authorize the release of your credit report for a period of time after the freeze is in place. To provide that authorization you must contact the consumer reporting agency and provide all of the following:

1. The personal identification number or password;
2. Proper identification to verify your identity; and
3. The proper information regarding the period of time for which the report shall be available.

A consumer reporting agency must authorize the release of your credit report no later than fifteen (15) minutes after receiving the above information.

A security freeze does not apply to a person or entity, or its affiliates, or collection agencies acting on behalf of the person or entity, with which you have an existing account, that requests information in your credit report for the purpose of fraud control, or, reviewing or collecting the account. Reviewing the account includes activities related to account maintenance.

You should consider filing a complaint regarding your identity theft situation with the Federal Trade Commission and the Tennessee department of commerce and insurance, division of consumer affairs, wither in writing or via their website.

You have a right to bring civil action against anyone, including a consumer reporting agency, who improperly obtains access to a file, misuses file data, or fails to correct inaccurate file data.

Unless you are a victim of identity theft with a police report, or other official document acceptable to a consumer reporting agency to verify the crimes, a consumer reporting agency has the right to charge you up to seven dollars and fifty cents ($7.50) to place a freeze on your credit report, but may not charge you to temporarily lift a freeze on your credit report. A consumer reporting agency may charge a consumer a reasonable fee not to exceed five dollars ($5.00) to permanently remove a security freeze, or to replace a personal identification number or password. A consumer reporting agency may increase these fees annually based on changes to a common measure of consumer prices. A consumer reporting agency may not charge a Tennessee consumer to place or permanently remove a security freeze if that Tennessee consumer is a victim of identity theft as defined in Tennessee law or federal law regarding identity theft and presents to the consumer reporting agency, at the time the request is made, a police report or other official documents acceptable to the consumer reporting agency detailing the theft.

CHAPTER 4
STEP II: REQUIREMENT OF PREPETITION CREDIT COUNSELING

CREDIT COUNSELING SERVICES

The law generally requires that you receive a credit counseling briefing from an approved credit counseling agency prior to filing bankruptcy [11 U.S.C. §109(h)]. If you are filing a joint case, both spouses must receive the briefing. With limited exceptions, you must receive it within 180 days before you file your bankruptcy petition. The briefing will outline the available opportunities for credit counseling and provide assistance in performing a budget analysis. The briefing may be conducted by telephone and must be provided by a nonprofit budget/credit counseling agency approved by the United States trustee or bankruptcy administrator.

In addition, *after* filing a bankruptcy case, you are required to complete a post-petition financial management instructional course before you can receive a discharge. You can use the same credit counseling agency as before. In fact, it would be best to make arrangements with them during the prepetition credit counseling briefing. Remember, if you are filing a joint case, both spouses must complete the course.

A debtor is not entitled to a waiver of the credit briefing requirement of 11 U.S.C. §109(h)(1) because of imprisonment; incarceration is not a disability under the statute. Also note the U.S. Bankruptcy Court for the District of Columbia held that debtor Sundari Karma Prasad failed to show that she is disabled and qualified for exemption. Prasad claimed "disabled" because she was in jail and didn't have access to internet. She also claimed medical disabilities, including diabetes, epilepsy, heart disease, and a history of alcohol abuse. Being in jail is not a physical impairment, the court said, noting her status as an inmate also does not qualify her for a disability under bankruptcy law. In addition Prasad's other medical disabilities did not show that she is "so physically impaired as to be unable, after reasonable effort, to participate in an in person, telephone, or internet briefing," and she didn't show how these disabilities would prevent her from participating in a pre-petition credit counseling course, the court said. Her ability to file a Chapter 7 case without an attorney is also "strong evidence" of no disability, the court said. [Case In re Prasad, 2018 BL 207762, Bankr. D.D.C., 18-00403 (Chapter 7), 06/11/18]

A credit counseling briefing generally can take from 15 to 30 minutes to complete, so you will need to have telephone access for that amount of time. Most credit counseling services require the briefing be conducted via telephone. Stand Sure Counseling Services, P.O. Box 418, Oneonta, AL 35121, (205)421-1590 or (877)240-1398, are willing and ready to provide assistance to inmates. My cost was $27 for the pre-petition credit counseling and $27 for the post-petition personal financial management. You may obtain both services for free, if you can demonstrate your inability to pay. All approved credit counseling agencies must provide their services without regard to the debtor's ability to pay the fees in accordance with 11 U.S.C. §111(c)(2)(b). Although my funds were extremely limited at the time, I was happy to pay the agency the requested amount. I sent out correspondence to ten different agencies, and other than a couple returned letters due to bad addresses, Stand Sure Counseling Services was the only one to acknowledge my request for assistance via a response letter. We know as inmates that although the law provides assistance, we can't force a business to respond to our letters or answer our phone calls. I was very grateful for their willingness to help me start the process.

OBTAINING PREPETITION CERTIFICATE

The credit counseling agency you use will send you a certificate when you complete the credit counseling briefing. With that certificate, you will be ready to prepare and file a petition for bankruptcy. An example of my certificate obtained can be located in this chapter. You may use the services of any of the approved credit counseling agencies listed below, even if they are not located in the bankruptcy district in which you will be filing your petition. You will need to write or call the agencies listed in this chapter for more information.

If needed you may also obtain a full list of agencies approved at http://justice.gov/ust/eo/hapcpa/ccde/cc_approved.html. In Alabama and North Carolina, go to http://www.uscourts.gov/federalcourts/bankruptcy/bankruptcyresources/approvedcreditanddebtcounselors.aspx. For those with no access to a computer, the clerk of the bankruptcy court may be able to help you obtain a list. To save you much time and trouble, I have provided many approved agencies for you to choose from.

APPROVED CREDIT COUNSELING AGENCIES

Consumer Credit Counseling Service of the Midwest, Inc.
690 Taylor Road Suite 110
Gahanna, OH 43230
800-355-2227
www.apprisen.com

Consumer Education Services, DBA Start Fresh Today/DBA Affordable Bankruptcy
3700 Barrett Drive
Raleigh, NC 27609
800-435-9138
www.startfreshtoday.com
English and Spanish

Credit Card Management Services, Inc. d/b/a Debthelper.com
1325 N. Congress Ave., Suite 201
West Palm Beach, FL 33401
800-920-2262
www.debthelper.com
English and Spanish

Credit Counseling Center
832 Second Street Pike
Richboro, PA 18954
215-348-8003
www.ccc-credit.com

Debt Counseling Corp.
3033 Express Drive North Suite 103
Hauppauge, NY 11749
888-354-6332
www.debtcounselingcorp.org
English and Spanish

Debt Education and Certification Foundation
112 Goliad Street
Benbrook, TX 76126
866-859-7323
www.bkcert.com
English and Spanish

Financial Education Services, Inc.
8956 Tuscan Valley Place
Orlando, FL 32825
877-460-7337
www.financialedservices.org
English and Spanish

Garden State Consumer Credit Counseling, Inc. d/b/a Navicore Solutions
200 U.S. Highway 9
Manalapan, NJ 07726
732-409-6281
www.navicoresolutions.org
English and Spanish

Greenpath, Inc.
36500 Corporate Drive
Farmington Hills, MI 48331
248-553-5400
www.greenpath.com
English and Spanish

Hananwill Financial Education Services
115 North Cross Street
Robinson, IL 62454
866-544-5557
www.hananwill.com

Incharge Debt Solutions
5750 Major Blvd Suite 300
Orlando, FL 32819
407-532-5716
www.personalfinanceeducation.com
English and Spanish

Money Management International, Inc.
14141 Southwest Freeway, Suite 1000
Sugar Land, TX 77478-3494
877-964-2227
www.moneymanagement.org
English and Spanish

MoneySharp Credit Counseling Inc.
1916 N. Fairfield Ave Suite 2
Chicago, IL 60647
866-200-6825
www.moneysharp.org
English and Spanish

National Debt Management, Inc.
17520 West 12 Mile Road Suite 105
Southfield, MI 48076
248-200-2106 or 855-378-8989
www.nationaldebtmgt.com

Northwest Michigan Community Action Agency, Inc.
3963 Three Mile Road
Traverse City, MI 49686
231-947-3780
www.nmcaa.net

Professional Financial Guidance, LLC
55 E Monroe #3400
Chicago, IL 60603
800-725-4734
www.pfged.com

Sage Personal Finance
4043 Contera Road
Encino, CA 91436
800-516-2759
www.sagepf.com
English and Spanish

Second Bankruptcy Course, LLC
4540 Honeywell Court
Dayton, OH 45424
800-214-7030 or 800-554-1147
www.secondbankruptcycourse.com
English and Spanish

Solid Start Financial Education Services, LLC
10121 SE Sunnyside Road, Suite 300
Clackamas, OR 97015
866-467-4147
www.solidstartfinancial.com
English and Spanish

Springboard Nonprofit Consumer Credit Management, Inc. dba credit.org
4351 Latham Street
Riverside, CA 92501
951-781-0114 or 888-425-3453
www.bkhelp.org or www.bancarrota.org
English and Spanish

Stand Sure Information Services, Inc.
406 5th Street North, Suite 1
Oneonta, AL 35121
877-240-1398 or 877-750-0851
www.standsuretoday.com
English and Spanish

Summit Financial Education, Inc.
4800 E. Flower Street
Tucson, AZ 85712
800-780-5965
www.summitFE.org

Take Charge America, Inc.
20620 North 19th Avenue
Phoenix, AZ 85027-3585
623-266-6100
www.bankruptcycounseling.org
English and Spanish

The Kingdom Ministries, Inc.
6094 Apple Tree Drive, Suite 1
Memphis, TN 38115
901-552-5131
www.thekingdomministries.com

The Mesquite Group, Inc.
463 W. Harwood Road
Hurst, TX 76054
877-769-4069
www.themesquitegroup.org
English and Spanish

Trustees' Education Network, Inc.
One Windsor Cove Suite 305
Columbia, SC. 29223
803-252-5646
www.trusteenet.org
English and Spanish

Certificate Number: 11504-TXN-CC-029881153

11504-TXN-CC-029881153

CERTIFICATE OF COUNSELING

I CERTIFY that on September 15, 2017, at 2:08 o'clock PM CDT, William J. Patterson received from Stand Sure Credit Counseling, a/k/a Biblical Financial Concepts, Inc., an agency approved pursuant to 11 U.S.C. § 111 to provide credit counseling in the Northern District of Texas, an individual [or group] briefing that complied with the provisions of 11 U.S.C. §§ 109(h) and 111.

A debt repayment plan was not prepared. If a debt repayment plan was prepared, a copy of the debt repayment plan is attached to this certificate.

This counseling session was conducted by telephone.

Date: September 15, 2017

By: /s/Carol McWaters

Name: Carol McWaters

Title: Administrator

* Individuals who wish to file a bankruptcy case under title 11 of the United States Bankruptcy Code are required to file with the United States Bankruptcy Court a completed certificate of counseling from the nonprofit budget and credit counseling agency that provided the individual the counseling services and a copy of the debt repayment plan, if any, developed through the credit counseling agency. *See* 11 U.S.C. §§ 109(h) and 521(b).

CHAPTER 5
STEP III: BANKRUPTCY PETITION PREPARATION

VOLUNTARY PETITION (FORM 101)
A Chapter 7 case begins with you filing a Voluntary Petition with the bankruptcy court in the area where you reside, more specifically, where you have resided the previous 180 days prior to your filing. It is important that you file in the correct district within your state. To find what district you are located in you may go to: http://www.uscourts.gov/courtlinks or look up your district by utilizing your law library resources. The Voluntary Petition form opens the case. The instructions are located on the form and are self-explanatory. An example of my Voluntary Petition form can be located in this chapter. This form will accompany other completed forms at the time of filing your bankruptcy.

FILING FEE (FORMS 103A OR 103B)
The fee for filing a bankruptcy case under Chapter 7 is currently $335. Normally, the fees must be paid to the clerk of the court upon filing. If you cannot afford to pay the full filing fee when you first file for bankruptcy, you may pay the fee in four installments by using the form: "Application for Individuals to Pay Filing Fee in Installments (103A)." However, in most cases you must pay the fee within 120 days after you file, and the court must approve your payment timetable. Your debts will not be discharged until you pay your entire fee. This form is only required if you cannot pay your full fee when filing.

If you are filing and cannot afford to pay the full filing fee at all, you may ask the court to waive your filing fee by filing this form: "Application to Have Chapter 7 Filing Fee Waived (103B)." An example of my "Application to Have Chapter 7 Filing Fee Waived" can be located in this chapter. When filing this form, you are petitioning the court to waive your fee. Your application will be reviewed by the court and a judge may render any of the following decisions: waive your fee, set a hearing for further investigation, or require you to pay the fee in installments or in full.

The waiver is based on both your inability to pay and if your income is less than 150 percent of the U.S. Government's poverty guidelines. This is not a difficult threshold to meet for inmates.

PREPARATION FOR FILING BANKRUPTCY

Remember, there are a number of things you must do before filing for bankruptcy. One is that you must receive a briefing about credit counseling from an approved agency within 180 days before you file. This was discussed in great detail in Chapter 4.

As we covered in Chapter 2, be sure to follow local rules. These local rules are important because they are specific to the district in which you are filing. Keep in mind that a bankruptcy court may require additional documents by local rule. You may choose to contact the clerk directly with a letter of inquiry prior to starting the process. Obviously, if any forms are missing once you file, the clerk will notify you; however, your time to respond and provide the document will be limited. If available, you may also check the local court's website for any specific local requirements that you might have to meet at: http://www.uscourts.gov/courtlinks.

Included in this chapter is "Notice Required by 11 U.S.C. § 342(b) for Individuals Filing for Bankruptcy (Form 2010)." Please read and review this form to make sure Chapter 7 bankruptcy is right for you.

As noted on (Form 2010), when filing bankruptcy, all forms must be filled out on time. I strongly encourage you to prepare in advance by having all your forms completed and ready to submit prior to filing. Section 521(a)(1) of the Bankruptcy Code requires that you promptly file detailed information about your creditors, assets, liabilities, income, expenses and general financial condition. The court may dismiss your bankruptcy case if you do not file this information within the deadlines set by the Bankruptcy Code, the Bankruptcy Rules, and the local rules of the court.

Make sure to keep your address current with the bankruptcy court. All correspondence from the court will be sent to the address listed on your "Voluntary Petition (Form 101)." To ensure that you receive information about your case, "Bankruptcy Rule 4002," requires that you notify the court of any changes in your address. In my letter submitted to the bankruptcy clerk at the time of my filing, I not only provided my address but requested to the clerk, to please include my inmate number on all correspondence sent to me.

FORMS REQUIRED AT TIME OF FILING

There are several initial forms and documents that you *must* give the court at the time you file; however, any additional forms and documents must be filed no later than 14 days after you file your bankruptcy, although these additional forms may be filed at the same time you file your case. Again, I cannot emphasize this enough about the importance of having all your documents prepared and ready beforehand to avoid any delays in your completion, or worst yet, a dismissal of your case. If you are unsure about something, please take time to write or contact the bankruptcy clerk's office before you file.

The initial forms listed below *must* be filed *on* the date you open your bankruptcy case. These forms are provided in Chapter 10 of this book or, if needed, they can also be located at: http://www.uscourts.gov/formsandfees/forms/bankruptcyforms.aspx.

1) Voluntary Petition (Form 101)
2) Filing Fee, Installments or Waiver thereof (Forms 103A or 103B)
3) Statement About Your Social Security Number (Form 121) (See Chapter 8)
4) Credit Counseling Certificate (Chapter 4)

5) Complete List of Creditors (Matrix Mailing List)
6) Bankruptcy Petition Preparer's Notice (Form 2800) If preparing your own petition, you will not need this form. However, a sample form has been provided in Chapter 10, if needed.

COMPLETE LIST OF CREDITORS

You will need to compile a complete list of names and addresses of all your creditors, formatted as a mailing list according to instructions from your bankruptcy court in which you file. Your court may refer to this list as a "creditor matrix" or "mailing matrix." This list must be thorough so that all creditors are made aware of your bankruptcy proceeding and are allowed to exercise their rights in the case. A debt owed to a creditor who is not given proper notice of the bankruptcy may not be discharged or forgiven, and you may continue to be liable for the payment of the debt despite having completed your bankruptcy case. Provided for you in the back of this chapter a copy of a mailing matrix. Also provided are instructions on how to create your own matrix list. Be sure to include all creditors when compiling your list.

ADDITIONAL FORMS REQUIRED

The initial forms previously discussed must be filed at the time of filing. However, the additional forms listed below may be filed at the time of filing your bankruptcy case or within 14 days after you file your "Voluntary Petition (Form 101)." Although it is possible to open your case without the below listed forms, I strongly recommend submitting all forms at same time to help your case proceed smoothly and without interruption.

Although some of the forms listed below may ask you similar questions, you must fill out all of the forms completely to protect your legal rights. All the forms listed below are required to accomplish filing your Chapter 7 bankruptcy. Sample forms are provided in Chapter 10, and blank forms, can be accessed at http://www.uscourts.gov/forms.
1) Schedule A/B: Property (Form 106AB) (Chapter 6)
2) Schedule C: Property Claimed As Exempt (Form 106C) (Chapter 6)
3) Schedule D: Creditors Who Have Claims Secured By Property (Form 106D) (Chapter 6)
4) Schedule E/F: Creditors Who Have Unsecured Claims (Form 106E/F) (Chapter 6)
5) Schedule G: Executory Contracts and Unexpired Leases (Form 106G) (Chapter 6)
6) Schedule H: Your Codebtors (Form 106H) (Chapter 6)
7) Schedule I: Your Income (Form 106I) (Chapter 6)
8) Schedule J: Your Expenses (Form 106J) (Chapter 6)
9) Summary of Your Assets, Liabilities and Statistical Information (Form 106Sum) (Chapter 6)
10) Declaration about an Individual Debtor's Schedules (Form 106Dec) (Chapter 6)
11) Statement of Financial Affairs (Form 107) (Chapter 8)
12) Statement of Intention for Individuals (Form 108) (Chapter 8)
13) Statement of Current Monthly Income (Form 122A-l) (Chapter 7)
14) Statement of Means Test (Form 122A-2) (If necessary) (Chapter 7)
15) Statement of Exemption from Presumption of Abuse (Form 122AI-Supp) (If necessary) (Chapter 7)

You may also be asked by the court to provide copies of all payment advances (payroll records) or other evidence of payment that you received within 60 days before you filed your bankruptcy case. Some local courts may require that you submit these documents to the trustee assigned to your case rather than filing them with the court. Check the local court rules or website to find out if local requirements apply, at: http://www.uscourts.gov/courtlinks.

In my particular filing, I did not file payroll records at the time of filing, instead I allowed the clerk to direct me to what documents were needed. By being prepared in advance, I was able to provide my B.O.P. payroll records or any other documents requested by the court.

After my initial filing I received a "Notice of Deficiency" from the bankruptcy clerk. I was informed that my "Schedule C" was not filed with my petition, which was an oversight on my part. The court also requested copies of my employee income records for the (14) days prior to my filing. Subsequently, I was able to provide them via my unit team counselor. Finally, the court requested a copy of my identification and Social Security card. Fortunately for me, I had copies of both. I am not sure if the court would have proceeded without my having a copy of my Social Security card, so this may be an important question to clarify with your clerk prior to filing. It may be that the court would accept a certified document from the institution that would verify both your identity and Social Security number. A copy of my "Notice of Deficiency" can be located in this chapter.

For an example I have included a copy of my letter written to the bankruptcy clerk, submitted at the time of my filing, to explain and clarify my status as an inmate and that I would be filing *pro se*. I also explained that I was without access to the internet or the ability to file electronically. As mentioned earlier, I failed to include my "Schedule C," which was brought to my attention. Another oversight on my part was including my "Statement of Social Security (Form 121)" with my initial filing documents. Per the filing instructions, it should be mailed separately. We will cover this again in Chapter 8. Be sure to request that your inmate number be included on all correspondence addressed to you. A copy of my initial filing letter can be located in this chapter.

Notice Required by 11 U.S.C. § 342(b) for Individuals Filing for Bankruptcy (Form 2010)

This notice is for you if:

You are an individual filing for bankruptcy, and

Your debts are primarily consumer debts. *Consumer debts* are defined in 11 U.S.C. § 101(8) as "incurred by an individual primarily for a personal, family, or household purpose."

The types of bankruptcy that are available to individuals

Individuals who meet the qualifications may file under one of four different chapters of the Bankruptcy Code:

- Chapter 7 — Liquidation
- Chapter 11— Reorganization
- Chapter 12— Voluntary repayment plan for family farmers or fishermen
- Chapter 13— Voluntary repayment plan for individuals with regular income

You should have an attorney review your decision to file for bankruptcy and the choice of chapter.

Chapter 7: Liquidation

$245	filing fee
$75	administrative fee
+ $15	trustee surcharge
$335	total fee

Chapter 7 is for individuals who have financial difficulty preventing them from paying their debts and who are willing to allow their non-exempt property to be used to pay their creditors. The primary purpose of filing under chapter 7 is to have your debts discharged. The bankruptcy discharge relieves you after bankruptcy from having to pay many of your pre-bankruptcy debts. Exceptions exist for particular debts, and liens on property may still be enforced after discharge. For example, a creditor may have the right to foreclose a home mortgage or repossess an automobile.

However, if the court finds that you have committed certain kinds of improper conduct described in the Bankruptcy Code, the court may deny your discharge.

You should know that even if you file chapter 7 and you receive a discharge, some debts are not discharged under the law. Therefore, you may still be responsible to pay:

- most taxes;
- most student loans;
- domestic support and property settlement obligations;

- most fines, penalties, forfeitures, and criminal restitution obligations; and
- certain debts that are not listed in your bankruptcy papers.

You may also be required to pay debts arising from:

- fraud or theft;
- fraud or defalcation while acting in breach of fiduciary capacity;
- intentional injuries that you inflicted; and
- death or personal injury caused by operating a motor vehicle, vessel, or aircraft while intoxicated from alcohol or drugs.

If your debts are primarily consumer debts, the court can dismiss your chapter 7 case if it finds that you have enough income to repay creditors a certain amount. You must file *Chapter 7 Statement of Your Current Monthly Income* (Official Form 122A–1) if you are an individual filing for bankruptcy under chapter 7. This form will determine your current monthly income and compare whether your income is more than the median income that applies in your state.

If your income is not above the median for your state, you will not have to complete the other chapter 7 form, the *Chapter 7 Means Test Calculation* (Official Form 122A–2).

If your income is above the median for your state, you must file a second form —the *Chapter 7 Means Test Calculation* (Official Form 122A–2). The calculations on the form— sometimes called the *Means Test*—deduct from your income living expenses and payments on certain debts to determine any amount available to pay unsecured creditors. If your income is more than the median income for your state of residence and family size, depending on the results of the *Means Test*, the U.S. trustee, bankruptcy administrator, or creditors can file a motion to dismiss your case under § 707(b) of the Bankruptcy Code. If a motion is filed, the court will decide if your case should be dismissed. To avoid dismissal, you may choose to proceed under another chapter of the Bankruptcy Code.

If you are an individual filing for chapter 7 bankruptcy, the trustee may sell your property to pay your debts, subject to your right to exempt the property or a portion of the proceeds from the sale of the property. The property, and the proceeds from property that your bankruptcy trustee sells or liquidates that you are entitled to, is called *exempt property*. Exemptions may enable you to keep your home, a car, clothing, and household items or to receive some of the proceeds if the property is sold.

Exemptions are not automatic. To exempt property, you must list it on *Schedule C: The Property You Claim as Exempt* (Official Form 106C). If you do not list the property, the trustee may sell it and pay all of the proceeds to your creditors.

Chapter 11: Reorganization

	$1,167	filing fee
+	$550	administrative fee
	$1,717	total fee

Chapter 11 is often used for reorganizing a business, but is also available to individuals. The provisions of chapter 11 are too complicated to summarize briefly.

Read These Important Warnings

Because bankruptcy can have serious long-term financial and legal consequences, including loss of your property, you should hire an attorney and carefully consider all of your options before you file. Only an attorney can give you legal advice about what can happen as a result of filing for bankruptcy and what your options are. If you do file for bankruptcy, an attorney can help you fill out the forms properly and protect you, your family, your home, and your possessions.

Although the law allows you to represent yourself in bankruptcy court, you should understand that many people find it difficult to represent themselves successfully. The rules are technical, and a mistake or inaction may harm you. If you file without an attorney, you are still responsible for knowing and following all of the legal requirements.

You should not file for bankruptcy if you are not eligible to file or if you do not intend to file the necessary documents.

Bankruptcy fraud is a serious crime; you could be fined and imprisoned if you commit fraud in your bankruptcy case. Making a false statement, concealing property, or obtaining money or property by fraud in connection with a bankruptcy case can result in fines up to $250,000, or imprisonment for up to 20 years, or both. 18 U.S.C. §§ 152, 1341, 1519, and 3571.

Chapter 12: Repayment plan for family farmers or fishermen

	$200	filing fee
+	$75	administrative fee
	$275	total fee

Similar to chapter 13, chapter 12 permits family farmers and fishermen to repay their debts over a period of time using future earnings and to discharge some debts that are not paid.

Chapter 13: Repayment plan for individuals with regular income

	$235	filing fee
+	$75	administrative fee
	$310	total fee

Chapter 13 is for individuals who have regular income and would like to pay all or part of their debts in installments over a period of time and to discharge some debts that are not paid. You are eligible for chapter 13 only if your debts are not more than certain dollar amounts set forth in 11 U.S.C. § 109.

Under chapter 13, you must file with the court a plan to repay your creditors all or part of the money that you owe them, usually using your future earnings. If the court approves your plan, the court will allow you to repay your debts, as adjusted by the plan, within 3 years or 5 years, depending on your income and other factors.

After you make all the payments under your plan, many of your debts are discharged. The debts that are not discharged and that you may still be responsible to pay include:

- domestic support obligations,
- most student loans,
- certain taxes,
- debts for fraud or theft,
- debts for fraud or defalcation while acting in a fiduciary capacity,
- most criminal fines and restitution obligations,
- certain debts that are not listed in your bankruptcy papers,
- certain debts for acts that caused death or personal injury, and
- certain long-term secured debts.

Warning: File Your Forms on Time

Section 521(a)(1) of the Bankruptcy Code requires that you promptly file detailed information about your creditors, assets, liabilities, income, expenses and general financial condition. The court may dismiss your bankruptcy case if you do not file this information within the deadlines set by the Bankruptcy Code, the Bankruptcy Rules, and the local rules of the court.

For more information about the documents and their deadlines, go to: http://www.uscourts.gov/forms/bankruptcy-forms

Bankruptcy crimes have serious consequences

- If you knowingly and fraudulently conceal assets or make a false oath or statement under penalty of perjury—either orally or in writing—in connection with a bankruptcy case, you may be fined, imprisoned, or both.
- All information you supply in connection with a bankruptcy case is subject to examination by the Attorney General acting through the Office of the U.S. Trustee, the Office of the U.S. Attorney, and other offices and employees of the U.S. Department of Justice.

Make sure the court has your mailing address

The bankruptcy court sends notices to the mailing address you list on *Voluntary Petition for Individuals Filing for Bankruptcy* (Official Form 101). To ensure that you receive information about your case, Bankruptcy Rule 4002 requires that you notify the court of any changes in your address.

A married couple may file a bankruptcy case together—called a *joint case*. If you file a joint case and each spouse lists the same mailing address on the bankruptcy petition, the bankruptcy court generally will mail you and your spouse one copy of each notice, unless you file a statement with the court asking that each spouse receive separate copies.

Understand which services you could receive from credit counseling agencies

The law generally requires that you receive a credit counseling briefing from an approved credit counseling agency. 11 U.S.C. § 109(h). If you are filing a joint case, both spouses must receive the briefing. With limited exceptions, you must receive it within the 180 days ***before*** you file your bankruptcy petition. This briefing is usually conducted by telephone or on the Internet.

In addition, after filing a bankruptcy case, you generally must complete a financial management instructional course before you can receive a discharge. If you are filing a joint case, both spouses must complete the course.

You can obtain the list of agencies approved to provide both the briefing and the instructional course from: http://www.uscourts.gov/services-forms/bankruptcy/credit-counseling-and-debtor-education-courses.

In Alabama and North Carolina, go to: http://www.uscourts.gov/services-forms/bankruptcy/credit-counseling-and-debtor-education-courses.

If you do not have access to a computer, the clerk of the bankruptcy court may be able to help you obtain the list.

Fill in this information to identify your case:

United States Bankruptcy Court for the:

Northern District of Texas

Case number (if known): ____________________

Chapter you are filing under:
- [x] Chapter 7
- [ ] Chapter 11
- [ ] Chapter 12
- [ ] Chapter 13

- [ ] Check if this is an amended filing

Official Form 101

Voluntary Petition for Individuals Filing for Bankruptcy

12/15

The bankruptcy forms use *you* and *Debtor 1* to refer to a debtor filing alone. A married couple may file a bankruptcy case together—called a *joint case*—and in joint cases, these forms use *you* to ask for information from both debtors. For example, if a form asks, "Do you own a car," the answer would be *yes* if either debtor owns a car. When information is needed about the spouses separately, the form uses *Debtor 1* and *Debtor 2* to distinguish between them. In joint cases, one of the spouses must report information as *Debtor 1* and the other as *Debtor 2*. The same person must be *Debtor 1* in all of the forms.

Be as complete and accurate as possible. If two married people are filing together, both are equally responsible for supplying correct information. If more space is needed, attach a separate sheet to this form. On the top of any additional pages, write your name and case number (if known). Answer every question.

Part 1: Identify Yourself

	About Debtor 1:	About Debtor 2 (Spouse Only in a Joint Case):
1. **Your full name** Write the name that is on your government-issued picture identification (for example, your driver's license or passport). Bring your picture identification to your meeting with the trustee.	William First name John Middle name Patterson Last name ______ Suffix (Sr., Jr., II, III)	______ First name ______ Middle name ______ Last name ______ Suffix (Sr., Jr., II, III)
2. **All other names you have used in the last 8 years** Include your married or maiden names.	None First name ______ Middle name ______ Last name ______ First name ______ Middle name ______ Last name	______ First name ______ Middle name ______ Last name ______ First name ______ Middle name ______ Last name
3. **Only the last 4 digits of your Social Security number or federal Individual Taxpayer Identification number (ITIN)**	xxx – xx – 1 2 3 4 OR 9xx – xx – __ __ __ __	xxx – xx – __ __ __ __ OR 9xx – xx – __ __ __ __

Official Form 101 **Voluntary Petition for Individuals Filing for Bankruptcy** page 1

Debtor 1 William John Patterson
First Name Middle Name Last Name

Case number (if known) ______

	About Debtor 1:	About Debtor 2 (Spouse Only in a Joint Case):
4. **Any business names and Employer Identification Numbers (EIN) you have used in the last 8 years** Include trade names and *doing business as* names	☒ I have not used any business names or EINs. ______ Business name ______ Business name __ – _______ EIN __ – _______ EIN	☐ I have not used any business names or EINs. ______ Business name ______ Business name __ – _______ EIN __ – _______ EIN
5. **Where you live**	2113 N. Hwy 175 Number Street ______ Seagoville TX 75159 City State ZIP Code Dallas County **If your mailing address is different from the one above, fill it in here.** Note that the court will send any notices to you at this mailing address. ______ Number Street P.O. Box 9000 P.O. Box Seagoville TX 75159 City State ZIP Code	**If Debtor 2 lives at a different address:** ______ Number Street ______ ______ City State ZIP Code ______ County **If Debtor 2's mailing address is different from yours, fill it in here.** Note that the court will send any notices to this mailing address. ______ Number Street ______ P.O. Box ______ City State ZIP Code
6. **Why you are choosing *this district* to file for bankruptcy**	*Check one:* ☒ Over the last 180 days before filing this petition, I have lived in this district longer than in any other district. ☐ I have another reason. Explain. (See 28 U.S.C. § 1408.) ______ ______ ______ ______	*Check one:* ☐ Over the last 180 days before filing this petition, I have lived in this district longer than in any other district. ☐ I have another reason. Explain. (See 28 U.S.C. § 1408.) ______ ______ ______ ______

Debtor 1 William John Patterson
First Name Middle Name Last Name

Case number (if known) ______________________

Part 2: Tell the Court About Your Bankruptcy Case

7. The chapter of the Bankruptcy Code you are choosing to file under

Check one. (For a brief description of each, see *Notice Required by 11 U.S.C. § 342(b) for Individuals Filing for Bankruptcy* (Form 2010)). Also, go to the top of page 1 and check the appropriate box.

- [x] Chapter 7
- [ ] Chapter 11
- [ ] Chapter 12
- [ ] Chapter 13

8. How you will pay the fee

- [ ] **I will pay the entire fee when I file my petition.** Please check with the clerk's office in your local court for more details about how you may pay. Typically, if you are paying the fee yourself, you may pay with cash, cashier's check, or money order. If your attorney is submitting your payment on your behalf, your attorney may pay with a credit card or check with a pre-printed address.
- [ ] **I need to pay the fee in installments.** If you choose this option, sign and attach the *Application for Individuals to Pay The Filing Fee in Installments* (Official Form 103A).
- [x] **I request that my fee be waived** (You may request this option only if you are filing for Chapter 7. By law, a judge may, but is not required to, waive your fee, and may do so only if your income is less than 150% of the official poverty line that applies to your family size and you are unable to pay the fee in installments). If you choose this option, you must fill out the *Application to Have the Chapter 7 Filing Fee Waived* (Official Form 103B) and file it with your petition.

9. Have you filed for bankruptcy within the last 8 years?

- [x] No
- [ ] Yes. District ______ When ______ (MM / DD / YYYY) Case number ______
  District ______ When ______ (MM / DD / YYYY) Case number ______
  District ______ When ______ (MM / DD / YYYY) Case number ______

10. Are any bankruptcy cases pending or being filed by a spouse who is not filing this case with you, or by a business partner, or by an affiliate?

- [x] No
- [ ] Yes. Debtor ______ Relationship to you ______
  District ______ When ______ (MM / DD / YYYY) Case number, if known ______
  Debtor ______ Relationship to you ______
  District ______ When ______ (MM / DD / YYYY) Case number, if known ______

11. Do you rent your residence?

- [x] No. Go to line 12.
- [ ] Yes. Has your landlord obtained an eviction judgment against you and do you want to stay in your residence?
  - [ ] No. Go to line 12.
  - [ ] Yes. Fill out *Initial Statement About an Eviction Judgment Against You* (Form 101A) and file it with this bankruptcy petition.

Official Form 101 **Voluntary Petition for Individuals Filing for Bankruptcy** page 3

Debtor 1 William John Patterson (First Name, Middle Name, Last Name) Case number (if known) ________

Part 3: Report About Any Businesses You Own as a Sole Proprietor

12. Are you a sole proprietor of any full- or part-time business?

A sole proprietorship is a business you operate as an individual, and is not a separate legal entity such as a corporation, partnership, or LLC.

If you have more than one sole proprietorship, use a separate sheet and attach it to this petition.

☒ No. Go to Part 4.

☐ Yes. Name and location of business

Name of business, if any ________

Number Street ________

____

City ________ State ________ ZIP Code ________

Check the appropriate box to describe your business:

☐ Health Care Business (as defined in 11 U.S.C. § 101(27A))

☐ Single Asset Real Estate (as defined in 11 U.S.C. § 101(51B))

☐ Stockbroker (as defined in 11 U.S.C. § 101(53A))

☐ Commodity Broker (as defined in 11 U.S.C. § 101(6))

☐ None of the above

13. Are you filing under Chapter 11 of the Bankruptcy Code and are you a *small business debtor*?

For a definition of *small business debtor*, see 11 U.S.C. § 101(51D).

If you are filing under Chapter 11, the court must know whether you are a small business debtor so that it can set appropriate deadlines. If you indicate that you are a small business debtor, you must attach your most recent balance sheet, statement of operations, cash-flow statement, and federal income tax return or if any of these documents do not exist, follow the procedure in 11 U.S.C. § 1116(1)(B).

☒ No. I am not filing under Chapter 11.

☐ No. I am filing under Chapter 11, but I am NOT a small business debtor according to the definition in the Bankruptcy Code.

☐ Yes. I am filing under Chapter 11 and I am a small business debtor according to the definition in the Bankruptcy Code.

Part 4: Report if You Own or Have Any Hazardous Property or Any Property That Needs Immediate Attention

14. Do you own or have any property that poses or is alleged to pose a threat of imminent and identifiable hazard to public health or safety? Or do you own any property that needs immediate attention?

For example, do you own perishable goods, or livestock that must be fed, or a building that needs urgent repairs?

☒ No

☐ Yes. What is the hazard? ________

____

If immediate attention is needed, why is it needed? ________

____

Where is the property? ________
Number Street

____

City ________ State ________ ZIP Code ________

Debtor 1 William John Patterson (First Name, Middle Name, Last Name) Case number (if known) ______

Part 5: Explain Your Efforts to Receive a Briefing About Credit Counseling

15. Tell the court whether you have received a briefing about credit counseling.

The law requires that you receive a briefing about credit counseling before you file for bankruptcy. You must truthfully check one of the following choices. If you cannot do so, you are not eligible to file.

If you file anyway, the court can dismiss your case, you will lose whatever filing fee you paid, and your creditors can begin collection activities again.

About Debtor 1:

You must check one:

☒ **I received a briefing from an approved credit counseling agency within the 180 days before I filed this bankruptcy petition, and I received a certificate of completion.**

Attach a copy of the certificate and the payment plan, if any, that you developed with the agency.

☐ **I received a briefing from an approved credit counseling agency within the 180 days before I filed this bankruptcy petition, but I do not have a certificate of completion.**

Within 14 days after you file this bankruptcy petition, you MUST file a copy of the certificate and payment plan, if any.

☐ **I certify that I asked for credit counseling services from an approved agency, but was unable to obtain those services during the 7 days after I made my request, and exigent circumstances merit a 30-day temporary waiver of the requirement.**

To ask for a 30-day temporary waiver of the requirement, attach a separate sheet explaining what efforts you made to obtain the briefing, why you were unable to obtain it before you filed for bankruptcy, and what exigent circumstances required you to file this case.

Your case may be dismissed if the court is dissatisfied with your reasons for not receiving a briefing before you filed for bankruptcy.

If the court is satisfied with your reasons, you must still receive a briefing within 30 days after you file. You must file a certificate from the approved agency, along with a copy of the payment plan you developed, if any. If you do not do so, your case may be dismissed.

Any extension of the 30-day deadline is granted only for cause and is limited to a maximum of 15 days.

☐ **I am not required to receive a briefing about credit counseling because of:**

☐ **Incapacity.** I have a mental illness or a mental deficiency that makes me incapable of realizing or making rational decisions about finances.

☐ **Disability.** My physical disability causes me to be unable to participate in a briefing in person, by phone, or through the internet, even after I reasonably tried to do so.

☐ **Active duty.** I am currently on active military duty in a military combat zone.

If you believe you are not required to receive a briefing about credit counseling, you must file a motion for waiver of credit counseling with the court.

About Debtor 2 (Spouse Only in a Joint Case):

You must check one:

☐ **I received a briefing from an approved credit counseling agency within the 180 days before I filed this bankruptcy petition, and I received a certificate of completion.**

Attach a copy of the certificate and the payment plan, if any, that you developed with the agency.

☐ **I received a briefing from an approved credit counseling agency within the 180 days before I filed this bankruptcy petition, but I do not have a certificate of completion.**

Within 14 days after you file this bankruptcy petition, you MUST file a copy of the certificate and payment plan, if any.

☐ **I certify that I asked for credit counseling services from an approved agency, but was unable to obtain those services during the 7 days after I made my request, and exigent circumstances merit a 30-day temporary waiver of the requirement.**

To ask for a 30-day temporary waiver of the requirement, attach a separate sheet explaining what efforts you made to obtain the briefing, why you were unable to obtain it before you filed for bankruptcy, and what exigent circumstances required you to file this case.

Your case may be dismissed if the court is dissatisfied with your reasons for not receiving a briefing before you filed for bankruptcy.

If the court is satisfied with your reasons, you must still receive a briefing within 30 days after you file. You must file a certificate from the approved agency, along with a copy of the payment plan you developed, if any. If you do not do so, your case may be dismissed.

Any extension of the 30-day deadline is granted only for cause and is limited to a maximum of 15 days.

☐ **I am not required to receive a briefing about credit counseling because of:**

☐ **Incapacity.** I have a mental illness or a mental deficiency that makes me incapable of realizing or making rational decisions about finances.

☐ **Disability.** My physical disability causes me to be unable to participate in a briefing in person, by phone, or through the internet, even after I reasonably tried to do so.

☐ **Active duty.** I am currently on active military duty in a military combat zone.

If you believe you are not required to receive a briefing about credit counseling, you must file a motion for waiver of credit counseling with the court.

Official Form 101 **Voluntary Petition for Individuals Filing for Bankruptcy** page 5

Debtor 1 William John Patterson
First Name Middle Name Last Name

Case number (If known) ____________

Part 6: Answer These Questions for Reporting Purposes

16. **What kind of debts do you have?**

16a. **Are your debts primarily consumer debts?** *Consumer debts* are defined in 11 U.S.C. § 101(8) as "incurred by an individual primarily for a personal, family, or household purpose."

- ☐ No. Go to line 16b.
- ☒ Yes. Go to line 17.

16b. **Are your debts primarily business debts?** *Business debts* are debts that you incurred to obtain money for a business or investment or through the operation of the business or investment.

- ☐ No. Go to line 16c.
- ☐ Yes. Go to line 17.

16c. State the type of debts you owe that are not consumer debts or business debts.

____

17. **Are you filing under Chapter 7?**

Do you estimate that after any exempt property is excluded and administrative expenses are paid that funds will be available for distribution to unsecured creditors?

- ☐ No. I am not filing under Chapter 7. Go to line 18.
- ☒ Yes. I am filing under Chapter 7. Do you estimate that after any exempt property is excluded and administrative expenses are paid that funds will be available to distribute to unsecured creditors?
  - ☒ No
  - ☐ Yes

18. **How many creditors do you estimate that you owe?**

☒ 1-49	☐ 1,000-5,000	☐ 25,001-50,000
☐ 50-99	☐ 5,001-10,000	☐ 50,001-100,000
☐ 100-199	☐ 10,001-25,000	☐ More than 100,000
☐ 200-999		

19. **How much do you estimate your assets to be worth?**

☒ \$0-\$50,000	☐ \$1,000,001-\$10 million	☐ \$500,000,001-\$1 billion
☐ \$50,001-\$100,000	☐ \$10,000,001-\$50 million	☐ \$1,000,000,001-\$10 billion
☐ \$100,001-\$500,000	☐ \$50,000,001-\$100 million	☐ \$10,000,000,001-\$50 billion
☐ \$500,001-\$1 million	☐ \$100,000,001-\$500 million	☐ More than \$50 billion

20. **How much do you estimate your liabilities to be?**

☐ \$0-\$50,000	☐ \$1,000,001-\$10 million	☐ \$500,000,001-\$1 billion
☒ \$50,001-\$100,000	☐ \$10,000,001-\$50 million	☐ \$1,000,000,001-\$10 billion
☐ \$100,001-\$500,000	☐ \$50,000,001-\$100 million	☐ \$10,000,000,001-\$50 billion
☐ \$500,001-\$1 million	☐ \$100,000,001-\$500 million	☐ More than \$50 billion

Part 7: Sign Below

For you

I have examined this petition, and I declare under penalty of perjury that the information provided is true and correct.

If I have chosen to file under Chapter 7, I am aware that I may proceed, if eligible, under Chapter 7, 11,12, or 13 of title 11, United States Code. I understand the relief available under each chapter, and I choose to proceed under Chapter 7.

If no attorney represents me and I did not pay or agree to pay someone who is not an attorney to help me fill out this document, I have obtained and read the notice required by 11 U.S.C. § 342(b).

I request relief in accordance with the chapter of title 11, United States Code, specified in this petition.

I understand making a false statement, concealing property, or obtaining money or property by fraud in connection with a bankruptcy case can result in fines up to \$250,000, or imprisonment for up to 20 years, or both. 18 U.S.C. §§ 152, 1341, 1519, and 3571.

✕ William John Patterson
Signature of Debtor 1

Executed on 10 / 18 / 2017
MM / DD / YYYY

✕ ____________
Signature of Debtor 2

Executed on ____________
MM / DD / YYYY

Debtor 1 William John Patterson
First Name Middle Name Last Name

Case number (if known) ______________

For your attorney, if you are represented by one

If you are not represented by an attorney, you do not need to file this page.

I, the attorney for the debtor(s) named in this petition, declare that I have informed the debtor(s) about eligibility to proceed under Chapter 7, 11, 12, or 13 of title 11, United States Code, and have explained the relief available under each chapter for which the person is eligible. I also certify that I have delivered to the debtor(s) the notice required by 11 U.S.C. § 342(b) and, in a case in which § 707(b)(4)(D) applies, certify that I have no knowledge after an inquiry that the information in the schedules filed with the petition is incorrect.

✗ N/A ______________ Date ______________
Signature of Attorney for Debtor MM / DD / YYYY

____
Printed name

____
Firm name

____
Number Street

____

______________ ______________ ______________
City State ZIP Code

Contact phone ______________ Email address ______________

______________ ______________
Bar number State

Debtor 1 Willaim John Patterson — First Name Middle Name Last Name   Case number (if known)

For you if you are filing this bankruptcy without an attorney

If you are represented by an attorney, you do not need to file this page.

The law allows you, as an individual, to represent yourself in bankruptcy court, but you **should understand that many people find it extremely difficult to represent themselves successfully. Because bankruptcy has long-term financial and legal consequences, you are strongly urged to hire a qualified attorney.**

To be successful, you must correctly file and handle your bankruptcy case. The rules are very technical, and a mistake or inaction may affect your rights. For example, your case may be dismissed because you did not file a required document, pay a fee on time, attend a meeting or hearing, or cooperate with the court, case trustee, U.S. trustee, bankruptcy administrator, or audit firm if your case is selected for audit. If that happens, you could lose your right to file another case, or you may lose protections, including the benefit of the automatic stay.

You must list all your property and debts in the schedules that you are required to file with the court. Even if you plan to pay a particular debt outside of your bankruptcy, you must list that debt in your schedules. If you do not list a debt, the debt may not be discharged. If you do not list property or properly claim it as exempt, you may not be able to keep the property. The judge can also deny you a discharge of all your debts if you do something dishonest in your bankruptcy case, such as destroying or hiding property, falsifying records, or lying. Individual bankruptcy cases are randomly audited to determine if debtors have been accurate, truthful, and complete. **Bankruptcy fraud is a serious crime; you could be fined and imprisoned.**

If you decide to file without an attorney, the court expects you to follow the rules as if you had hired an attorney. The court will not treat you differently because you are filing for yourself. To be successful, you must be familiar with the United States Bankruptcy Code, the Federal Rules of Bankruptcy Procedure, and the local rules of the court in which your case is filed. You must also be familiar with any state exemption laws that apply.

Are you aware that filing for bankruptcy is a serious action with long-term financial and legal consequences?

- ☐ No
- ☒ Yes

Are you aware that bankruptcy fraud is a serious crime and that if your bankruptcy forms are inaccurate or incomplete, you could be fined or imprisoned?

- ☐ No
- ☒ Yes

Did you pay or agree to pay someone who is not an attorney to help you fill out your bankruptcy forms?

- ☒ No
- ☐ Yes. Name of Person_______________________________________
  Attach *Bankruptcy Petition Preparer's Notice, Declaration, and Signature* (Official Form 119).

By signing here, I acknowledge that I understand the risks involved in filing without an attorney. I have read and understood this notice, and I am aware that filing a bankruptcy case without an attorney may cause me to lose my rights or property if I do not properly handle the case.

✕ William John Patter	✕
Signature of Debtor 1	Signature of Debtor 2
Date 10/18/2017 MM / DD / YYYY	Date MM / DD / YYYY
Contact phone	Contact phone
Cell phone	Cell phone
Email address	Email address

Application for Individuals to Pay the Filing Fee in Installments (Official Form 103A)

If you cannot afford to pay the full filing fee when you first file for bankruptcy, you may pay the fee in installments. However, in most cases, you must pay the entire fee within 120 days after you file, and the court must approve your payment timetable. Your debts will not be discharged until you pay your entire fee.

Do not file this form if you can afford to pay your full fee when you file.

If you are filing under chapter 7 and cannot afford to pay the full filing fee at all, you may be qualified to ask the court to waive your filing fee. See *Application to Have Your Chapter 7 Filing Fee Waived* (Official Form 103B).

If a bankruptcy petition preparer helped you complete this form, make sure that person fills out the *Bankruptcy Petition Preparer's Notice, Declaration, and Signature* (Official Form 119); include a copy of it when you file this application.

Fill in this information to identify your case:

Debtor 1 Your Name Here
First Name Middle Name Last Name

Debtor 2
(Spouse, if filing) First Name Middle Name Last Name

United States Bankruptcy Court for the ? ? District of Your State

Case number
(If known)

☐ Check if this is an amended filing

Official Form 103A

Application for Individuals to Pay the Filing Fee in Installments 12/15

Be as complete and accurate as possible. If two married people are filing together, both are equally responsible for supplying correct information.

Part 1: Specify Your Proposed Payment Timetable

1. **Which chapter of the Bankruptcy Code are you choosing to file under?**

   ☒ Chapter 7
   ☐ Chapter 11
   ☐ Chapter 12
   ☐ Chapter 13

2. **You may apply to pay the filing fee in up to four installments. Fill in the amounts you propose to pay and the dates you plan to pay them. Be sure all dates are business days. Then add the payments you propose to pay.**

   You must propose to pay the entire fee no later than 120 days after you file this bankruptcy case. If the court approves your application, the court will set your final payment timetable.

You propose to pay...	
$ 83.75	☒ With the filing of the petition ☐ On or before this date........ MM / DD / YYYY
$ 83.75	On or before this date.......... You choose date (MM / DD / YYYY)
$ 83.75	On or before this date.......... Choose date (MM / DD / YYYY)
+ $ 83.75	On or before this date.......... Choose date (MM / DD / YYYY)
Total $ 335.00	◀ Your total must equal the entire fee for the chapter you checked in line 1.

Part 2: Sign Below

By signing here, you state that you are unable to pay the full filing fee at once, that you want to pay the fee in installments, and that you understand that:

- You must pay your entire filing fee before you make any more payments or transfer any more property to an attorney, bankruptcy petition preparer, or anyone else for services in connection with your bankruptcy case.
- You must pay the entire fee no later than 120 days after you first file for bankruptcy, unless the court later extends your deadline. Your debts will not be discharged until your entire fee is paid.
- If you do not make any payment when it is due, your bankruptcy case may be dismissed, and your rights in other bankruptcy proceedings may be affected.

✗ Sign Here	✗	✗
Signature of Debtor 1	Signature of Debtor 2	Your attorney's name and signature, if you used one
Date Date Here (MM / DD / YYYY)	Date MM / DD / YYYY	Date MM / DD / YYYY

Application to Have the Chapter 7 Filing Fee Waived (Official Form 103B)

The fee for filing a bankruptcy case under chapter 7 is $335. If you cannot afford to pay the entire fee now in full or in installments within 120 days, use this form. If you can afford to pay your filing fee in installments, see *Application for Individuals to Pay the Filing Fee in Installments* (Official Form 103A).

If you file this form, you are asking the court to waive your fee. After reviewing your application, the court may waive your fee, set a hearing for further investigation, or require you to pay the fee in installments or in full.

For your fee to be waived, all of these statements must be true:

- You are filing for bankruptcy under chapter 7.
- You are an individual.
- The total combined monthly income for your family is less than 150% of the official poverty guideline last published by the U.S. Department of Health and Human Services (DHHS). (For more information about the guidelines, go to http://www.uscourts.gov.)
- You cannot afford to pay the fee in installments.

Your family includes you, your spouse, and any dependents listed on *Schedule I*. Your family may be different from your *household*, referenced on *Schedules I* and *J*. Your household may include your unmarried partner and others who live with you and with whom you share income and expenses.

If a bankruptcy petition preparer helped you complete this form, make sure that person fills out *Bankruptcy Petition Preparer's Notice, Declaration, and Signature* (Official Form 119); include a copy of it when you file this application.

If you have already completed the following forms, the information on them may help you when you fill out this application:

- *Schedule A/B: Property* (Official Form 106A/B)
- *Schedule I: Your Income* (Official Form 106I)
- *Schedule J: Your Expenses* (Official Form 106J)

This form includes a proposed order for use by the court in considering the application. The court may modify the form of the order or use its own version of the order.

Fill in this information to identify your case:

Debtor 1 William John Patterson
First Name Middle Name Last Name

Debtor 2
(Spouse, if filing) First Name Middle Name Last Name

United States Bankruptcy Court for the: Northern District of Texas (State)

Case number (If known)

☐ Check if this is an amended filing

Official Form B 3B

Application to Have the Chapter 7 Filing Fee Waived

06/14

Be as complete and accurate as possible. If two married people are filing together, both are equally responsible for supplying correct information. If more space is needed, attach a separate sheet to this form. On the top of any additional pages, write your name and case number (if known).

Part 1: Tell the Court About Your Family and Your Family's Income

1. **What is the size of your family?**
   Your family includes you, your spouse, and any dependents listed on *Schedule J: Current Expenditures of Individual Debtor(s)* (Official Form 6J).

   Check all that apply:
   ☒ You
   ☐ Your spouse
   ☐ Your dependents ______ How many dependents? ______ Total number of people

2. **Fill in your family's average monthly income.**
   Include your spouse's income if your spouse is living with you, even if your spouse is not filing.
   Do not include your spouse's income if you are separated and your spouse is not filing with you.

   Add your income and your spouse's income. Include the value (if known) of any non-cash governmental assistance that you receive, such as food stamps (benefits under the Supplemental Nutrition Assistance Program) or housing subsidies.
   If you have already filled out *Schedule I: Your Income*, see line 10 of that schedule.

	That person's average monthly net income (take-home pay)
You	$ 5.25
Your spouse ... +	$
Subtotal	$ 5.25
Subtract any non-cash governmental assistance that you included above. −	$
Your family's average monthly net income — Total	$ 5.25

3. **Do you receive non-cash governmental assistance?**
   ☒ No
   ☐ Yes. Describe. **Type of assistance**

4. **Do you expect your family's average monthly net income to increase or decrease by more than 10% during the next 6 months?**
   ☒ No
   ☐ Yes. Explain.

5. **Tell the court why you are unable to pay the filing fee in installments within 120 days.** If you have some additional circumstances that cause you to not be able to pay your filing fee in installments, explain them.

   Inmate income of $5.25 per moth and lack of savings and current family support don't allow me to pay any portion of filing fee.

Debtor 1 William John Patterson
First Name Middle Name Last Name

Case number (if known)

Part 2: Tell the Court About Your Monthly Expenses

6. **Estimate your average monthly expenses.**
Include amounts paid by any government assistance that you reported on line 2. $ 128.30

If you have already filled out *Schedule J, Your Expenses*, copy line 22 from that form.

7. **Do these expenses cover anyone who is not included in your family as reported in line 1?**
☒ No
☐ Yes. Identify who........

8. **Does anyone other than you regularly pay any of these expenses?**
If you have already filled out *Schedule I: Your Income*, copy the total from line 11.
☒ No
☐ Yes. How much do you regularly receive as contributions? $________ monthly

9. **Do you expect your average monthly expenses to increase or decrease by more than 10% during the next 6 months?**
☒ No
☐ Yes. Explain..............

Part 3: Tell the Court About Your Property

If you have already filled out *Schedule A: Real Property (Official Form B 6A)* and *Schedule B: Personal Property (Official Form B 6B)*, attach copies to this application and go to Part 4.

10. **How much cash do you have?**
Examples: Money you have in your wallet, in your home, and on hand when you file this application
Cash: $ 0.00

11. **Bank accounts and other deposits of money?**
Examples: Checking, savings, money market, or other financial accounts; certificates of deposit; shares in banks, credit unions, brokerage houses, and other similar institutions. If you have more than one account with the same institution, list each. Do not include 401(k) and IRA accounts.

	Institution name:	Amount:
Checking account:		$
Savings account:		$
Other financial accounts:	Federal Inmate Account	$ 95.00
Other financial accounts:		$

12. **Your home?** (if you own it outright or are purchasing it)
Examples: House, condominium, manufactured home, or mobile home
N/A
Number Street
City State ZIP Code
Current value: $
Amount you owe on mortgage and liens: $

13. **Other real estate?**
N/A
Number Street
City State ZIP Code
Current value: $
Amount you owe on mortgage and liens: $

14. **The vehicles you own?**
Examples: Cars, vans, trucks, sports utility vehicles, motorcycles, tractors, boats
Make: N/A
Model:
Year:
Mileage
Current value: $
Amount you owe on liens: $

Make:
Model:
Year:
Mileage
Current value: $
Amount you owe on liens: $

Official Form B 3B **Application to Have the Chapter 7 Filing Fee Waived** page 2

Debtor 1 William John Patterson
First Name Middle Name Last Name

Case number (if known) ______

15. **Other assets?** N/A

Do not include household items and clothing.

Describe the other assets:

Current value: $______

Amount you owe on liens: $______

16. **Money or property due you?**

Examples: Tax refunds, past due or lump sum alimony, spousal support, child support, maintenance, divorce or property settlements, Social Security benefits, Workers' compensation, personal injury recovery

Who owes you the money or property?

How much is owed? $______ $______

Do you believe you will likely receive payment in the next 180 days?

☐ No

☐ Yes. Explain: N/A

Part 4: Answer These Additional Questions

17. **Have you paid anyone for services for this case, including filling out this application, the bankruptcy filing package, or the schedules?**

☒ No

☐ Yes. **Whom did you pay?** *Check all that apply:*

☐ An attorney

☐ A bankruptcy petition preparer, paralegal, or typing service

☐ Someone else ______

How much did you pay? $______

18. **Have you promised to pay or do you expect to pay someone for services for your bankruptcy case?**

☒ No

☐ Yes. **Whom do you expect to pay?** *Check all that apply:*

☐ An attorney

☐ A bankruptcy petition preparer, paralegal, or typing service

☐ Someone else ______

How much do you expect to pay? $______

19. **Has anyone paid someone on your behalf for services for this case?**

☒ No

☐ Yes. **Who was paid on your behalf?** *Check all that apply:*

☐ An attorney

☐ A bankruptcy petition preparer, paralegal, or typing service

☐ Someone else ______

Who paid? *Check all that apply:*

☐ Parent

☐ Brother or sister

☐ Friend

☐ Pastor or clergy

☐ Someone else ______

How much did someone else pay? $______

20. **Have you filed for bankruptcy within the last 8 years?**

☒ No

☐ Yes. District ______ When ______ MM/ DD/ YYYY Case number ______

District ______ When ______ MM/ DD/ YYYY Case number ______

District ______ When ______ MM/ DD/ YYYY Case number ______

Part 5: Sign Below

By signing here under penalty of perjury, I declare that I cannot afford to pay the filing fee either in full or in installments I also declare that the information I provided in this application is true and correct.

✘ William John Patterson
Signature of Debtor 1
William John Patterson
Date 10/18/2017
MM / DD / YYYY

✘ ______
Signature of Debtor 2
Date ______
MM / DD / YYYY

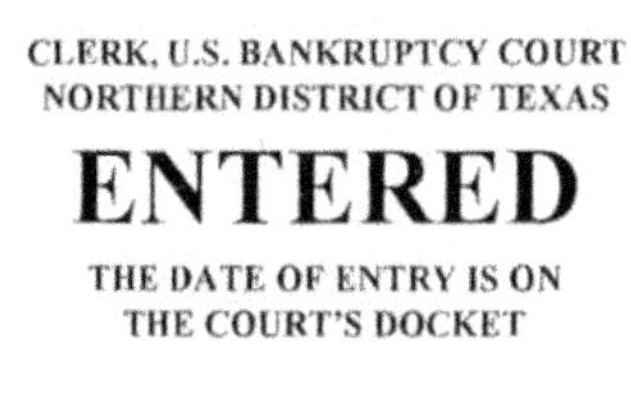
CLERK, U.S. BANKRUPTCY COURT
NORTHERN DISTRICT OF TEXAS
ENTERED
THE DATE OF ENTRY IS ON
THE COURT'S DOCKET

The following constitutes the ruling of the court and has the force and effect therein described.

Signed October 24, 2017

United States Bankruptcy Judge

B3B (rev. 04/13)

UNITED STATES BANKRUPTCY COURT
NORTHERN DISTRICT OF TEXAS

In Re: §
William John Patterson § Case No.: 17–33972–bjh7
§ Chapter No.: 7
Debtor(s) §

ORDER ON DEBTOR'S APPLICATION FOR WAIVER OF THE CHAPTER 7 FILING FEE

Upon consideration of the debtor's "Application for Waiver of the Chapter 7 Filing Fee," the court orders that the application be:

☑ GRANTED.

It is further ordered that all subsequent filing fees to be paid by the debtor shall be waived in the above referenced case until such time the case is closed. This order is subject to being vacated at a later time if developments in the administration of the bankruptcy case demonstrate that the waiver was unwarranted.

☐ DENIED.

Comments:

The debtor shall pay the chapter 7 filing fee according to the following terms:

$ on or before
$ on or before
$ on or before
$ on or before

The Debtor(s) shall make payment by cash, money order or cashier's check to the:

US BANKRUPTCY COURT
1100 Commerce Street
Room 1254
Dallas, TX 75242

Until the filing fee is paid in full, the debtor shall not make any additional payment or transfer any additional property to an attorney or any other person for services in connection with this case.

IF THE DEBTOR FAILS TO TIMELY PAY THE FILING FEE IN FULL OR TO TIMELY MAKE INSTALLMENT PAYMENTS, THE COURT MAY DISMISS THE DEBTOR'S CHAPTER 7 CASE.

☐ SCHEDULED FOR HEARING.
A hearing to consider the debtor's "Application for Waiver of the Chapter 7 Filing Fee" shall be held on at am at .

IF THE DEBTOR FAILS TO APPEAR AT THE SCHEDULED HEARING, THE COURT MAY DEEM SUCH FAILURE TO BE THE DEBTOR'S CONSENT TO THE ENTRY OF AN ORDER DENYING THE FEE WAIVER APPLICATION BY DEFAULT.

End of Order # #

HOW TO CREATE A MATRIX FOR PRO SE DEBTORS PAPER FILING

Common rules for properly formatting a creditor-mailing matrix:
1. Prepare a typed list of the names and addresses of all your creditors.
2. Creditors must be listed in a single, left column containing as many pages as are required to list all creditors. Do not include page numbers or headings in the list.
3. Margin at the top and bottom of the page must be at least one inch.
4. Use either a typewriter or computer printer with standard type.
5. Separate each creditor by at least one blank line.
6. Name and address of each creditor is limited to (5) lines. The creditor's name must be on the first line. Put the first name first, any middle initial and then the last name. Use the second line for % (care of) or Attention: [Collections Department].
7. If you have a physical address and post office box information, list both the P.O. Box information and the physical address.
8. The city/town and state abbreviation as well as the zip code must be on the last line. All states must be the standard two-letter abbreviations. Separate any nine-digit zip codes with a hyphen.
9. *Do not* include any account numbers.

Examples are as follows:

ABC Corporation
123 Main Street
Any town, TX 01010

Dr. John Doe
Medical Diagnostics and Recovery
321 First Avenue, Suite 123
Pleasantville, CO 12345

Mr. and Mrs. XYZ
500 Happy Boulevard
Anywhere, TX 12345

United States Bankruptcy Court
Northern District of Texas

In Re: William John Patterson | Case Number:

Debtor(s) | Chapter: 7

VERIFICATION OF CREDITOR MATRIX

The above named Debtors hereby verify that the attached list of creditors is true and correct to the best of their knowledge.

Date: 10/18/2017 Signature of Debtor(s): /s/ William John Patterson
/s/

MAILING MATRIX

Bank of Nashville
401 Church Street
Nashville, TN 37219

Columbus B and T/Synovus Bank
P.O. Box 120
Columbus, GA 31902

Discover Financial Services
P.O. Box 15316
Wilmington, DE 19850

FAMS
P.O. Box 1729
Woodstock, GA 30188

F.H. Cann and Associates Inc.
1600 Osgood Street Suite 20-2/120
North Andover, MA 01845

Home Depot Credit Services
P.O. Box 790328
St. Lou is, MO 63179

JH Portfolio Debt Equity
5757 Phantom Drive Suite 225
Hazelwood, MO 63042

MPD Community Credit Union
2711 Old Lebanon Rd
Nashville, TN 37214

Nashville Electric Service
1214 Church Street
Nashville, TN 37246

National Enterprise Systems
2479 Edison Boulevard, Unit A
Twinsburg, OH 44087

Penn Credit Corporation
916 South 14th Street
Harrisburg, PA 17104

Portfolio Recovery Associates
120 Corporate Boulevard, Suite 120
Norfolk, VA 23502

Portfolio Recovery Associates
P.O. Box 4115, Department 922
Concord, CA 94524

Portfolio Recovery Associates
P.O. Box 12914
Norfolk, VA 23541

Robinson, Reagan and Young, PLLC
Attorney
446 James Robertson Parkway
Nashville, TN 37246

Sallie Mae
123 Justison Street, 3rd Floor
Wilmington, DE 19801

SAM'S Club
P.O. Box 530942
Atlanta, GA 30353

SYNCB/SAM'S
P.O. Box 965005
Orlando, FL 32896

SYNOVUS BANK
1111 Bay Ave
Columbus, GA 31901

Synovus Bank
P.O. Box 120
Columbus, GA 31902

USA Funds
P.O. Box 6180
Indianapolis, IN 46206

BTXN 036 (rev. 11/16)

UNITED STATES BANKRUPTCY COURT
NORTHERN DISTRICT OF TEXAS

In Re: §
William John Patterson § Case No.: 17-33972-bjh7
§ Chapter No.: 7
Debtor(s) §

NOTICE OF DEFICIENCY

Notice is hereby given to the Debtor(s) that the Original Petition and/or Other Document(s) filed is/are deficient for one or more of the following reasons:

- ☐ A mailing matrix containing an alphabetical listing of all creditors, was not filed with the petition as required by N.D. TX L.B.R. 1007-1(a). The mailing matrix must be filed **within 48 hours** of the date of this notice.
- ☐ Tax ID Number must be provided **within 48 hours** of the date of this notice.
- ☐ Debtor(s)' chapter 13 plan or plan summary was not filed with the petition. The plan or plan summary in a form acceptable to the Trustee must be filed **within 14 days** of the date of the filing of the petition (Bankruptcy Rule 3015).
- ☐ Debtor(s)' chapter 13 plan or plan summary must be filed **within 14 days** from the date of the order of conversion (Bankruptcy Rule 3015).
- ☑ Debtor(s)' schedules C were not filed with the petition. The schedules must be filed **within 14 days** of the date of the filing of the petition (Bankruptcy Rule 1007(c)).
- ☐ Debtor(s)' statement of financial affairs was not filed with the petition. The statement of financial affairs must be filed **within 14 days** of the date of filing of the petition (Bankruptcy Rule 1007(c)).
- ☐ Attorney Fee Disclosure must be filed **within 14 days** of the date of the filing of the petition.
- ☐ Adversary Cover Sheet (Form 1040) not filed with the complaint. Form 1040 must be filed with the court **within 2 days** from the date of this notice.
- ☐ Summary of Assets and Liabilities (Official Form 106Sum or 206Sum) not provided at the time of filing. Official Form 106Sum or 206Sum must be filed **within 14 days** of the date of the filing of the petition.
- ☐ Portions of the original petition were not answered or provided at the time of filing. An amended petition including the items indicated below must be filed **within 3 days** from the issuance of this notice.
- ☐ Twenty Largest Unsecured Creditors must be filed **within 48 hours** of the date of the filing of the petition.
- ☐ This case was filed without docketing a Form 121 Statement of Social Security Number. Form 121 must be filed with the court within 48 hours of the date of the petition pursuant to L.B.R. 1007-1(d). If a debtor Social Security Number was erroneously entered by you in this case, you must notify all parties and credit reporting agencies of the correct Social Security Number information.
- ☐ Certificate from an approved credit counselor of completion of a briefing received **prior to the filing** of the petition must be provided **within ### days** of the date of the filing of the petition. If the briefing was not completed prior to the petition date, the debtor must submit to the court a certification that complies with the requirements of 11 USC 109(h)(3)(A).
- ☑ Copies of employee income records must be provided **within 14 days** of the date of the filing of the petition.
- ☐ Statement of Current Monthly Income must be provided **within 14 days** of the date of the filing of the petition.
- ☐ Chapter 15 Service List must be provided **within 14 days** of the date of the filing of the petition.

– continued –

☐ Cash flow statement must be provided **within 7 days** from the issuance of this notice.

☐ Statement of operations must be provided **within 7 days** from the issuance of this notice.

☐ Balance sheet must be provided **within 7 days** from the issuance of this notice.

☐ Other:

Failure to comply with the N.D. TX L.B.R.'s and 11 U.S.C. § 521 to cure any or all of the deficiencies noted above shall subject this petition to dismissal without further notice.

BTXN 027 (rev. 06/13)

UNITED STATES BANKRUPTCY COURT
NORTHERN DISTRICT OF TEXAS

In Re:	§	
William John Patterson	§	Case No.: 17−33972−bjh7
	§	Chapter No.: 7
Debtor(s)	§	

Dear William:

The above referenced case has been reviewed as part of the Clerk's Office continuing effort to identify cases that are deficient for specific documents. Our review indicates that this case requires:

- ☐ Interim Report
- ☐ Trustee's Final Account
- ☐ Trustee's Final Report
- ☐ 341 Meeting Minute Sheet and Exempt Property Report
- ☐ Report of Trustee in No−Asset Case and Application for Closing
- ☐ Motion to Dismiss debtor's Failure to Attend 341 Meeting
- ☑ Other: The Clerk's will need a copy of a ID and your Social Security Card. You will also need to turn in the cover sheet for the verification of mailing matrix

Please electronically file the requested documents, provide a specific date for which this information will be provided to the Court, or provide information as to why this case should remain open. Failure to respond within 5 days from the date of this letter may result in the Court setting a status conference to determine why the document(s) has not been filed or the matter may be denied for want of prosecution.

DATED: 10/23/17

FOR THE COURT:
Jed G. Weintraub, Clerk of Court

by: /s/Bill Rielly, Deputy Clerk
bill_rielly@txnb.uscourts.gov

Clerk of the United States Bankruptcy Court
Northern District of Texas, Dallas Division
1100 Commerce Street, Room 1254
Dallas, TX 75242

October 18, 2017

Re: WILLIAM JOHN PATTERSON, pro se
Chapter 7 filing

Dear Clerk:

I am an incarcerated inmate without access to the internet or the ability to create pdf electronic files or email them to you. Accordingly, I request leave to commence this Chapter 7 case via paper filing and submit the enclosed documents to do so. I have studied the local rules of court and believe the enclosed papers should be sufficient to comply with all filing and service requirments. Please do not hesitate to contact me by U.S. Mail at the address below should you require anything additional from me. Please include my Federal inmate number #21450-075 in my mailing address or I will be unable to receive and respond to correspondence from your office.

Enclosed for filing are:
(1) Voluntary Petition, Form 101;
(2) Application to Have the Chapter 7 Filing Fee Waived, Form 103B;
(3) Statement about your SSN, Form 121 -- **to be filed under seal**;
(4) Summary of your Assets and liabilities, etc., Form 106Sum;
(5) Declaration about an Individual Debtor's Schedules, Form 106Dec;
(6) Schedule A/B: Property, Form 106A/B;
(7) Schedule D: Creditors who have claims secured by Prop., Form 106D;
(8) Schedule E/F: Creditors who have unsecured claims, Form 106E/F;
(9) Schedule G: Executory contracts and unexpired leases, Form 106G;
(10) Schedule H: Your Codebtors, Form 106H;
(11) Schedule I: Your income, Form B6I;
(12) Schedule J: Your expenses, Form B6J;
(13) Statement of Financial Affairs for Individuals, From 107;
(14) Statement of Current Monthly Income, Form 122A-1;
(15) Mailing Matrix; and
(16) Certificate of Counseling.

Thank you for filing this material and please send me acknowledgment of your office doing so.

Sincerely,
William John Patterson

William John Patterson, #215450-075
Federal Correctional Institution
P. O. Box 9000
Seagoville, TX 75159-9000

CHAPTER 6:
STEP IV: SCHEDULES

OVERVIEW AND INSTRUCTIONS

When a bankruptcy is filed, the U.S. Bankruptcy Court opens a case. It is important that the answers to the questions on the forms be complete and accurate so that the case proceeds smoothly. You should understand that filing a bankruptcy is not private. Anyone has a right to see your bankruptcy forms after you file them, unless the court orders otherwise under 11 U.S.C. §107. Certain information in court filings, however, must be protected from public disclosure under Bankruptcy Rule 9037.

Things to remember when filling out these forms:

- Be as complete and accurate as possible.
- If more space is needed, attach a separate sheet to the form. On the top of any additional pages, write your name and case number (if known). Also identify the form and line numbers to which the additional information applies.
- Do not list a minor child's full name. Instead fill in only the child's initials and the full name and address of the child's parent or guardian. 11 U.S.C. §112; Bankruptcy Rule 1007(m) and 9037.
- For your records, be sure to keep a copy of your bankruptcy documents and all attachments to your file.

When a debt was incurred on a single date, fill in the actual date the debt was incurred. When a debt was incurred on multiple dates, fill in the range of dates. For example, if the debt is from a credit card, fill in the month and year of the first and last transaction. Note: You'll notice when reviewing my example forms that many of the form numbers may differ slightly from the current forms provided in Chapter 10. I have attempted to provide you with the most up to date sample forms and information related to each schedule.

SCHEDULE A/B: PROPERTY (FORM 106A/B)

All property interests that are involved in a bankruptcy case are listed on a "Schedule A/B: Property (Form 106 A/B)." All individuals filing for a bankruptcy must list everything they own or have a legal or equitable interest in. "Legal or equitable interests" is a broad term and includes all kinds of property interests in both tangible and intangible property, whether or not anyone else has an interest in that property.

The information in this form is grouped by category and includes several examples for many items: Note that those examples are meant to give you an idea of what to include in the categories. They are not intended to be complete lists of everything within that category. Make sure you list everything you own or have an interest in.

You must verify under penalty of perjury that the information you provide is complete and accurate. Making a false statement, concealing property, or obtaining money or property by fraud in connection with a bankruptcy case can result in fines up to $250,000, or imprisonment for up to 20 years, or both. 18 U.S.C. §§152, 1341, 1519, and 3571.

To make sure you understand the terms used on this form, I recommend you review both "community property" and "current value" located in the glossary.

For each question, report the current value of the portion of the property that you own. To do this, you would usually determine the current value of the entire property and the percentage of the property that you own. Multiply the current value of the property by the percentage that you own. Report the result where the form asks for Current value of the portion you own. For example:

- If you own a house by yourself, you own 100% of that house. Report the entire current value of the house.
- If you and a sister own the house equally, report 50% of the value of the house (or half of the value of the house).

In certain categories, current value may be difficult to figure out. When you cannot find the value from a reputable source (such as a pricing guide for your car), estimate the value, and be prepared to explain how you determined it.

List items only once on this form; do not list them in more than one category. List all real estate in Part 1 and other property in the other parts of the form.

Where you list similar items of minimal value (such as clothing), add the value of the items, and report a total.

Be specific when you describe each item. If you have an item that you think could fit into more than one category, select the most suitable category, and list the item there.

Separately describe and list individual items worth more than $500.

Make sure that the values you report on this form match the values you report on "Schedule D: Creditors Who Have Claims Secured by Your Property (Form 106)" and "Schedule C: The Property You Claim as Exempt (Form 106C)."

An example of my schedule A/B can be found at the end of this chapter.

SCHEDULE C: PROPERTY CLAIMED AS EXEMPT (FORM 106C)
If you are an individual filing for bankruptcy, the law may allow you to keep some property, or it may entitle you to part of the proceeds if the property is sold after your case is filed. Property that the law permits you to keep is called exempt property. For example, exemptions may enable you to keep your home, a car, clothing, and household items.

Exemptions are not automatic. For property to be considered exempt, you must list the property on "Schedule C: The Property You Claim as Exempt (Form 106C)." If you do not list the property, the trustee may sell it and pay all of the proceeds to your creditors. You may unnecessarily lose property if you do not claim exemptions to which you are entitled. This is when hiring a qualified attorney may be beneficial.

Before you fill out this form, you must learn which set of exemptions you can use. In general, exemptions are determined on a state-by-state basis. Some states permit you to use the exemptions provided by the Bankruptcy Code 11 U.S.C. §522.

The Bankruptcy Code provides that you use the exemptions in the law of the state where you had your legal home for 730 days before you file for bankruptcy. Special rules may apply if you did not have the same home state for 730 days before you file. You may lose property if you do not use the best set of exemptions for your situation.

If your spouse is filing with you and you are filing in a state in which you may choose between state and federal sets of bankruptcy exemptions, you both must use the same set of exemptions.

Using the property and values that you list on "Schedule A/B: Property (Form 106A/B)" as your source, list on this form the property that you claim as exempt. For each item of property you claim as exempt, you must specify the amount of the exemption you claim. Usually, a specific dollar amount is claimed as exempt, but in some circumstances the amount of the exemption claimed might be indicated as 100% of fair market value. For example, you might claim 100% of fair market value for an exemption that is unlimited in dollar amount, such as some exemptions for health aids.

In the last column of the form, you must identify the laws that allow you to claim the property as exempt. If you have additional questions about exemptions you may want to consult a qualified attorney. An example of my Schedule C can be found at the end of this chapter.

SCHEDULE D: CREDITORS WITH SECURED CLAIMS (FORM 106D)
The people or organizations to which you owe money are called your creditors. A claim is a creditor's right to payment. When you file for bankruptcy, the court needs to know who all your creditors are and what types of claims they have against you.

Typically, in bankruptcy cases, there are more debts than assets to pay those debts. The court must know as much as possible about your creditors to make sure that their claims are properly treated according to the rules.

Creditors may have different types of claims:

• Secured Claims – Report these on "Schedule D: Creditors Who Have Claims Secured by Property (Form 106D)."
• Unsecured Claims – Report these on "Schedule E/F: Creditors Who Have Unsecured Claims (Form 106E/F)."

If your debts are not paid, a creditor with a secured claim may be able to get paid from specific property in which that creditor has an interest, such as a mortgage or a lien. That property is sometimes called "collateral" and could include items such as your house, your car, or your furniture. Creditors with unsecured claims do not have rights against specific property.

Many creditors' claims have a specific amount, which you do not dispute. However, some claims are uncertain when you file for bankruptcy, or they become due only after you file. You must list the claims of all your creditors in your schedules, even if the claims are contingent, unliquidated, or disputed

Claims may be: Contingent, Unliquidated, or Disputed. The definitions of each can be located in the glossary. A single claim can have one, more than one, or none of these characteristics. On your "Schedule D (Form 106D)" list all creditors who have a claim that is secured by your property.

Do not leave out any secured creditors. In alphabetical order (as much as possible), list anyone who has judgment liens, garnishments, statutory liens, mortgage, deeds of trust, and other security interests against your property. When listing creditors who have secured claims, be sure to include all of them. For example, include the following:
• Your relatives or friends who have a lien or security interest in your property;
• Vehicle lenders, stores, banks, credit unions, and others who made loans to enable you to finance the purchase of property and who have a lien against that property;
• Anyone who has a mortgage or deed of trust on real estate that you own;
• Contractors or mechanics that have liens on property you own because they did work on the property and were not paid;
• Someone who won a lawsuit against you and has a judgment lien;
• Another parent or government agency that has a lien for unpaid child support;
• Doctors or attorneys who have liens on the outcome of a lawsuit;
• Federal, state or local government agencies such as the IRS that have tax liens against property for unpaid taxes; and
• Anyone who is trying to collect a secured debt from you, such as collection agencies and attorneys.

List the debt in Part 1 only once and list any others that should be notified about the debt in Part 2. For example, if a collection agency or an attorney is trying to collect from you for a debt you owe to someone else, list the person whom you owe the debt in Part 1, and list the collection agency in Part 2. If you are not sure who the creditor is, list the person you are paying in Part 1 and list anyone else who has contacted you in about this in Part 2.

If a creditor's full claim is more than the value of your property securing that claim – for instance, a car loan in an amount greater than the value of the car – the creditor's claim may be partly secured and partly unsecured. In that situation, list the claim only once on "Schedule

D (Form 106D)." Do not repeat it on "Schedule E/F (Form 106E/F)." List a creditor in "Schedule D," even if it appears that there is no value to support that creditor's secured claim.

To determine the amount of a secured claim, compare the amount of the claim to the value of your portion of the property that supports the claim. If that value is greater than the amount of the claim, then the entire amount of the claim is secured. But if that value is less than the amount of the claim, the difference is an unsecured portion. For example, if the outstanding balance of a vehicle loan is $10,000 and the vehicle is worth $8,000, the vehicle loan has a $2,000 unsecured portion.

If there is more than one secured claim against the same property, the claim that is entitled to be paid first must be subtracted from the property value to determine how much value remains for the next claim. For example, if a home worth $300,000 has a first mortgage of $200,000 and a second mortgage of $150,000, the first mortgage would be fully secured, and there would be $100,000 of property value for the second mortgage, which would have an unsecured portion of $50,000.

An example of my "Schedule D" can be found at the end of this chapter.

SCHEDULE E/F: CREDITORS WITH UNSECURED CLAIMS (FORM 106E/F)

As discussed in the previous section, the people or organizations to which you owe money are called your creditors. A claim is a creditor's right to payment. When you file for bankruptcy, the court needs to know who all your creditors are and what types of claims they have against you.

Use "Schedule E/F: Creditors Who Have Unsecured Claims (Form 106E/F)" to identify everyone who has an unsecured claim against you when you file your bankruptcy petition, unless you have already listed them on "Schedule D: Creditors Who Have Claims Secured by Your Property (Form 106D)."

In the case of unsecured claims there is no property used as collateral for your debt. Creditors with unsecured claims do not have rights against specific property.

Many creditors' claims have a specific amount, which you do not dispute. However, some claims are uncertain when you file for bankruptcy, or they become due only after you file. You must list the claims of all your creditors in your schedules, even if the claims are contingent, unliquidated, or disputed. Again, as stated previously, claims may be: Contingent, Unliquidated, or Disputed. The definition of all 3 of these can be located in the glossary. A single claim can have *one*, *more than one*, or *none* of these characteristics.

Creditors with unsecured claims do not have liens on or other security interests in your property. It is secured creditors that have a right to take property if you do not pay them. Common examples are lenders for your vehicle, your home, or your furniture.

List all unsecured creditors in each part of the form in alphabetical order as much as possible. Do to the vast number of unsecured creditors, I had to make multiple page copies of Part 2 in order to list them all. Even if you plan to pay a creditor, you must list that creditor. When listing creditors who have unsecured claims, be sure to include all of them. For instance, include the following:

• Your relatives or friends to whom you owe money;

• Your ex-spouse, if you are still obligated under a divorce decree or settlement agreement to pay joint debts;

• A credit card company, even if you intend to fully pay your credit card bill;

• A lender, even if the loan is cosigned;

• Anyone who has a loan or promissory note that you cosigned for someone else;

• Anyone who has sued or may sue you because of an accident, dispute, or similar event that has occurred; or

• Anyone who is trying to collect a debt from you such as a bill collector or attorney.

In bankruptcy cases, priority unsecured claims are those debts that the Bankruptcy Code requires to be paid before most other unsecured claims are paid. The most common priority unsecured claims are certain income tax debts and past due alimony or child support. Priority unsecured claims include those you owe for:

• Domestic support obligations – If you owe domestic support to a spouse or former spouse; a child or the parent, legal guardian, or responsible relative of a child; or a governmental unit to whom such a domestic support claim has been assigned. 11 U.S.C. §507 (a)(1).

• Taxes and certain other debts you owe the government – If you owe certain federal, state, or local government taxes, customs duties, or penalties. 11 U.S.C. §507 (a)(8).

• Claims for death or personal injury that you caused while you were intoxicated – If you have a claim against you for death or personal injury that resulted from you unlawfully operating a motor vehicle or vessel while you were unlawfully intoxicated from alcohol, drugs, or another substance. This priority does not apply to claims for property damage. 11 U.S.C. §507 (a)(10).

• Other:

1. Deposits by individuals – If you received money from someone for the purchase, lease, or rental of your property or the use of your services but you never delivered or performed. For the debt to have priority, the property or services must have been intended for personal, family, or household use (only the first $2,850 per person is a priority debt).[1] [11 U.S.C. §507 (a)(7)]

2. Wages, salaries, and commissions – If you owe wages, salaries, and commissions, including vacation, severance, and sick leave pay and those amounts were earned within 180 days before you filed your bankruptcy petition or ceased business. In either instance, on the first $12,850 per claim is a priority debt.[2] [11 U.S.C. §507 (a)(4)]

3. Contributions to employee benefit plans – If you owe contributions to an employee benefit plan for services an employee rendered within 180 days before you file your bankruptcy petition, or within 180 days before your business ends. Count only the first $12,850 per employee, less any amounts owed for wages, salaries, and commissions.[3] [11 U.S.C. §507 (a)(5)]

---

[1] Subject to adjustment on 04/01/19, and every 3 years after that for cases begun on or after the date of adjustment.

[2] Subject to adjustment on 04/01/19, and every 3 years after that for cases begun on or after the date of adjustment.

[3] Subject to adjustment on 04/01/19, and every 3 years after that for cases begun on or after the date of adjustment.

Nonpriority unsecured claims are those debts that generally will be paid after priority unsecured claims are paid. The most common examples of nonpriority unsecured claims are credit card bills, medical bills, and educational loans.

If a claim has both priority and nonpriority amounts, list that claim in Part 2 and show both priority and nonpriority amounts. Do not list it again in Part 3.

In Part 3 list all of the creditors you have not listed before. You must list every creditor that you owe and even if you plan to pay a particular debt. If you do not list a debt, it may not be discharged.

An example of my “Schedule E/F” can be found at the end of this chapter.

SCHEDULE G: EXECUTORY CONTRACTS AND UNEXPIRED LEASES (FORM 106G)
Use “Schedule G” to identify your ongoing leases and certain contracts. List all of your executory contracts and unexpired leases. Executory contracts are contracts between you and someone else in which neither you nor the other party has performed all the requirements by the time you file for bankruptcy. Unexpired leases are leases that are still in effect; the lease period has not yet ended.

You must list all agreements that may be executory contracts or unexpired leases, even if they are listed on “Schedule A/B: Property (Form 106A/B)” including the following:

- Residential leases (for example, a rental agreement for a place where you live or vacation, even if it is only a verbal or month-to-month arrangement);
- Service provider agreements (for example, contracts for cell phones) and personal electronic devices);
- Internet and cable contracts;
- Vehicle leases;
- Supplier or service contracts (for example, contracts for lawn care or home alarm or security systems);
- Timeshare contracts or leases;
- Rent-to-own contracts;
- Employment contracts;
- Real estate listing agreements;
- Contracts to sell a residence, building, land, or other real property
- Equipment leases;
- Leases for business or investment property;
- Supplier and service contracts for your business;
- Copyright and patent license agreements; and
- Development contracts.

An example of my “Schedule G” can be found at the end of this chapter.

SCHEDULE H: CODEBTORS (FORM 106H)
If you have any debts that someone else may also be responsible for paying these people or entities are called codebtors. Use “Schedule H” to list any codebtors who are responsible for any debts you have listed on the other schedules. To help fill out this form, use both “Schedule D” and “Schedule E/F”. List all your codebtors and the creditors to whom you owe the debt.

For example, if someone cosigned for the vehicle loan that you owe, you must list that person on this form. Note: If you are filing a joint case, do not list either spouse as a codebtor.

Other codebtors could include the following: cosigner, guarantor, former spouse, unmarried partner, joint contractor, or a nonfiling spouse – even if the spouse is not a cosigner – where the debt is for necessities (such as food or medical care) if state law makes the nonfiling spouse legally responsible for debts for necessities. An example of my "Schedule H" can be found at the end of this chapter.

SCHEDULE I: CURRENT INCOME (FORM 106I)

In "Schedule I" you will give the details about your employment and monthly income as of the date you file this form. If you are married and your spouse is living with you, include information about your spouse even if your spouse is not filing with you. If you are separated and your spouse is not filing with you, do not include information about your spouse.
It will be your decision and contingent on your interpretation on how to best answer the employment income question while incarcerated. Although I received a very small payment each month at the time of my filing, I did not consider it employment because of my incarceration status. However, I acknowledged my monthly income in the "other monthly income" section. Since, choosing that option, I should have specified it as "maintenance pay" next to the "other monthly income" line. Either of these should be acceptable since the most important issue is the disclosure of all your income. If you have nothing to report for a line, write $0.

In Part 1, line 1, fill in employment information for you and, if appropriate, for a non-filing spouse. If either person has more than one employer, attach a separate page with information about the additional employment.

In Part 2, give details about your monthly income you currently expect to receive. Show all totals as monthly payments, even if income is not received in monthly payments. If your income is received in another time period, such as daily, weekly, quarterly, annually, or irregularly, calculate how much income would be by month. One easy way to calculate how much income per month is to total the payments earned in a year, then divide by 12 to get a monthly figure.

In Part 2, line 11, fill in the amounts that other people provide to pay the expenses you list on "Schedule J." In most cases this will not apply to inmates. An example would be if you and a person to whom you are not married pay all household expenses together and you list all your joint household expenses on "Schedule J," you must list the amounts that person contributes monthly to pay the household expenses on line 11. Do not list on line 11 contributions that you already disclosed elsewhere on the form.

Note that the income you report on "Schedule I" may be different from the income you report on the other bankruptcy forms. For example, the Chapter 7 "Statement of Your Current Monthly Income (Form 122A-1)" uses a different definition of income and applies that definition to a different period of time. "Schedule I" asks about the income that you are now receiving, while the other forms ask about income you received in the applicable time period before filing. So, the amount of income reported in any of those forms may be different from the amount reported here. An example of my "Schedule I" can be found at the end of this chapter.

SCHEDULE J: CURRENT EXPENSES (FORM 106J AND 106J-2)
Your "Schedule J" provides an estimate of the monthly expenses, as of the date you file for bankruptcy, for you, your dependents, and the other people (if any) in your household whose income is included on your "Schedule I." If you are married and are filing individually, include your non-filing spouse's expenses unless you are separated. If you are filing jointly and you and Debtor 2 keep separate households, Debtor 2 must complete and include a "Schedule J-2 (Form 106J-2)."

Do not include expenses that other members of your household (if any) pay directly from their income if you did not include that income on your "Schedule I." Show all totals as monthly payments. If you have weekly, quarterly, or annual payments, calculate how much you would spend on those items every month. I reached my monthly total expenses by reviewing my prior six months of commissary receipts and phone costs in order to calculate my monthly average of expenses.

Do not list as expenses any payments on credit card debts incurred before filing bankruptcy. Do not include business expenses on this form. You have already accounted for those expenses as part of determining net business income on "Schedule I."

On line 20, do not include expenses for your residence (if any) or for any rental or business property. You have already listed expenses for those items on lines 4 and 5 of this form as well as line 8a on "Schedule I." If you have nothing to report for a line, write $0. An example of my "Schedule J" can be found at the end of this chapter.

SUMMARY OF ASSETS, LIABILITIES, AND STATISTICAL INFORMATION (FORM 106SUM)

When you file for bankruptcy, you must summarize certain information from the following forms:
- Schedule A/B (Form 106A/B)
- Schedule E/F (Form 106E/F)
- Schedule J (Form 106J)
- Schedule D (Form 106D)
- Schedule I (Form 106I)
- Statement of Your Current Monthly Income (Form 122A-1)

After you fill out all of these forms, complete "Summary of Your Assets and Liabilities and Certain Statistical Information (Form 106Sum)" to report the totals of certain information that you listed on the forms. If you are filing an amended version of any of these forms at some time after you file your original forms, you must fill out a new "Summary (Form 106Sum)" to ensure that your information is up to date and you must check the box at the top. An example of my "Summary (Form 106Sum)" can be found at the end of this chapter.

DECLARATION OF DEBTOR'S SCHEDULES (FORM 106DEC)

Once you have completed all the required schedules, sign and date the "Declaration about an Individuals Debtors Schedules," thereby declaring under penalty of perjury that you have read the foregoing summary and schedules and they are true and correct to the best of your knowledge, information, and belief. An example of my "Declaration of Debtor's Schedule" can be found at the end of this chapter.

Fill in this information to identify your case and this filing:

Debtor 1 William John Patterson
First Name Middle Name Last Name

Debtor 2
(Spouse, if filing) First Name Middle Name Last Name

United States Bankruptcy Court for the: Northern District of Texas

Case number ______

☐ Check if this is an amended filing

Official Form 106A/B

Schedule A/B: Property

12/15

In each category, separately list and describe items. List an asset only once. If an asset fits in more than one category, list the asset in the category where you think it fits best. Be as complete and accurate as possible. If two married people are filing together, both are equally responsible for supplying correct information. If more space is needed, attach a separate sheet to this form. On the top of any additional pages, write your name and case number (if known). Answer every question.

Part 1: Describe Each Residence, Building, Land, or Other Real Estate You Own or Have an Interest In

1. **Do you own or have any legal or equitable interest in any residence, building, land, or similar property?**

☒ No. Go to Part 2.
☐ Yes. Where is the property?

1.1. ______
Street address, if available, or other description
______
City State ZIP Code
______
County

What is the property? Check all that apply.
☐ Single-family home
☐ Duplex or multi-unit building
☐ Condominium or cooperative
☐ Manufactured or mobile home
☐ Land
☐ Investment property
☐ Timeshare
☐ Other ______

Who has an interest in the property? Check one.
☐ Debtor 1 only
☐ Debtor 2 only
☐ Debtor 1 and Debtor 2 only
☐ At least one of the debtors and another

Other information you wish to add about this item, such as local property identification number: ______

Do not deduct secured claims or exemptions. Put the amount of any secured claims on Schedule D: Creditors Who Have Claims Secured by Property.

Current value of the entire property? $______
Current value of the portion you own? $______

Describe the nature of your ownership interest (such as fee simple, tenancy by the entireties, or a life estate), if known. ______

☐ **Check if this is community property** (see instructions)

If you own or have more than one, list here:

1.2. ______
Street address, if available, or other description
______
City State ZIP Code
______
County

What is the property? Check all that apply.
☐ Single-family home
☐ Duplex or multi-unit building
☐ Condominium or cooperative
☐ Manufactured or mobile home
☐ Land
☐ Investment property
☐ Timeshare
☐ Other ______

Who has an interest in the property? Check one.
☐ Debtor 1 only
☐ Debtor 2 only
☐ Debtor 1 and Debtor 2 only
☐ At least one of the debtors and another

Other information you wish to add about this item, such as local property identification number: ______

Do not deduct secured claims or exemptions. Put the amount of any secured claims on Schedule D: Creditors Who Have Claims Secured by Property.

Current value of the entire property? $______
Current value of the portion you own? $______

Describe the nature of your ownership interest (such as fee simple, tenancy by the entireties, or a life estate), if known. ______

☐ **Check if this is community property** (see instructions)

Debtor 1 William John Patterson
First Name Middle Name Last Name

Case number (if known) ______

1.3. ______
Street address, if available, or other description

______

City State ZIP Code

______
County

What is the property? Check all that apply.
- ☐ Single-family home
- ☐ Duplex or multi-unit building
- ☐ Condominium or cooperative
- ☐ Manufactured or mobile home
- ☐ Land
- ☐ Investment property
- ☐ Timeshare
- ☐ Other ______

Who has an interest in the property? Check one.
- ☐ Debtor 1 only
- ☐ Debtor 2 only
- ☐ Debtor 1 and Debtor 2 only
- ☐ At least one of the debtors and another

Other information you wish to add about this item, such as local property identification number: ______

Do not deduct secured claims or exemptions. Put the amount of any secured claims on *Schedule D: Creditors Who Have Claims Secured by Property.*

Current value of the entire property? $______

Current value of the portion you own? $______

Describe the nature of your ownership interest (such as fee simple, tenancy by the entireties, or a life estate), if known.

______

☐ Check if this is community property (see instructions)

2. **Add the dollar value of the portion you own for all of your entries from Part 1, including any entries for pages you have attached for Part 1. Write that number here.** .... → $0.00

Part 2: Describe Your Vehicles

Do you own, lease, or have legal or equitable interest in any vehicles, whether they are registered or not? Include any vehicles you own that someone else drives. If you lease a vehicle, also report it on *Schedule G: Executory Contracts and Unexpired Leases.*

3. **Cars, vans, trucks, tractors, sport utility vehicles, motorcycles**
- ☒ No
- ☐ Yes

3.1. Make: ______
Model: ______
Year: ______
Approximate mileage: ______
Other information:

Who has an interest in the property? Check one.
- ☐ Debtor 1 only
- ☐ Debtor 2 only
- ☐ Debtor 1 and Debtor 2 only
- ☐ At least one of the debtors and another

☐ Check if this is community property (see instructions)

Do not deduct secured claims or exemptions. Put the amount of any secured claims on *Schedule D: Creditors Who Have Claims Secured by Property.*

Current value of the entire property? $______

Current value of the portion you own? $______

If you own or have more than one, describe here:

3.2. Make: ______
Model: ______
Year: ______
Approximate mileage: ______
Other information:

Who has an interest in the property? Check one.
- ☐ Debtor 1 only
- ☐ Debtor 2 only
- ☐ Debtor 1 and Debtor 2 only
- ☐ At least one of the debtors and another

☐ Check if this is community property (see instructions)

Do not deduct secured claims or exemptions. Put the amount of any secured claims on *Schedule D: Creditors Who Have Claims Secured by Property.*

Current value of the entire property? $______

Current value of the portion you own? $______

Official Form 106A/B **Schedule A/B: Property** page 2

Debtor 1 William John Patterson (First Name, Middle Name, Last Name) Case number (if known) ____________

3.3. Make: ________
Model: ________
Year: ________
Approximate mileage: ________
Other information:

Who has an interest in the property? Check one.
- ❑ Debtor 1 only
- ❑ Debtor 2 only
- ❑ Debtor 1 and Debtor 2 only
- ❑ At least one of the debtors and another

❑ Check if this is community property (see instructions)

Do not deduct secured claims or exemptions. Put the amount of any secured claims on *Schedule D: Creditors Who Have Claims Secured by Property.*

Current value of the entire property? $________
Current value of the portion you own? $________

3.4. Make: ________
Model: ________
Year: ________
Approximate mileage: ________
Other information:

Who has an interest in the property? Check one.
- ❑ Debtor 1 only
- ❑ Debtor 2 only
- ❑ Debtor 1 and Debtor 2 only
- ❑ At least one of the debtors and another

❑ Check if this is community property (see instructions)

Do not deduct secured claims or exemptions. Put the amount of any secured claims on *Schedule D: Creditors Who Have Claims Secured by Property.*

Current value of the entire property? $________
Current value of the portion you own? $________

4. **Watercraft, aircraft, motor homes, ATVs and other recreational vehicles, other vehicles, and accessories**
Examples: Boats, trailers, motors, personal watercraft, fishing vessels, snowmobiles, motorcycle accessories

☒ No
❑ Yes

4.1. Make: ________
Model: ________
Year: ________
Other information:

Who has an interest in the property? Check one.
- ❑ Debtor 1 only
- ❑ Debtor 2 only
- ❑ Debtor 1 and Debtor 2 only
- ❑ At least one of the debtors and another

❑ Check if this is community property (see instructions)

Do not deduct secured claims or exemptions. Put the amount of any secured claims on *Schedule D: Creditors Who Have Claims Secured by Property.*

Current value of the entire property? $________
Current value of the portion you own? $________

If you own or have more than one, list here:

4.2. Make: ________
Model: ________
Year: ________
Other information:

Who has an interest in the property? Check one.
- ❑ Debtor 1 only
- ❑ Debtor 2 only
- ❑ Debtor 1 and Debtor 2 only
- ❑ At least one of the debtors and another

❑ Check if this is community property (see instructions)

Do not deduct secured claims or exemptions. Put the amount of any secured claims on *Schedule D: Creditors Who Have Claims Secured by Property.*

Current value of the entire property? $________
Current value of the portion you own? $________

5. **Add the dollar value of the portion you own for all of your entries from Part 2, including any entries for pages you have attached for Part 2. Write that number here** .... → $ 0.00

Debtor 1 William John Patterson — First Name, Middle Name, Last Name

Case number (if known) ______

Part 3: Describe Your Personal and Household Items

Do you own or have any legal or equitable interest in any of the following items?

Current value of the portion you own? Do not deduct secured claims or exemptions.

6. **Household goods and furnishings**
Examples: Major appliances, furniture, linens, china, kitchenware
☒ No
☐ Yes. Describe........ $______

7. **Electronics**
Examples: Televisions and radios; audio, video, stereo, and digital equipment; computers, printers, scanners; music collections; electronic devices including cell phones, cameras, media players, games
☒ No
☐ Yes. Describe........ $______

8. **Collectibles of value**
Examples: Antiques and figurines; paintings, prints, or other artwork; books, pictures, or other art objects; stamp, coin, or baseball card collections; other collections, memorabilia, collectibles
☒ No
☐ Yes. Describe........ $______

9. **Equipment for sports and hobbies**
Examples: Sports, photographic, exercise, and other hobby equipment; bicycles, pool tables, golf clubs, skis; canoes and kayaks; carpentry tools; musical instruments
☒ No
☐ Yes. Describe........ $______

10. **Firearms**
Examples: Pistols, rifles, shotguns, ammunition, and related equipment
☒ No
☐ Yes. Describe........ $______

11. **Clothes**
Examples: Everyday clothes, furs, leather coats, designer wear, shoes, accessories
☒ No
☐ Yes. Describe........ $______

12. **Jewelry**
Examples: Everyday jewelry, costume jewelry, engagement rings, wedding rings, heirloom jewelry, watches, gems, gold, silver
☒ No
☐ Yes. Describe........ $______

13. **Non-farm animals**
Examples: Dogs, cats, birds, horses
☒ No
☐ Yes. Describe........ $______

14. **Any other personal and household items you did not already list, including any health aids you did not list**
☒ No
☐ Yes. Give specific information. .... $______

15. **Add the dollar value of all of your entries from Part 3, including any entries for pages you have attached for Part 3. Write that number here** .... → $ 0.00

Debtor 1 William John Patterson — Case number (if known) ____

First Name / Middle Name / Last Name

Part 4: Describe Your Financial Assets

Do you own or have any legal or equitable interest in any of the following?

Current value of the portion you own?
Do not deduct secured claims or exemptions.

16. Cash

Examples: Money you have in your wallet, in your home, in a safe deposit box, and on hand when you file your petition

- [x] No
- [ ] Yes .... Cash: .... $____

17. Deposits of money

Examples: Checking, savings, or other financial accounts; certificates of deposit; shares in credit unions, brokerage houses, and other similar institutions. If you have multiple accounts with the same institution, list each.

- [ ] No
- [x] Yes .... Institution name:

	Institution name	
17.1. Checking account:		$
17.2. Checking account:		$
17.3. Savings account:		$
17.4. Savings account:		$
17.5. Certificates of deposit:		$
17.6. Other financial account:	Federal inmate account	$ 95.00
17.7. Other financial account:		$
17.8. Other financial account:		$
17.9. Other financial account:		$

18. Bonds, mutual funds, or publicly traded stocks

Examples: Bond funds, investment accounts with brokerage firms, money market accounts

- [x] No
- [ ] Yes .... Institution or issuer name:

Institution or issuer name	
	$
	$
	$

19. Non-publicly traded stock and interests in incorporated and unincorporated businesses, including an interest in an LLC, partnership, and joint venture

- [x] No
- [ ] Yes. Give specific information about them........

Name of entity:	% of ownership:	
	0% %	$
	0% %	$
	0% %	$

Official Form 106A/B — Schedule A/B: Property — page 5

Debtor 1 William John Patterson
First Name Middle Name Last Name
Case number (if known)

20. Government and corporate bonds and other negotiable and non-negotiable instruments

Negotiable instruments include personal checks, cashiers' checks, promissory notes, and money orders.
Non-negotiable instruments are those you cannot transfer to someone by signing or delivering them.

☒ No

☐ Yes. Give specific information about them.......... Issuer name:

$
$
$

21. Retirement or pension accounts

Examples: Interests in IRA, ERISA, Keogh, 401(k), 403(b), thrift savings accounts, or other pension or profit-sharing plans

☒ No

☐ Yes. List each account separately. Type of account: Institution name:

401(k) or similar plan: $
Pension plan: $
IRA: $
Retirement account: $
Keogh: $
Additional account: $
Additional account: $

22. Security deposits and prepayments

Your share of all unused deposits you have made so that you may continue service or use from a company
Examples: Agreements with landlords, prepaid rent, public utilities (electric, gas, water), telecommunications companies, or others

☒ No

☐ Yes.......... Institution name or individual:

Electric: $
Gas: $
Heating oil: $
Security deposit on rental unit: $
Prepaid rent: $
Telephone: $
Water: $
Rented furniture: $
Other: $

23. Annuities (A contract for a periodic payment of money to you, either for life or for a number of years)

☒ No

☐ Yes.......... Issuer name and description:

$
$
$

Official Form 106A/B Schedule A/B: Property page 6

Debtor 1 William John Patterson (First Name, Middle Name, Last Name) Case number (if known) ____

24. Interests in an education IRA, in an account in a qualified ABLE program, or under a qualified state tuition program.
26 U.S.C. §§ 530(b)(1), 529A(b), and 529(b)(1).

☒ No
☐ Yes .... Institution name and description. Separately file the records of any interests.11 U.S.C. § 521(c):

$____
$____
$____

25. Trusts, equitable or future interests in property (other than anything listed in line 1), and rights or powers exercisable for your benefit

☒ No
☐ Yes. Give specific information about them.... $____

26. Patents, copyrights, trademarks, trade secrets, and other intellectual property
Examples: Internet domain names, websites, proceeds from royalties and licensing agreements

☒ No
☐ Yes. Give specific information about them.... $____

27. Licenses, franchises, and other general intangibles
Examples: Building permits, exclusive licenses, cooperative association holdings, liquor licenses, professional licenses

☒ No
☐ Yes. Give specific information about them.... $____

Money or property owed to you?

Current value of the portion you own?
Do not deduct secured claims or exemptions.

28. Tax refunds owed to you

☒ No
☐ Yes. Give specific information about them, including whether you already filed the returns and the tax years. ....

Federal: $____
State: $____
Local: $____

29. Family support
Examples: Past due or lump sum alimony, spousal support, child support, maintenance, divorce settlement, property settlement

☒ No
☐ Yes. Give specific information.........

Alimony: $____
Maintenance: $____
Support: $____
Divorce settlement: $____
Property settlement: $____

30. Other amounts someone owes you
Examples: Unpaid wages, disability insurance payments, disability benefits, sick pay, vacation pay, workers' compensation, Social Security benefits; unpaid loans you made to someone else

☒ No
☐ Yes. Give specific information........ $____

Debtor 1 William John Patterson
First Name Middle Name Last Name

Case number (if known) ______

31. **Interests in insurance policies**
Examples: Health, disability, or life insurance; health savings account (HSA); credit, homeowner's, or renter's insurance

☒ No
☐ Yes. Name the insurance company of each policy and list its value. ...

Company name:	Beneficiary:	Surrender or refund value:
		$
		$
		$

32. **Any interest in property that is due you from someone who has died**
If you are the beneficiary of a living trust, expect proceeds from a life insurance policy, or are currently entitled to receive property because someone has died.

☒ No
☐ Yes. Give specific information.............. $______

33. **Claims against third parties, whether or not you have filed a lawsuit or made a demand for payment**
Examples: Accidents, employment disputes, insurance claims, or rights to sue

☒ No
☐ Yes. Describe each claim. .... $______

34. **Other contingent and unliquidated claims of every nature, including counterclaims of the debtor and rights to set off claims**

☒ No
☐ Yes. Describe each claim. .... $______

35. **Any financial assets you did not already list**

☒ No
☐ Yes. Give specific information............ $______

36. **Add the dollar value of all of your entries from Part 4, including any entries for pages you have attached for Part 4. Write that number here** .... → $ 95.00

Part 5: Describe Any Business-Related Property You Own or Have an Interest In. List any real estate in Part 1.

37. **Do you own or have any legal or equitable interest in any business-related property?**

☒ No. Go to Part 6.
☐ Yes. Go to line 38.

Current value of the portion you own?
Do not deduct secured claims or exemptions.

38. **Accounts receivable or commissions you already earned**

☒ No
☐ Yes. Describe....... $______

39. **Office equipment, furnishings, and supplies**
Examples: Business-related computers, software, modems, printers, copiers, fax machines, rugs, telephones, desks, chairs, electronic devices

☒ No
☐ Yes. Describe ...... $______

Official Form 106A/B   Schedule A/B: Property   page 8

Debtor 1 William John Patterson — First Name / Middle Name / Last Name — Case number (if known) ______

40. **Machinery, fixtures, equipment, supplies you use in business, and tools of your trade**

- ☐ No
- ☐ Yes. Describe...... $______

41. **Inventory**

- ☐ No
- ☐ Yes. Describe...... $______

42. **Interests in partnerships or joint ventures**

- ☐ No
- ☐ Yes. Describe......

Name of entity:	% of ownership:	
______	____%	$______
______	____%	$______
______	____%	$______

43. **Customer lists, mailing lists, or other compilations**

- ☐ No
- ☐ Yes. **Do your lists include personally identifiable information** (as defined in 11 U.S.C. § 101(41A))?
  - ☐ No
  - ☐ Yes. Describe....... $______

44. **Any business-related property you did not already list**

- ☐ No
- ☐ Yes. Give specific information ....

$______
$______
$______
$______
$______
$______

45. **Add the dollar value of all of your entries from Part 5, including any entries for pages you have attached for Part 5. Write that number here** ...... → $______

Part 6: Describe Any Farm- and Commercial Fishing-Related Property You Own or Have an Interest In.
If you own or have an interest in farmland, list it in Part 1.

46. **Do you own or have any legal or equitable interest in any farm- or commercial fishing-related property?**

- ☒ No. Go to Part 7.
- ☐ Yes. Go to line 47.

Current value of the portion you own?
Do not deduct secured claims or exemptions.

47. **Farm animals**
Examples: Livestock, poultry, farm-raised fish

- ☐ No
- ☐ Yes...................... $______

Debtor 1 William John Patterson
First Name Middle Name Last Name

Case number (if known) ______

48. Crops—either growing or harvested

☐ No
☐ Yes. Give specific information. ______ $______

49. Farm and fishing equipment, implements, machinery, fixtures, and tools of trade

☐ No
☐ Yes ______ $______

50. Farm and fishing supplies, chemicals, and feed

☐ No
☐ Yes ______ $______

51. Any farm- and commercial fishing-related property you did not already list

☐ No
☐ Yes. Give specific information. ______ $______

52. Add the dollar value of all of your entries from Part 6, including any entries for pages you have attached for Part 6. Write that number here → $______

Part 7: Describe All Property You Own or Have an Interest in That You Did Not List Above

53. Do you have other property of any kind you did not already list?
Examples: Season tickets, country club membership

☒ No
☐ Yes. Give specific information. ______ $______ $______ $______

54. Add the dollar value of all of your entries from Part 7. Write that number here → $ 0.00

Part 8: List the Totals of Each Part of this Form

55. Part 1: Total real estate, line 2 → $ ~~0.00~~

56. Part 2: Total vehicles, line 5 $ 0.00

57. Part 3: Total personal and household items, line 15 $ 0.00

58. Part 4: Total financial assets, line 36 $ 95.00

59. Part 5: Total business-related property, line 45 $ 0.00

60. Part 6: Total farm- and fishing-related property, line 52 $ 0.00

61. Part 7: Total other property not listed, line 54 + $ 0.00

62. Total personal property. Add lines 56 through 61. $ 95.00 Copy personal property total → + $ 95.00

63. Total of all property on Schedule A/B. Add line 55 + line 62. $ ~~95.00~~

Fill in this information to identify your case:

Debtor 1 William John Patterson
First Name Middle Name Last Name

Debtor 2 (Spouse, if filing) First Name Middle Name Last Name

United States Bankruptcy Court for the Northern District of Texas

Case number (If known)

☐ Check if this is an amended filing

Official Form 106C

Schedule C: The Property You Claim as Exempt

04/16

Be as complete and accurate as possible. If two married people are filing together, both are equally responsible for supplying correct information. Using the property you listed on *Schedule A/B: Property* (Official Form 106A/B) as your source, list the property that you claim as exempt. If more space is needed, fill out and attach to this page as many copies of *Part 2: Additional Page* as necessary. On the top of any additional pages, write your name and case number (if known).

For each item of property you claim as exempt, you must specify the amount of the exemption you claim. One way of doing so is to state a specific dollar amount as exempt. Alternatively, you may claim the full fair market value of the property being exempted up to the amount of any applicable statutory limit. Some exemptions—such as those for health aids, rights to receive certain benefits, and tax-exempt retirement funds—may be unlimited in dollar amount. However, if you claim an exemption of 100% of fair market value under a law that limits the exemption to a particular dollar amount and the value of the property is determined to exceed that amount, your exemption would be limited to the applicable statutory amount.

Part 1: Identify the Property You Claim as Exempt

1. **Which set of exemptions are you claiming?** *Check one only, even if your spouse is filing with you.*
   - ☐ You are claiming state and federal nonbankruptcy exemptions. 11 U.S.C. § 522(b)(3)
   - ☐ You are claiming federal exemptions. 11 U.S.C. § 522(b)(2)

2. **For any property you list on *Schedule A/B* that you claim as exempt, fill in the information below.**

Brief description of the property and line on *Schedule A/B* that lists this property	Current value of the portion you own Copy the value from *Schedule A/B*	Amount of the exemption you claim *Check only one box for each exemption*	Specific laws that allow exemption
Brief description: ______ Line from *Schedule A/B*: ____	$______	☐ $______ ☐ 100% of fair market value, up to any applicable statutory limit	______
Brief description: ______ Line from *Schedule A/B*: ____	$______	☐ $______ ☐ 100% of fair market value, up to any applicable statutory limit	______
Brief description: ______ Line from *Schedule A/B*: ____	$______	☐ $______ ☐ 100% of fair market value, up to any applicable statutory limit	______

3. **Are you claiming a homestead exemption of more than $160,375?**
   (Subject to adjustment on 4/01/19 and every 3 years after that for cases filed on or after the date of adjustment.)
   - ☐ No
   - ☐ Yes. Did you acquire the property covered by the exemption within 1,215 days before you filed this case?
     - ☐ No
     - ☐ Yes

Debtor 1 William John Patterson
First Name Middle Name Last Name

Case number (if known)

Part 2: Additional Page

Brief description of the property and line on *Schedule A/B* that lists this property	Current value of the portion you own Copy the value from *Schedule A/B*	Amount of the exemption you claim *Check only one box for each exemption*	Specific laws that allow exemption
Brief description: ______ Line from *Schedule A/B*: ____	$______	☐ $______ ☐ 100% of fair market value, up to any applicable statutory limit	______
Brief description: ______ Line from *Schedule A/B*: ____	$______	☐ $______ ☐ 100% of fair market value, up to any applicable statutory limit	______
Brief description: ______ Line from *Schedule A/B*: ____	$______	☐ $______ ☐ 100% of fair market value, up to any applicable statutory limit	______
Brief description: ______ Line from *Schedule A/B*: ____	$______	☐ $______ ☐ 100% of fair market value, up to any applicable statutory limit	______
Brief description: ______ Line from *Schedule A/B*: ____	$______	☐ $______ ☐ 100% of fair market value, up to any applicable statutory limit	______
Brief description: ______ Line from *Schedule A/B*: ____	$______	☐ $______ ☐ 100% of fair market value, up to any applicable statutory limit	______
Brief description: ______ Line from *Schedule A/B*: ____	$______	☐ $______ ☐ 100% of fair market value, up to any applicable statutory limit	______
Brief description: ______ Line from *Schedule A/B*: ____	$______	☐ $______ ☐ 100% of fair market value, up to any applicable statutory limit	______
Brief description: ______ Line from *Schedule A/B*: ____	$______	☐ $______ ☐ 100% of fair market value, up to any applicable statutory limit	______
Brief description: ______ Line from *Schedule A/B*: ____	$______	☐ $______ ☐ 100% of fair market value, up to any applicable statutory limit	______
Brief description: ______ Line from *Schedule A/B*: ____	$______	☐ $______ ☐ 100% of fair market value, up to any applicable statutory limit	______
Brief description: ______ Line from *Schedule A/B*: ____	$______	☐ $______ ☐ 100% of fair market value, up to any applicable statutory limit	______

Official Form 106C **Schedule C: The Property You Claim as Exempt** page 2 of 2

Fill in this information to identify your case:

Debtor 1 William John Patterson
First Name / Middle Name / Last Name

Debtor 2
(Spouse, if filing) First Name / Middle Name / Last Name

United States Bankruptcy Court for the: Northern District of Texas

Case number
(If known)

☐ Check if this is an amended filing

Official Form 106D

Schedule D: Creditors Who Have Claims Secured by Property

12/15

Be as complete and accurate as possible. If two married people are filing together, both are equally responsible for supplying correct information. If more space is needed, copy the Additional Page, fill it out, number the entries, and attach it to this form. On the top of any additional pages, write your name and case number (if known).

1. **Do any creditors have claims secured by your property?**
   ☒ No. Check this box and submit this form to the court with your other schedules. You have nothing else to report on this form.
   ☐ Yes. Fill in all of the information below.

Part 1: List All Secured Claims

2. **List all secured claims.** If a creditor has more than one secured claim, list the creditor separately for each claim. If more than one creditor has a particular claim, list the other creditors in Part 2. As much as possible, list the claims in alphabetical order according to the creditor's name.

Column A **Amount of claim** Do not deduct the value of collateral. | *Column B* **Value of collateral that supports this claim** | *Column C* **Unsecured portion** If any

2.1 Creditor's Name / Number Street / City State ZIP Code

Describe the property that secures the claim: $______ $______ $______

As of the date you file, the claim is: Check all that apply.
☐ Contingent
☐ Unliquidated
☐ Disputed

Who owes the debt? Check one.
☐ Debtor 1 only
☐ Debtor 2 only
☐ Debtor 1 and Debtor 2 only
☐ At least one of the debtors and another
☐ Check if this claim relates to a community debt

Nature of lien. Check all that apply.
☐ An agreement you made (such as mortgage or secured car loan)
☐ Statutory lien (such as tax lien, mechanic's lien)
☐ Judgment lien from a lawsuit
☐ Other (including a right to offset) ______

Date debt was incurred ______ Last 4 digits of account number ___ ___ ___ ___

2.2 Creditor's Name / Number Street / City State ZIP Code

Describe the property that secures the claim: $______ $______ $______

As of the date you file, the claim is: Check all that apply.
☐ Contingent
☐ Unliquidated
☐ Disputed

Who owes the debt? Check one.
☐ Debtor 1 only
☐ Debtor 2 only
☐ Debtor 1 and Debtor 2 only
☐ At least one of the debtors and another
☐ Check if this claim relates to a community debt

Nature of lien. Check all that apply.
☐ An agreement you made (such as mortgage or secured car loan)
☐ Statutory lien (such as tax lien, mechanic's lien)
☐ Judgment lien from a lawsuit
☐ Other (including a right to offset) ______

Date debt was incurred ______ Last 4 digits of account number ___ ___ ___ ___

Add the dollar value of your entries in Column A on this page. Write that number here: $______

Official Form 106D Schedule D: Creditors Who Have Claims Secured by Property page 1 of 1

Debtor 1 William John Patterson
First Name Middle Name Last Name

Case number (if known) ____________________

Part 1: **Additional Page**

After listing any entries on this page, number them beginning with 2.3, followed by 2.4, and so forth.

Column A Amount of claim Do not deduct the value of collateral.	Column B Value of collateral that supports this claim	Column C Unsecured portion If any

☐ ____________________ Creditor's Name

Number Street ____________________

____

City State ZIP Code

Describe the property that secures the claim: $________ $________ $________

As of the date you file, the claim is: Check all that apply.
- ☐ Contingent
- ☐ Unliquidated
- ☐ Disputed

Who owes the debt? Check one.
- ☐ Debtor 1 only
- ☐ Debtor 2 only
- ☐ Debtor 1 and Debtor 2 only
- ☐ At least one of the debtors and another
- ☐ Check if this claim relates to a community debt

Nature of lien. Check all that apply.
- ☐ An agreement you made (such as mortgage or secured car loan)
- ☐ Statutory lien (such as tax lien, mechanic's lien)
- ☐ Judgment lien from a lawsuit
- ☐ Other (including a right to offset) ____________

Date debt was incurred ________ Last 4 digits of account number __ __ __ __

☐ ____________________ Creditor's Name

Number Street ____________________

____

City State ZIP Code

Describe the property that secures the claim: $________ $________ $________

As of the date you file, the claim is: Check all that apply.
- ☐ Contingent
- ☐ Unliquidated
- ☐ Disputed

Who owes the debt? Check one.
- ☐ Debtor 1 only
- ☐ Debtor 2 only
- ☐ Debtor 1 and Debtor 2 only
- ☐ At least one of the debtors and another
- ☐ Check if this claim relates to a community debt

Nature of lien. Check all that apply.
- ☐ An agreement you made (such as mortgage or secured car loan)
- ☐ Statutory lien (such as tax lien, mechanic's lien)
- ☐ Judgment lien from a lawsuit
- ☐ Other (including a right to offset) ____________

Date debt was incurred ________ Last 4 digits of account number __ __ __ __

☐ ____________________ Creditor's Name

Number Street ____________________

____

City State ZIP Code

Describe the property that secures the claim: $________ $________ $________

As of the date you file, the claim is: Check all that apply.
- ☐ Contingent
- ☐ Unliquidated
- ☐ Disputed

Who owes the debt? Check one.
- ☐ Debtor 1 only
- ☐ Debtor 2 only
- ☐ Debtor 1 and Debtor 2 only
- ☐ At least one of the debtors and another
- ☐ Check if this claim relates to a community debt

Nature of lien. Check all that apply.
- ☐ An agreement you made (such as mortgage or secured car loan)
- ☐ Statutory lien (such as tax lien, mechanic's lien)
- ☐ Judgment lien from a lawsuit
- ☐ Other (including a right to offset) ____________

Date debt was incurred ________ Last 4 digits of account number __ __ __ __

Add the dollar value of your entries in Column A on this page. Write that number here: $________

If this is the last page of your form, add the dollar value totals from all pages. Write that number here: $________

Official Form 106D Additional Page of Schedule D: Creditors Who Have Claims Secured by Property page 2 of 3

Debtor 1 William John Patterson
First Name Middle Name Last Name

Case number (if known) ____

Part 2: List Others to Be Notified for a Debt That You Already Listed

Use this page only if you have others to be notified about your bankruptcy for a debt that you already listed in Part 1. For example, if a collection agency is trying to collect from you for a debt you owe to someone else, list the creditor in Part 1, and then list the collection agency here. Similarly, if you have more than one creditor for any of the debts that you listed in Part 1, list the additional creditors here. If you do not have additional persons to be notified for any debts in Part 1, do not fill out or submit this page.

☐ ____
Name
____
Number Street
____
City State ZIP Code

On which line in Part 1 did you enter the creditor? ____
Last 4 digits of account number ___ ___ ___ ___

☐ ____
Name
____
Number Street
____
City State ZIP Code

On which line in Part 1 did you enter the creditor? ____
Last 4 digits of account number ___ ___ ___ ___

☐ ____
Name
____
Number Street
____
City State ZIP Code

On which line in Part 1 did you enter the creditor? ____
Last 4 digits of account number ___ ___ ___ ___

☐ ____
Name
____
Number Street
____
City State ZIP Code

On which line in Part 1 did you enter the creditor? ____
Last 4 digits of account number ___ ___ ___ ___

☐ ____
Name
____
Number Street
____
City State ZIP Code

On which line in Part 1 did you enter the creditor? ____
Last 4 digits of account number ___ ___ ___ ___

☐ ____
Name
____
Number Street
____
City State ZIP Code

On which line in Part 1 did you enter the creditor? ____
Last 4 digits of account number ___ ___ ___ ___

Print | Save As... | Add Attachment | Reset

Official Form 106D — Part 2 of Schedule D: Creditors Who Have Claims Secured by Property — page 3 of 3

Fill in this information to identify your case:

Debtor 1 William John Patterson
First Name Middle Name Last Name

Debtor 2
(Spouse, if filing) First Name Middle Name Last Name

United States Bankruptcy Court for the: Northern District of Texas

Case number
(If known)

☐ Check if this is an amended filing

Official Form 106E/F

Schedule E/F: Creditors Who Have Unsecured Claims

12/15

Be as complete and accurate as possible. Use Part 1 for creditors with PRIORITY claims and Part 2 for creditors with NONPRIORITY claims. List the other party to any executory contracts or unexpired leases that could result in a claim. Also list executory contracts on *Schedule A/B: Property* (Official Form 106A/B) and on *Schedule G: Executory Contracts and Unexpired Leases* (Official Form 106G). Do not include any creditors with partially secured claims that are listed in *Schedule D: Creditors Who Have Claims Secured by Property*. If more space is needed, copy the Part you need, fill it out, number the entries in the boxes on the left. Attach the Continuation Page to this page. On the top of any additional pages, write your name and case number (if known).

Part 1: List All of Your PRIORITY Unsecured Claims

1. **Do any creditors have priority unsecured claims against you?**
   ☒ No. Go to Part 2.
   ☐ Yes.

2. **List all of your priority unsecured claims.** If a creditor has more than one priority unsecured claim, list the creditor separately for each claim. For each claim listed, identify what type of claim it is. If a claim has both priority and nonpriority amounts, list that claim here and show both priority and nonpriority amounts. As much as possible, list the claims in alphabetical order according to the creditor's name. If you have more than two priority unsecured claims, fill out the Continuation Page of Part 1. If more than one creditor holds a particular claim, list the other creditors in Part 3.
   (For an explanation of each type of claim, see the instructions for this form in the instruction booklet.)

		Total claim	Priority amount	Nonpriority amount

2.1

Priority Creditor's Name

Number Street

City State ZIP Code

Who incurred the debt? Check one.
☐ Debtor 1 only
☐ Debtor 2 only
☐ Debtor 1 and Debtor 2 only
☐ At least one of the debtors and another
☐ **Check if this claim is for a community debt**

Is the claim subject to offset?
☐ No
☐ Yes

Last 4 digits of account number _ _ _ _ $____ $____ $____

When was the debt incurred? ____

As of the date you file, the claim is: Check all that apply
☐ Contingent
☐ Unliquidated
☐ Disputed

Type of PRIORITY unsecured claim:
☐ Domestic support obligations
☐ Taxes and certain other debts you owe the government
☐ Claims for death or personal injury while you were intoxicated
☐ Other. Specify ____

2.2

Priority Creditor's Name

Number Street

City State ZIP Code

Who incurred the debt? Check one.
☐ Debtor 1 only
☐ Debtor 2 only
☐ Debtor 1 and Debtor 2 only
☐ At least one of the debtors and another
☐ **Check if this claim is for a community debt**

Is the claim subject to offset?
☐ No
☐ Yes

Last 4 digits of account number _ _ _ _ $____ $____ $____

When was the debt incurred? ____

As of the date you file, the claim is: Check all that apply
☐ Contingent
☐ Unliquidated
☐ Disputed

Type of PRIORITY unsecured claim:
☐ Domestic support obligations
☐ Taxes and certain other debts you owe the government
☐ Claims for death or personal injury while you were intoxicated
☐ Other. Specify ____

Official Form 106E/F **Schedule E/F: Creditors Who Have Unsecured Claims** page 1 of 8

Debtor 1 William John Patterson
First Name Middle Name Last Name

Case number (if known)

Part 2: List All of Your NONPRIORITY Unsecured Claims

3. **Do any creditors have nonpriority unsecured claims against you?**

☐ No. You have nothing to report in this part. Submit this form to the court with your other schedules.
☒ Yes

4. **List all of your nonpriority unsecured claims in the alphabetical order of the creditor who holds each claim.** If a creditor has more than one nonpriority unsecured claim, list the creditor separately for each claim. For each claim listed, identify what type of claim it is. Do not list claims already included in Part 1. If more than one creditor holds a particular claim, list the other creditors in Part 3. If you have more than three nonpriority unsecured claims fill out the Continuation Page of Part 2.

Total claim

4.1 Bank Of Nashville
Nonpriority Creditor's Name
401 Church St.
Number Street
Nashville Tn 37219
City State ZIP Code

Last 4 digits of account number 1 2 3 4 — $31,425
When was the debt incurred? 2008-2012

As of the date you file, the claim is: Check all that apply
☐ Contingent
☐ Unliquidated
☐ Disputed

Who incurred the debt? Check one
☒ Debtor 1 only
☐ Debtor 2 only
☐ Debtor 1 and Debtor 2 only
☐ At least one of the debtors and another

☐ **Check if this claim is for a community debt**

Is the claim subject to offset?
☒ No
☐ Yes

Type of NONPRIORITY unsecured claim:
☐ Student loans
☐ Obligations arising out of a separation agreement or divorce that you did not report as priority claims
☐ Debts to pension or profit-sharing plans, and other similar debts
☒ Other. Specify Judgment on personal loan (HELOC)

4.2 Discover Financial
Nonpriority Creditor's Name
P.O. Box 15316
Number Street
Wilmington DE 19850
City State ZIP Code

Last 4 digits of account number 1 2 3 4 — $1,455
When was the debt incurred? 01/2012

As of the date you file, the claim is: Check all that apply
☐ Contingent
☐ Unliquidated
☐ Disputed

Who incurred the debt? Check one
☒ Debtor 1 only
☐ Debtor 2 only
☐ Debtor 1 and Debtor 2 only
☐ At least one of the debtors and another

☐ **Check if this claim is for a community debt**

Is the claim subject to offset?
☒ No
☐ Yes

Type of NONPRIORITY unsecured claim:
☐ Student loans
☐ Obligations arising out of a separation agreement or divorce that you did not report as priority claims
☐ Debts to pension or profit-sharing plans, and other similar debts
☒ Other. Specify Credit card

4.3 Home Depot
Nonpriority Creditor's Name
P.O. Box 790328
Number Street
St. Louis MO 63179
City State ZIP Code

Last 4 digits of account number 8 0 7 4 — $3,075
When was the debt incurred? 2012

As of the date you file, the claim is: Check all that apply
☐ Contingent
☐ Unliquidated
☐ Disputed

Who incurred the debt? Check one
☒ Debtor 1 only
☐ Debtor 2 only
☐ Debtor 1 and Debtor 2 only
☐ At least one of the debtors and another

☐ **Check if this claim is for a community debt**

Is the claim subject to offset?
☒ No
☐ Yes

Type of NONPRIORITY unsecured claim:
☐ Student loans
☐ Obligations arising out of a separation agreement or divorce that you did not report as priority claims
☐ Debts to pension or profit-sharing plans, and other similar debts
☒ Other. Specify Credit Card

Debtor 1 William John Patterson
First Name Middle Name Last Name

Case number (if known)

Part 2: Your NONPRIORITY Unsecured Claims — Continuation Page

After listing any entries on this page, number them beginning with 4.4, followed by 4.5, and so forth. **Total claim**

4.4 MPD Credit Union
Nonpriority Creditor's Name
2711 Old Lebanon Rd.
Number Street
Nashville TN 37214
City State ZIP Code

Who incurred the debt? Check one.
- [x] Debtor 1 only
- [ ] Debtor 2 only
- [ ] Debtor 1 and Debtor 2 only
- [ ] At least one of the debtors and another
- [ ] **Check if this claim is for a community debt**

Is the claim subject to offset?
- [x] No
- [ ] Yes

Last 4 digits of account number 2 0 1 0 — $6,781

When was the debt incurred? 11/2012

As of the date you file, the claim is: Check all that apply.
- [ ] Contingent
- [ ] Unliquidated
- [ ] Disputed

Type of **NONPRIORITY** unsecured claim:
- [ ] Student loans
- [ ] Obligations arising out of a separation agreement or divorce that you did not report as priority claims
- [ ] Debts to pension or profit-sharing plans, and other similar debts
- [x] Other. Specify Personal loan/ motorcycle

4.5 MPD Credit Union
Nonpriority Creditor's Name
2711 Old Lebanon Rd
Number Street
Nashville TN 37214
City State ZIP Code

Who incurred the debt? Check one.
- [x] Debtor 1 only
- [ ] Debtor 2 only
- [ ] Debtor 1 and Debtor 2 only
- [ ] At least one of the debtors and another
- [ ] **Check if this claim is for a community debt**

Is the claim subject to offset?
- [x] No
- [ ] Yes

Last 4 digits of account number 6 3 S 0 — $93.00

When was the debt incurred? 2012

As of the date you file, the claim is: Check all that apply.
- [ ] Contingent
- [ ] Unliquidated
- [ ] Disputed

Type of **NONPRIORITY** unsecured claim:
- [ ] Student loans
- [ ] Obligations arising out of a separation agreement or divorce that you did not report as priority claims
- [ ] Debts to pension or profit-sharing plans, and other similar debts
- [x] Other. Specify Unknown

4.6 MPD Credit Union
Nonpriority Creditor's Name
2711 Old Lebanon Rd
Number Street
Nashville TN 37214
City State ZIP Code

Who incurred the debt? Check one.
- [x] Debtor 1 only
- [ ] Debtor 2 only
- [ ] Debtor 1 and Debtor 2 only
- [ ] At least one of the debtors and another
- [ ] **Check if this claim is for a community debt**

Is the claim subject to offset?
- [x] No
- [ ] Yes

Last 4 digits of account number 1 9 8 7 — $15,283

When was the debt incurred? 09/2012

As of the date you file, the claim is: Check all that apply.
- [ ] Contingent
- [ ] Unliquidated
- [ ] Disputed

Type of **NONPRIORITY** unsecured claim:
- [ ] Student loans
- [ ] Obligations arising out of a separation agreement or divorce that you did not report as priority claims
- [ ] Debts to pension or profit-sharing plans, and other similar debts
- [x] Other. Specify Credit Account

Debtor 1 William John Patterson (First Name, Middle Name, Last Name) Case number (if known)

Part 2: Your NONPRIORITY Unsecured Claims – Continuation Page

After listing any entries on this page, number them beginning with 4.4, followed by 4.5, and so forth. **Total claim**

4.7 Nashville Electric Service
Nonpriority Creditor's Name
1214 Church St
Number Street
Nashville TN 37214
City State ZIP Code

Last 4 digits of account number 4 4 4 4 — $ 286.00

When was the debt incurred? 2012

As of the date you file, the claim is: Check all that apply.
- ☐ Contingent
- ☐ Unliquidated
- ☐ Disputed

Who incurred the debt? Check one.
- ☒ Debtor 1 only
- ☐ Debtor 2 only
- ☐ Debtor 1 and Debtor 2 only
- ☐ At least one of the debtors and another

☐ **Check if this claim is for a community debt**

Is the claim subject to offset?
- ☒ No
- ☐ Yes

Type of **NONPRIORITY** unsecured claim:
- ☐ Student loans
- ☐ Obligations arising out of a separation agreement or divorce that you did not report as priority claims
- ☐ Debts to pension or profit-sharing plans, and other similar debts
- ☒ Other. Specify Public Utility

4.8 Sams Club
Nonpriority Creditor's Name
P.O. Box 530942
Number Street
Atlanta GA 30353
City State ZIP Code

Last 4 digits of account number 4 5 1 4 — $1,400

When was the debt incurred? 2008-2012

As of the date you file, the claim is: Check all that apply.
- ☐ Contingent
- ☐ Unliquidated
- ☐ Disputed

Who incurred the debt? Check one.
- ☒ Debtor 1 only
- ☐ Debtor 2 only
- ☐ Debtor 1 and Debtor 2 only
- ☐ At least one of the debtors and another

☐ **Check if this claim is for a community debt**

Is the claim subject to offset?
- ☒ No
- ☐ Yes

Type of **NONPRIORITY** unsecured claim:
- ☐ Student loans
- ☐ Obligations arising out of a separation agreement or divorce that you did not report as priority claims
- ☐ Debts to pension or profit-sharing plans, and other similar debts
- ☒ Other. Specify Credit Card

4.9 Sallie Mae
Nonpriority Creditor's Name
P.O. Box 9500
Number Street
Wilkes Barre PA 18773
City State ZIP Code

Last 4 digits of account number 2 0 0 2 — $2,123

When was the debt incurred? 2002-2012

As of the date you file, the claim is: Check all that apply.
- ☐ Contingent
- ☐ Unliquidated
- ☐ Disputed

Who incurred the debt? Check one.
- ☒ Debtor 1 only
- ☐ Debtor 2 only
- ☐ Debtor 1 and Debtor 2 only
- ☐ At least one of the debtors and another

☐ **Check if this claim is for a community debt**

Is the claim subject to offset?
- ☒ No
- ☐ Yes

Type of **NONPRIORITY** unsecured claim:
- ☒ Student loans
- ☐ Obligations arising out of a separation agreement or divorce that you did not report as priority claims
- ☐ Debts to pension or profit-sharing plans, and other similar debts
- ☐ Other. Specify

Debtor 1 William John Patterson
First Name Middle Name Last Name

Case number (if known)

Part 2: Your NONPRIORITY Unsecured Claims – Continuation Page

After listing any entries on this page, number them beginning with 4.4, followed by 4.5, and so forth. **Total claim**

4.10 Wells Fargo
Nonpriority Creditor's Name
P.O. Box 10335
Number Street
Des Moines IA 50306
City State ZIP Code

Who incurred the debt? Check one.

- ☒ Debtor 1 only
- ☐ Debtor 2 only
- ☐ Debtor 1 and Debtor 2 only
- ☐ At least one of the debtors and another

☐ **Check if this claim is for a community debt**

Is the claim subject to offset?

- ☒ No
- ☐ Yes

Last 4 digits of account number 8 4 5 2 — $103,200

When was the debt incurred? 2008-2012

As of the date you file, the claim is: Check all that apply.

- ☐ Contingent
- ☐ Unliquidated
- ☐ Disputed

Type of **NONPRIORITY** unsecured claim:

- ☐ Student loans
- ☐ Obligations arising out of a separation agreement or divorce that you did not report as priority claims
- ☐ Debts to pension or profit-sharing plans, and other similar debts
- ☒ Other. Specify Home Mortgage

4.11 World Finance
Nonpriority Creditor's Name
P.O. Box 6429
Number Street
Greenville SC 29606
City State ZIP Code

Who incurred the debt? Check one.

- ☒ Debtor 1 only
- ☐ Debtor 2 only
- ☐ Debtor 1 and Debtor 2 only
- ☐ At least one of the debtors and another

☐ **Check if this claim is for a community debt**

Is the claim subject to offset?

- ☒ No
- ☐ Yes

Last 4 digits of account number 8 9 7 7 — $3,888

When was the debt incurred? 2012

As of the date you file, the claim is: Check all that apply.

- ☐ Contingent
- ☐ Unliquidated
- ☐ Disputed

Type of **NONPRIORITY** unsecured claim:

- ☐ Student loans
- ☐ Obligations arising out of a separation agreement or divorce that you did not report as priority claims
- ☐ Debts to pension or profit-sharing plans, and other similar debts
- ☒ Other. Specify Personal Loan

☐ ____________________
Nonpriority Creditor's Name
____
Number Street
____
City State ZIP Code

Who incurred the debt? Check one.

- ☐ Debtor 1 only
- ☐ Debtor 2 only
- ☐ Debtor 1 and Debtor 2 only
- ☐ At least one of the debtors and another

☐ **Check if this claim is for a community debt**

Is the claim subject to offset?

- ☐ No
- ☐ Yes

Last 4 digits of account number ___ ___ ___ ___ — $________

When was the debt incurred? ________

As of the date you file, the claim is: Check all that apply.

- ☐ Contingent
- ☐ Unliquidated
- ☐ Disputed

Type of **NONPRIORITY** unsecured claim:

- ☐ Student loans
- ☐ Obligations arising out of a separation agreement or divorce that you did not report as priority claims
- ☐ Debts to pension or profit-sharing plans, and other similar debts
- ☐ Other. Specify________

Official Form 106E/F **Schedule E/F: Creditors Who Have Unsecured Claims** page 5 of 8

Debtor 1 William John Patterson (First Name, Middle Name, Last Name) Case number (if known)

Part 3: List Others to Be Notified About a Debt That You Already Listed

5. **Use this page only if you have others to be notified about your bankruptcy, for a debt that you already listed in Parts 1 or 2. For example, if a collection agency is trying to collect from you for a debt you owe to someone else, list the original creditor in Parts 1 or 2, then list the collection agency here.** Similarly, if you have more than one creditor for any of the debts that you listed in Parts 1 or 2, list the additional creditors here. **If you do not have additional persons to be notified for any debts in Parts 1 or 2, do not fill out or submit this page.**

Columbus B&T / Synovus Bank
P.O. Box 120
Columbus GA 31902

On which entry in Part 1 or Part 2 did you list the original creditor?
Line 4.1 of (*Check one*): ☐ Part 1: Creditors with Priority Unsecured Claims
☒ Part 2: Creditors with Nonpriority Unsecured Claims
Last 4 digits of account number 1 2 3 4

FAMS
P.O. Box 1729
Woodstock GA 30188

On which entry in Part 1 or Part 2 did you list the original creditor?
Line 4.9 of (*Check one*): ☐ Part 1: Creditors with Priority Unsecured Claims
☒ Part 2: Creditors with Nonpriority Unsecured Claims
Last 4 digits of account number 2 5 0 3

F.H. Cann & Associates
1600 Osgood St. Suite 20-12/120
North Andover MD 01845

On which entry in Part 1 or Part 2 did you list the original creditor?
Line 4.9 of (*Check one*): ☐ Part 1: Creditors with Priority Unsecured Claims
☒ Part 2: Creditors with Nonpriority Unsecured Claims
Last 4 digits of account number 1 0 2 7

JH Portfolio Debt Equity
5757 Phantom Dr. Suite 225
Hazelwood MO 63042

On which entry in Part 1 or Part 2 did you list the original creditor?
Line 4.11 of (*Check one*): ☐ Part 1: Creditors with Priority Unsecured Claims
☒ Part 2: Creditors with Nonpriority Unsecured Claims
Last 4 digits of account number P 1 3 2

National Enterprise System
2479 Edison Blvd. Unit A
Twinsburg OH 44087-2340

On which entry in Part 1 or Part 2 did you list the original creditor?
Line 4.9 of (*Check one*): ☐ Part 1: Creditors with Priority Unsecured Claims
☒ Part 2: Creditors with Nonpriority Unsecured Claims
Last 4 digits of account number 2 0 0 2

Penn Credit Corp
916 S. 14th Street
Harrisburg PA 17104

On which entry in Part 1 or Part 2 did you list the original creditor?
Line 4.7 of (*Check one*): ☐ Part 1: Creditors with Priority Unsecured Claims
☒ Part 2: Creditors with Nonpriority Unsecured Claims
Last 4 digits of account number 8 0 5 1

Portfolio Recovery
120 Corporate Blvd Ste 100
Norfolk VA 23502

On which entry in Part 1 or Part 2 did you list the original creditor?
Line 4.8 of (*Check one*): ☐ Part 1: Creditors with Priority Unsecured Claims
☒ Part 2: Creditors with Nonpriority Unsecured Claims
Last 4 digits of account number 4 5 1 5

Debtor 1 William John Patterson (First Name / Middle Name / Last Name)   Case number (if known) ______

Part 3: List Others to Be Notified About a Debt That You Already Listed

5. Use this page only if you have others to be notified about your bankruptcy, for a debt that you already listed in Parts 1 or 2. For example, if a collection agency is trying to collect from you for a debt you owe to someone else, list the original creditor in Parts 1 or 2, then list the collection agency here. Similarly, if you have more than one creditor for any of the debts that you listed in Parts 1 or 2, list the additional creditors here. If you do not have additional persons to be notified for any debts in Parts 1 or 2, do not fill out or submit this page.

Name / Address	On which entry in Part 1 or Part 2 did you list the original creditor?
Name: Portfolio Recovery Number Street: 120 Corporate Blvd Ste 100 City: Norfolk State: VA ZIP Code: 23502	Line 4.3 of (Check one): ☐ Part 1: Creditors with Priority Unsecured Claims ☒ Part 2: Creditors with Nonpriority Unsecured Claims Last 4 digits of account number 4 3 4 4
Name: Robinson Attorney At Law Number Street: 446 James Robertson Pkwy City: Nashville State: TN ZIP Code: 37219	Line 4.7 of (Check one): ☐ Part 1: Creditors with Priority Unsecured Claims ☒ Part 2: Creditors with Nonpriority Unsecured Claims Last 4 digits of account number 3 6 4 4
Name: Selene Finance Number Street: 120 Gibralar Rd Ste 300 City: Horsham State: PA ZIP Code: 19044	Line 4.10 of (Check one): ☐ Part 1: Creditors with Priority Unsecured Claims ☒ Part 2: Creditors with Nonpriority Unsecured Claims Last 4 digits of account number 1 2 4 7
Name: SYNCB/SAMS Number Street: P.O. Box 965005 City: Orlando State: FL ZIP Code: 32896	Line 4.8 of (Check one): ☐ Part 1: Creditors with Priority Unsecured Claims ☒ Part 2: Creditors with Nonpriority Unsecured Claims Last 4 digits of account number 4 5 1 4
Name: Synovus Bank Number Street: 111 Bay Avenue City: Columbus State: GA ZIP Code: 31901	Line 4.1 of (Check one): ☐ Part 1: Creditors with Priority Unsecured Claims ☒ Part 2: Creditors with Nonpriority Unsecured Claims Last 4 digits of account number 9 2 7 0
Name: USA Funds Number Street: P.O. Box 6180 City: Indianapolis State: IN ZIP Code: 46206	Line 4.9 of (Check one): ☐ Part 1: Creditors with Priority Unsecured Claims ☒ Part 2: Creditors with Nonpriority Unsecured Claims Last 4 digits of account number 7 4 0 4
Name: ______ Number Street: ______ City ______ State ______ ZIP Code ______	Line ____ of (Check one): ☐ Part 1: Creditors with Priority Unsecured Claims ☐ Part 2: Creditors with Nonpriority Unsecured Claims Last 4 digits of account number __ __ __ __

Debtor 1 William John Patterson Case number (if known)
First Name Middle Name Last Name

Part 4: Add the Amounts for Each Type of Unsecured Claim

6. **Total the amounts of certain types of unsecured claims. This information is for statistical reporting purposes only. 28 U.S.C. § 159. Add the amounts for each type of unsecured claim.**

			Total claim
Total claims from Part 1	6a. Domestic support obligations	6a.	$
	6b. Taxes and certain other debts you owe the government	6b.	$
	6c. Claims for death or personal injury while you were intoxicated	6c.	$
	6d. Other. Add all other priority unsecured claims. Write that amount here.	6d.	+ $
	6e. Total. Add lines 6a through 6d.	6e.	$ 0.00

			Total claim
Total claims from Part 2	6f. Student loans	6f.	$ 2,123.00
	6g. Obligations arising out of a separation agreement or divorce that you did not report as priority claims	6g.	$
	6h. Debts to pension or profit-sharing plans, and other similar debts	6h.	$
	6i. Other. Add all other nonpriority unsecured claims. Write that amount here.	6i.	+ $ 166,886.00
	6j. Total. Add lines 6f through 6i.	6j.	$ 169,009.00

Fill in this information to identify your case:

Debtor: William John Patterson
First Name / Middle Name / Last Name

Debtor 2 (Spouse if filing): First Name / Middle Name / Last Name

United States Bankruptcy Court for the: Northern District of Texas

Case number (If known): ____________

☐ Check if this is an amended filing

Official Form 106G

Schedule G: Executory Contracts and Unexpired Leases

12/15

Be as complete and accurate as possible. If two married people are filing together, both are equally responsible for supplying correct information. If more space is needed, copy the additional page, fill it out, number the entries, and attach it to this page. On the top of any additional pages, write your name and case number (if known).

1. **Do you have any executory contracts or unexpired leases?**
   ☒ No. Check this box and file this form with the court with your other schedules. You have nothing else to report on this form.
   ☐ Yes. Fill in all of the information below even if the contracts or leases are listed on *Schedule A/B: Property* (Official Form 106A/B).

2. **List separately each person or company with whom you have the contract or lease. Then state what each contract or lease is for (for example, rent, vehicle lease, cell phone).** See the instructions for this form in the instruction booklet for more examples of executory contracts and unexpired leases.

	Person or company with whom you have the contract or lease	State what the contract or lease is for
2.1	Name Number Street City State ZIP Code	
2.2	Name Number Street City State ZIP Code	
2.3	Name Number Street City State ZIP Code	
2.4	Name Number Street City State ZIP Code	
2.5	Name Number Street City State ZIP Code	

Official Form 106G Schedule G: Executory Contracts and Unexpired Leases page 1 of 1

Fill in this information to identify your case:

Debtor 1 William John Patterson
First Name Middle Name Last Name

Debtor 2
(Spouse, if filing) First Name Middle Name Last Name

United States Bankruptcy Court for the: Northern District of Texas

Case number
(If known)

☐ Check if this is an amended filing

Official Form 106H

Schedule H: Your Codebtors

1.2/15

Codebtors are people or entities who are also liable for any debts you may have. Be as complete and accurate as possible. If two married people are filing together, both are equally responsible for supplying correct information. If more space is needed, copy the Additional Page, fill it out, and number the entries in the boxes on the left. Attach the Additional Page to this page. On the top of any Additional Pages, write your name and case number (if known). Answer every question.

1. **Do you have any codebtors?** (If you are filing a joint case, do not list either spouse as a codebtor.)
   - ☒ No
   - ☐ Yes
2. **Within the last 8 years, have you lived in a community property state or territory?** (*Community property states and territories* include Arizona, California, Idaho, Louisiana, Nevada, New Mexico, Puerto Rico, Texas, Washington, and Wisconsin.)
   - ☐ No. Go to line 3.
   - ☒ Yes. Did your spouse, former spouse, or legal equivalent live with you at the time?
     - ☒ No
     - ☐ Yes. In which community state or territory did you live? Texas. Fill in the name and current address of that person.

     Name of your spouse, former spouse, or legal equivalent

     Number Street

     City State ZIP Code
3. **In Column 1, list all of your codebtors. Do not include your spouse as a codebtor if your spouse is filing with you. List the person shown in line 2 again as a codebtor only if that person is a guarantor or cosigner. Make sure you have listed the creditor on *Schedule D* (Official Form 106D), *Schedule E/F* (Official Form 106E/F), or *Schedule G* (Official Form 106G). Use *Schedule D, Schedule E/F, or Schedule G* to fill out Column 2.**

	Column 1: Your codebtor	*Column 2:* The creditor to whom you owe the debt Check all schedules that apply:
3.1	Name Number Street City State ZIP Code	☐ Schedule D, line ____ ☐ Schedule E/F, line ____ ☐ Schedule G, line ____
3.2	Name Number Street City State ZIP Code	☐ Schedule D, line ____ ☐ Schedule E/F, line ____ ☐ Schedule G, line ____
3.3	Name Number Street City State ZIP Code	☐ Schedule D, line ____ ☐ Schedule E/F, line ____ ☐ Schedule G, line ____

Fill in this information to identify your case:

Debtor 1 William John Patterson
First Name Middle Name Last Name

Debtor 2
(Spouse, if filing) First Name Middle Name Last Name

United States Bankruptcy Court for the: Northern District of Texas

Case number
(If known)

Check if this is:

☐ An amended filing

☐ A supplement showing post-petition chapter 13 income as of the following date:

MM / DD / YYYY

Official Form B 6I

Schedule I: Your Income

12/13

Be as complete and accurate as possible. If two married people are filing together (Debtor 1 and Debtor 2), both are equally responsible for supplying correct information. If you are married and not filing jointly, and your spouse is living with you, include information about your spouse. If you are separated and your spouse is not filing with you, do not include information about your spouse. If more space is needed, attach a separate sheet to this form. On the top of any additional pages, write your name and case number (if known). Answer every question.

Part 1: Describe Employment

1. **Fill in your employment information.**

If you have more than one job, attach a separate page with information about additional employers.

Include part-time, seasonal, or self-employed work.

Occupation may include student or homemaker, if it applies.

	Debtor 1	Debtor 2 or non-filing spouse
Employment status	☐ Employed ☒ Not employed	☐ Employed ☐ Not employed
Occupation	Federal inmate	
Employer's name		
Employer's address	Number Street City State ZIP Code	Number Street City State ZIP Code
How long employed there?		

Part 2: Give Details About Monthly Income

Estimate monthly income as of the date you file this form. If you have nothing to report for any line, write $0 in the space. Include your non-filing spouse unless you are separated.

If you or your non-filing spouse have more than one employer, combine the information for all employers for that person on the lines below. If you need more space, attach a separate sheet to this form.

		For Debtor 1	For Debtor 2 or non-filing spouse
2. **List monthly gross wages, salary, and commissions** (before all payroll deductions). If not paid monthly, calculate what the monthly wage would be.	2.	$ 0.00	$
3. **Estimate and list monthly overtime pay.**	3.	+$ 0.00	+ $
4. **Calculate gross income.** Add line 2 + line 3.	4.	$ 0.00	$

Debtor 1 William John Patterson
First Name Middle Name Last Name

Case number (if known)

		For Debtor 1	For Debtor 2 or non-filing spouse
Copy line 4 here	→ 4.	$ 0.00	$
5. List all payroll deductions:			
5a. **Tax, Medicare, and Social Security deductions**	5a.	$ 0.00	$
5b. **Mandatory contributions for retirement plans**	5b.	$ 0.00	$
5c. **Voluntary contributions for retirement plans**	5c.	$ 0.00	$
5d. **Required repayments of retirement fund loans**	5d.	$ 0.00	$
5e. **Insurance**	5e.	$ 0.00	$
5f. **Domestic support obligations**	5f.	$ 0.00	$
5g. **Union dues**	5g.	$ 0.00	$
5h. **Other deductions.** Specify:	5h.	+ $ 0.00	+ $
6. **Add the payroll deductions.** Add lines 5a + 5b + 5c + 5d + 5e +5f + 5g +5h.	6.	$ 0.00	$
7. **Calculate total monthly take-home pay.** Subtract line 6 from line 4.	7.	$ 0.00	$
8. List all other income regularly received:			
8a. **Net income from rental property and from operating a business, profession, or farm** Attach a statement for each property and business showing gross receipts, ordinary and necessary business expenses, and the total monthly net income.	8a.	$ 0.00	$
8b. **Interest and dividends**	8b.	$ 0.00	$
8c. **Family support payments that you, a non-filing spouse, or a dependent regularly receive** Include alimony, spousal support, child support, maintenance, divorce settlement, and property settlement.	8c.	$ 0.00	$
8d. **Unemployment compensation**	8d.	$ 0.00	$
8e. **Social Security**	8e.	$ 0.00	$
8f. **Other government assistance that you regularly receive** Include cash assistance and the value (if known) of any non-cash assistance that you receive, such as food stamps (benefits under the Supplemental Nutrition Assistance Program) or housing subsidies. Specify:	8f.	$ 0.00	$
8g. **Pension or retirement income**	8g.	$ 0.00	$
8h. **Other monthly income.** Specify:	8h.	+ $ 5.25	+ $
9. **Add all other income.** Add lines 8a + 8b + 8c + 8d + 8e + 8f +8g + 8h.	9.	$ 5.25	$
10. **Calculate monthly income.** Add line 7 + line 9. Add the entries in line 10 for Debtor 1 and Debtor 2 or non-filing spouse.	10.	$ 5.25 +	$ = $ 5.25

11. **State all other regular contributions to the expenses that you list in *Schedule J*.**
Include contributions from an unmarried partner, members of your household, your dependents, your roommates, and other friends or relatives.
Do not include any amounts already included in lines 2-10 or amounts that are not available to pay expenses listed in *Schedule J*.
Specify: 11. + $ 0.00

12. **Add the amount in the last column of line 10 to the amount in line 11.** The result is the combined monthly income. Write that amount on the *Summary of Schedules* and *Statistical Summary of Certain Liabilities and Related Data*, if it applies 12. $ 5.25
Combined monthly income

13. **Do you expect an increase or decrease within the year after you file this form?**
[X] No.
[ ] Yes. Explain:

Fill in this information to identify your case:

Debtor 1 William John Patterson
First Name Middle Name Last Name

Debtor 2
(Spouse, if filing) First Name Middle Name Last Name

United States Bankruptcy Court for the: Northern District of Texas

Case number
(If known)

Check if this is:

☐ An amended filing

☐ A supplement showing post-petition chapter 13 expenses as of the following date:
MM / DD / YYYY

☐ A separate filing for Debtor 2 because Debtor 2 maintains a separate household

Official Form B 6J

Schedule J: Your Expenses

12/13

Be as complete and accurate as possible. If two married people are filing together, both are equally responsible for supplying correct information. If more space is needed, attach another sheet to this form. On the top of any additional pages, write your name and case number (if known). Answer every question.

Part 1: Describe Your Household

1. **Is this a joint case?**

☒ No. Go to line 2.

☐ Yes. **Does Debtor 2 live in a separate household?**

☐ No

☐ Yes. Debtor 2 must file a separate Schedule J.

2. **Do you have dependents?**

Do not list Debtor 1 and Debtor 2.

Do not state the dependents' names.

☐ No

☒ Yes. Fill out this information for each dependent.........................

Dependent's relationship to Debtor 1 or Debtor 2	Dependent's age	Does dependent live with you?
Son	11	☒ No ☐ Yes
Son	13	☒ No ☐ Yes
		☐ No ☐ Yes
		☐ No ☐ Yes
		☐ No ☐ Yes

3. **Do your expenses include expenses of people other than yourself and your dependents?**

☒ No

☐ Yes

Part 2: Estimate Your Ongoing Monthly Expenses

Estimate your expenses as of your bankruptcy filing date unless you are using this form as a supplement in a Chapter 13 case to report expenses as of a date after the bankruptcy is filed. If this is a supplemental *Schedule J*, check the box at the top of the form and fill in the applicable date.

Include expenses paid for with non-cash government assistance if you know the value of such assistance and have included it on *Schedule I: Your Income* (Official Form B 6I.)

			Your expenses
4.	**The rental or home ownership expenses for your residence.** Include first mortgage payments and any rent for the ground or lot.	4.	$ 0.00
	If not included in line 4:		
4a.	Real estate taxes	4a.	$ 0.00
4b.	Property, homeowner's, or renter's insurance	4b.	$ 0.00
4c.	Home maintenance, repair, and upkeep expenses	4c.	$ 0.00
4d.	Homeowner's association or condominium dues	4d.	$ 0.00

Official Form B 6J **Schedule J: Your Expenses** page 1

Debtor 1 William John Patterson — First Name / Middle Name / Last Name — Case number (if known) ______

		Your expenses
5. **Additional mortgage payments for your residence**, such as home equity loans	5.	$ 0.00
6. **Utilities:**		
6a. Electricity, heat, natural gas	6a.	$ 0.00
6b. Water, sewer, garbage collection	6b.	$ 0.00
6c. Telephone, cell phone, Internet, satellite, and cable services	6c.	$ 18.00
6d. Other. Specify: ______	6d.	$ 0.00
7. **Food and housekeeping supplies**	7.	$ 78.65
8. **Childcare and children's education costs**	8.	$ 0.00
9. **Clothing, laundry, and dry cleaning**	9.	$ 0.00
10. **Personal care products and services**	10.	$ 9.18
11. **Medical and dental expenses**	11.	$ 0.00
12. **Transportation.** Include gas, maintenance, bus or train fare. Do not include car payments.	12.	$ 0.00
13. **Entertainment, clubs, recreation, newspapers, magazines, and books**	13.	$ 0.00
14. **Charitable contributions and religious donations**	14.	$ 0.00
15. **Insurance.** Do not include insurance deducted from your pay or included in lines 4 or 20.		
15a. Life insurance	15a.	$ 0.00
15b. Health insurance	15b.	$ 0.00
15c. Vehicle insurance	15c.	$ 0.00
15d. Other insurance. Specify: ______	15d	$ 0.00
16. **Taxes.** Do not include taxes deducted from your pay or included in lines 4 or 20. Specify: ______	16.	$ 0.00
17. **Installment or lease payments:**		
17a. Car payments for Vehicle 1	17a.	$ 0.00
17b. Car payments for Vehicle 2	17b.	$ 0.00
17c. Other. Specify: ______	17c.	$ 0.00
17d. Other. Specify: ______	17d.	$ 0.00
18. **Your payments of alimony, maintenance, and support that you did not report as deducted from your pay on line 5, *Schedule I, Your Income* (Official Form B 6I).**	18.	$ 0.00
19. **Other payments you make to support others who do not live with you.** Specify: ______	19.	$ 0.00
20. **Other real property expenses not included in lines 4 or 5 of this form or on *Schedule I: Your Income*.**		
20a. Mortgages on other property	20a.	$ 0.00
20b. Real estate taxes	20b.	$ 0.00
20c. Property, homeowner's, or renter's insurance	20c.	$ 0.00
20d. Maintenance, repair, and upkeep expenses	20d.	$ 0.00
20e. Homeowner's association or condominium dues	20e.	$ 0.00

Debtor 1 William John Patterson
First Name Middle Name Last Name

Case number (if known) ____________

21. **Other.** Specify: ~~Stationary/stamps~~ — 21. +$ 15.97

22. **Your monthly expenses.** Add lines 4 through 21.
The result is your monthly expenses. — 22. $ 128.30

23. **Calculate your monthly net income.**

23a. Copy line 12 (*your combined monthly income*) from *Schedule I.* — 23a. $ 5.25

23b. Copy your monthly expenses from line 22 above. — 23b. −$ 128.30

23c. Subtract your monthly expenses from your monthly income.
The result is your *monthly net income.* — 23c. $ -123.05

24. **Do you expect an increase or decrease in your expenses within the year after you file this form?**

For example, do you expect to finish paying for your car loan within the year or do you expect your mortgage payment to increase or decrease because of a modification to the terms of your mortgage?

☐ No.

☒ Yes. Explain here: Without receiving any future gifts from outside sources, my total expenses will decrease to my monthly prison income of $5.25.

Fill in this information to identify your case:

Debtor 1 William John Patterson
First Name / Middle Name / Last Name

Debtor 2
(Spouse, if filing) First Name / Middle Name / Last Name

United States Bankruptcy Court for the: Northern District of Texas

Case number
(If known)

☐ Check if this is an amended filing

Official Form 106Sum

Summary of Your Assets and Liabilities and Certain Statistical Information 12/15

Be as complete and accurate as possible. If two married people are filing together, both are equally responsible for supplying correct information. Fill out all of your schedules first; then complete the information on this form. If you are filing amended schedules after you file your original forms, you must fill out a new *Summary* and check the box at the top of this page.

Part 1: Summarize Your Assets

	Your assets Value of what you own
1. *Schedule A/B: Property* (Official Form 106A/B)	
1a. Copy line 55, Total real estate, from *Schedule A/B*	$ 0.00
1b. Copy line 62, Total personal property, from *Schedule A/B*	$ 95.00
1c. Copy line 63, Total of all property on *Schedule A/B*	$ 95.00

Part 2: Summarize Your Liabilities

	Your liabilities Amount you owe
2. *Schedule D: Creditors Who Have Claims Secured by Property* (Official Form 106D)	
2a. Copy the total you listed in Column A, *Amount of claim*, at the bottom of the last page of Part 1 of *Schedule D*	$ 0.00
3. *Schedule E/F: Creditors Who Have Unsecured Claims* (Official Form 106E/F)	
3a. Copy the total claims from Part 1 (priority unsecured claims) from line 6e of *Schedule E/F*	$ 0.00
3b. Copy the total claims from Part 2 (nonpriority unsecured claims) from line 6j of *Schedule E/F*	+ $ 169,009.00
Your total liabilities	$ 169,009.00

Part 3: Summarize Your Income and Expenses

4. *Schedule I: Your Income* (Official Form 106I) Copy your combined monthly income from line 12 of *Schedule I*	$ 5.25
5. *Schedule J: Your Expenses* (Official Form 106J) Copy your monthly expenses from line 22c of *Schedule J*	$ 123.05

Debtor 1 William John Patterson (First Name, Middle Name, Last Name) Case number (if known) ____________

Part 4: Answer These Questions for Administrative and Statistical Records

6. Are you filing for bankruptcy under Chapters 7, 11, or 13?

☐ No. You have nothing to report on this part of the form. Check this box and submit this form to the court with your other schedules.
☒ Yes

7. What kind of debt do you have?

☒ **Your debts are primarily consumer debts.** *Consumer debts* are those "incurred by an individual primarily for a personal, family, or household purpose." 11 U.S.C. § 101(8). Fill out lines 8-9g for statistical purposes. 28 U.S.C. § 159.

☐ **Your debts are not primarily consumer debts.** You have nothing to report on this part of the form. Check this box and submit this form to the court with your other schedules.

8. From the *Statement of Your Current Monthly Income*: Copy your total current monthly income from Official Form 122A-1 Line 11; OR, Form 122B Line 11; OR, Form 122C-1 Line 14. $ 5.25

9. Copy the following special categories of claims from Part 4, line 6 of *Schedule E/F*:

From Part 4 on *Schedule E/F*, copy the following:	Total claim 0.00
9a. Domestic support obligations (Copy line 6a.)	$ 0.00
9b. Taxes and certain other debts you owe the government. (Copy line 6b.)	$ 0.00
9c. Claims for death or personal injury while you were intoxicated. (Copy line 6c.)	$ 0.00
9d. Student loans. (Copy line 6f.)	$ 2,123.00
9e. Obligations arising out of a separation agreement or divorce that you did not report as priority claims. (Copy line 6g.)	$ 0.00
9f. Debts to pension or profit-sharing plans, and other similar debts. (Copy line 6h.)	+ $ 0.00
9g. Total. Add lines 9a through 9f.	$2,123.00

Fill in this information to identify your case:

Debtor 1 William John Patterson
First Name Middle Name Last Name

Debtor 2
(Spouse, if filing) First Name Middle Name Last Name

United States Bankruptcy Court for the: Northern District of Texas

Case number
(If known)

☐ Check if this is an amended filing

Official Form 106Dec

Declaration About an Individual Debtor's Schedules

12/15

If two married people are filing together, both are equally responsible for supplying correct information.

You must file this form whenever you file bankruptcy schedules or amended schedules. Making a false statement, concealing property, or obtaining money or property by fraud in connection with a bankruptcy case can result in fines up to $250,000, or imprisonment for up to 20 years, or both. 18 U.S.C. §§ 152, 1341, 1519, and 3571.

Sign Below

Did you pay or agree to pay someone who is NOT an attorney to help you fill out bankruptcy forms?

☒ No

☐ Yes. Name of person________________________. Attach *Bankruptcy Petition Preparer's Notice, Declaration, and Signature* (Official Form 119).

Under penalty of perjury, I declare that I have read the summary and schedules filed with this declaration and that they are true and correct.

✕ William John Patterson
Signature of Debtor 1
William John Patterson
Date 10 / 18 / 2017
MM / DD / YYYY

✕ ________________
Signature of Debtor 2
Date ________
MM / DD / YYYY

CHAPTER 7:
STEP V: CURRENT MONTHLY INCOME AND MEANS TEST

OVERVIEW AND INSTRUCTIONS

Under Chapter 7 the statement of your monthly income and means test calculation includes the following forms, "(122A-1, 122A-1 Supp, and 122A-2)." Official forms "122A-1" and "122A-2" determine whether your income and expenses create a presumption of abuse that may prevent you from obtaining relief from your debts under Chapter 7 of the Bankruptcy Code. Chapter 7 relief can be denied to a person who has primarily consumer debts if the court finds that the person has enough income to repay creditors an amount that under the Bankruptcy Code, would be a sufficient portion of their claims.

As an individual filing Chapter 7, you must complete and submit a "Statement of Your Current Monthly Income (Form 122A-1)." This form will determine your current monthly income and compare whether your income is more than the median income for households of the same size in your state. If your income is not above the median, there is no presumption of abuse and you will not have to fill out the second form.

I have provided a copy of my "122A-1" in this chapter, and it indicates my income was below the median; therefore, no presumption of abuse and no other form was required. Note that my debts were primarily consumer debts. If your debts are not primarily consumer debts the next paragraph may apply to you.

Statement of Exemption from Presumption of Abuse under §707(b)(2), form "122A-1Supp" determines whether you may be exempted from the presumption of abuse because you do not have primarily consumer debts or because you have provided certain military or homeland defense services. If one of these exemptions applies, you should file a supplement, form "122A-1Supp", and verify the supplement by completing Part 3 of form "122A-1." If you qualify for an exemption, you are not required to fill out any part of form "122A-1" other than the verification/signature. If the exemptions do not apply, you should complete all the parts of form "122A-1" and file it without the supplemental form.

If you and your spouse are filing together, you and your spouse may file a single form "122A-1." However, if an exemption on form "122A-1Supp" applies to only one of you, separate forms may be required. 11 U.S.C. §707(b)(2)(C).

If your completed form "122A-1" shows income above the median you must file the second form, "Chapter 7 Means Test Calculation (Form 122A-2)." The calculation on this form – sometimes called the Means Test – reduces your income by living expenses and payment of certain debts, resulting in an amount available to pay other debts. If this amount is high enough, it will give rise to a presumption of abuse. A presumption of abuse does not mean you are actually trying to abuse the bankruptcy system. Rather, the presumption simply means that you are presumed to have enough income that you should not be granted relief under Chapter 7. You may overcome the presumption by showing special circumstances that reduce your income or increase your expenses.

If you cannot obtain relief under Chapter 7, you may be eligible to continue under another chapter of the Bankruptcy Code and pay creditors over a period of time.

Read each question carefully. You may not be required to answer every question on this form. For example, your military status may determine whether you must fill out the entire form. The instructions will alert you if you may skip questions. If you have nothing to report for a line, write $0.

To fill out several lines of the forms, you must look up information provided on websites or from other sources. For information to complete line 13 of form "122A-1" and lines 6-15, 30, and 36 of form "122A-2", go to: www.justice.gov/ust/eo/bapcpa/meanstesting.htm. This information is published by the Census Bureau, and the data is updated each year. The link provides the median family income reproduced in a format that is designed for ease of use in completing the bankruptcy forms. The "Census Bureau's 2018 Median Family Income" chart is located in this chapter for your convenience.

If your case is filed in Alabama or North Carolina, the administrative expense multiplier mentioned at line 36 can be found at: www.uscourts.gov/federalcourts/bankruptcy/bankruptcyresources/administrative expensesmultiplier.aspx.

For the bankruptcy basics information referred to on line 36 of form "122A-2", go to: www.uscourts.gov/federalcourts/bankruptcy/bankruptcybasics.aspx.

Fill in this information to identify your case:

Debtor 1 William John Patterson
First Name Middle Name Last Name

Debtor 2
(Spouse, if filing) First Name Middle Name Last Name

United States Bankruptcy Court for the: Northern District of Texas

Case number
(If known)

Check one box only as directed in this form and in Form 122A-1Supp:

☒ 1. There is no presumption of abuse.

☐ 2. The calculation to determine if a presumption of abuse applies will be made under *Chapter 7 Means Test Calculation* (Official Form 122A–2).

☐ 3. The Means Test does not apply now because of qualified military service but it could apply later.

☐ Check if this is an amended filing

Official Form 122A–1

Chapter 7 Statement of Your Current Monthly Income

12/15

Be as complete and accurate as possible. If two married people are filing together, both are equally responsible for being accurate. If more space is needed, attach a separate sheet to this form. Include the line number to which the additional information applies. On the top of any additional pages, write your name and case number (if known). If you believe that you are exempted from a presumption of abuse because you do not have primarily consumer debts or because of qualifying military service, complete and file *Statement of Exemption from Presumption of Abuse Under § 707(b)(2)* (Official Form 122A-1Supp) with this form.

Part 1: Calculate Your Current Monthly Income

1. **What is your marital and filing status?** Check one only.

☒ **Not married.** Fill out Column A, lines 2-11.

☐ **Married and your spouse is filing with you.** Fill out both Columns A and B, lines 2-11.

☐ **Married and your spouse is NOT filing with you. You and your spouse are:**

☐ **Living in the same household and are not legally separated.** Fill out both Columns A and B, lines 2-11.

☐ **Living separately or are legally separated.** Fill out Column A, lines 2-11; do not fill out Column B. By checking this box, you declare under penalty of perjury that you and your spouse are legally separated under nonbankruptcy law that applies or that you and your spouse are living apart for reasons that do not include evading the Means Test requirements. 11 U.S.C. § 707(b)(7)(B).

Fill in the average monthly income that you received from all sources, derived during the 6 full months before you file this bankruptcy case. 11 U.S.C. § 101(10A). For example, if you are filing on September 15, the 6-month period would be March 1 through August 31. If the amount of your monthly income varied during the 6 months, add the income for all 6 months and divide the total by 6. Fill in the result. Do not include any income amount more than once. For example, if both spouses own the same rental property, put the income from that property in one column only. If you have nothing to report for any line, write $0 in the space.

	Debtor 1	Debtor 2		Column A Debtor 1	Column B Debtor 2 or non-filing spouse
2. **Your gross wages, salary, tips, bonuses, overtime, and commissions** (before all payroll deductions).				$ 0.00	$
3. **Alimony and maintenance payments.** Do not include payments from a spouse if Column B is filled in.				$ 0.00	$
4. **All amounts from any source which are regularly paid for household expenses of you or your dependents, including child support.** Include regular contributions from an unmarried partner, members of your household, your dependents, parents, and roommates. Include regular contributions from a spouse only if Column B is not filled in. Do not include payments you listed on line 3.				$ 0.00	$
5. **Net income from operating a business, profession, or farm**	Debtor 1	Debtor 2			
Gross receipts (before all deductions)	$	$			
Ordinary and necessary operating expenses	– $	– $			
Net monthly income from a business, profession, or farm	$	$	Copy here →	$ 0.00	$
6. **Net income from rental and other real property**	Debtor 1	Debtor 2			
Gross receipts (before all deductions)	$	$			
Ordinary and necessary operating expenses	– $	– $			
Net monthly income from rental or other real property	$	$	Copy here →	$ 0.00	$
7. **Interest, dividends, and royalties**				$ 0.00	$

Debtor 1 William John Patterson — Case number (if known)
First Name Middle Name Last Name

	Column A Debtor 1	Column B Debtor 2 or non-filing spouse
8. **Unemployment compensation**	$ 0.00	$
Do not enter the amount if you contend that the amount received was a benefit under the Social Security Act. Instead, list it here:		
For you ... $		
For your spouse ... $		
9. **Pension or retirement income.** Do not include any amount received that was a benefit under the Social Security Act.	$ 0.00	$
10. **Income from all other sources not listed above.** Specify the source and amount. Do not include any benefits received under the Social Security Act or payments received as a victim of a war crime, a crime against humanity, or international or domestic terrorism. If necessary, list other sources on a separate page and put the total below.		
Inmate maintenance pay	$ 5.25	$
	$	$
Total amounts from separate pages, if any.	+ $	+ $
11. **Calculate your total current monthly income.** Add lines 2 through 10 for each column. Then add the total for Column A to the total for Column B.	$ 5.25	+ $ = $ 5.25 Total current monthly income

Part 2: Determine Whether the Means Test Applies to You

12. **Calculate your current monthly income for the year.** Follow these steps:

12a. Copy your total current monthly income from line 11. ... Copy line 11 here→ $ 5.25

Multiply by 12 (the number of months in a year). x 12

12b. The result is your annual income for this part of the form. 12b. $63.00

13. **Calculate the median family income that applies to you.** Follow these steps:

Fill in the state in which you live. Texas

Fill in the number of people in your household. 1

Fill in the median family income for your state and size of household. ... 13. $46,709.00

To find a list of applicable median income amounts, go online using the link specified in the separate instructions for this form. This list may also be available at the bankruptcy clerk's office.

14. **How do the lines compare?**

14a. ☒ Line 12b is less than or equal to line 13. On the top of page 1, check box 1, *There is no presumption of abuse.* Go to Part 3.

14b. ☐ Line 12b is more than line 13. On the top of page 1, check box 2, *The presumption of abuse is determined by Form 122A-2.* Go to Part 3 and fill out Form 122A–2.

Part 3: Sign Below

By signing here, I declare under penalty of perjury that the information on this statement and in any attachments is true and correct.

✘ William John Patterson — Signature of Debtor 1

William John Patterson

Date 10/18/2017 MM / DD / YYYY

✘ ________ Signature of Debtor 2

Date ________ MM / DD / YYYY

If you checked line 14a, do NOT fill out or file Form 122A–2.

If you checked line 14b, fill out Form 122A–2 and file it with this form.

Census Bureau Median Family Income By Family Size

(Cases Filed On or After May 1, 2018)

The following table provides median family income data reproduced in a format designed for ease of use in completing Bankruptcy Forms 122A-1 and 122C-1.

STATE	1 EARNER	FAMILY SIZE		
		2 PEOPLE	3 PEOPLE	4 PEOPLE *
ALABAMA	$46,400	$54,339	$62,033	$77,597
ALASKA	$63,524	$87,745	$87,745	$105,191
ARIZONA	$48,369	$62,055	$63,334	$75,900
ARKANSAS	$42,041	$51,672	$58,649	$71,294
CALIFORNIA	$54,787	$73,162	$79,061	$91,349
COLORADO	$57,906	$75,888	$84,952	$96,485
CONNECTICUT	$64,152	$84,005	$98,666	$119,844
DELAWARE	$52,900	$66,207	$78,993	$92,828
DISTRICT OF COLUMBIA	$56,509	$109,379	$109,379	$109,379
FLORIDA	$46,677	$57,968	$62,912	$74,512
GEORGIA	$46,104	$59,606	$67,304	$80,038
HAWAII	$64,482	$74,419	$90,596	$99,934
IDAHO	$50,142	$59,219	$66,271	$73,839
ILLINOIS	$52,410	$68,687	$80,233	$96,485
INDIANA	$47,799	$60,657	$70,710	$80,985
IOWA	$50,205	$65,589	$76,491	$92,945
KANSAS	$50,687	$65,112	$73,760	$85,507
KENTUCKY	$43,720	$53,314	$62,696	$77,023
LOUISIANA	$43,243	$51,813	$60,009	$77,861
MAINE	$50,866	$61,473	$78,688	$93,127
MARYLAND	$65,723	$86,063	$98,152	$118,294
MASSACHUSETTS	$62,660	$80,180	$98,758	$123,864
MICHIGAN	$49,662	$60,809	$72,083	$88,925
MINNESOTA	$54,613	$74,283	$87,811	$107,902
MISSISSIPPI	$40,067	$49,973	$54,615	$63,897
MISSOURI	$46,488	$58,796	$70,089	$83,180
MONTANA	$49,237	$61,984	$73,475	$84,217
NEBRASKA	$46,813	$68,974	$78,281	$87,715
NEVADA	$49,170	$62,204	$67,101	$77,397
NEW HAMPSHIRE	$64,531	$75,856	$92,263	$115,926
NEW JERSEY	$66,284	$81,054	$98,174	$121,226
NEW MEXICO	$42,905	$57,701	$57,701	$63,841
NEW YORK	$53,132	$68,087	$80,840	$98,583
NORTH CAROLINA	$46,438	$57,951	$66,361	$78,009
NORTH DAKOTA	$51,700	$73,641	$80,273	$97,936
OHIO	$48,596	$60,834	$70,529	$85,294
OKLAHOMA	$46,169	$58,426	$64,977	$71,638
OREGON	$53,501	$65,190	$76,603	$90,332
PENNSYLVANIA	$53,067	$63,687	$78,953	$93,645
RHODE ISLAND	$51,680	$69,090	$82,224	$107,693
SOUTH CAROLINA	$45,740	$58,348	$61,473	$77,564
SOUTH DAKOTA	$45,950	$64,326	$75,564	$88,294
TENNESSEE	$45,842	$55,759	$63,865	$75,172

TEXAS	$47,238	$63,148	$69,294	$78,572
UTAH	$59,002	$64,832	$76,066	$83,537
VERMONT	$53,531	$67,517	$81,076	$91,567
VIRGINIA	$60,011	$74,299	$87,009	$103,549
WASHINGTON	$63,376	$75,012	$86,630	$102,418
WEST VIRGINIA	$45,804	$52,033	$61,696	$74,317
WISCONSIN	$49,555	$65,097	$78,005	$95,492
WYOMING	$57,020	$69,993	$72,378	$92,193

* *Add $8,400 for each individual in excess of 4.*

COMMONWEALTH OR U.S. TERRITORY	1 EARNER	FAMILY SIZE		
		2 PEOPLE	3 PEOPLE	4 PEOPLE *
GUAM	$41,007	$49,031	$55,873	$67,614
NORTHERN MARIANA ISLANDS	$27,538	$27,538	$32,038	$47,122
PUERTO RICO	$24,455	$24,455	$24,555	$33,027
VIRGIN ISLANDS	$32,536	$39,104	$41,694	$45,678

* *Add $8,400 for each individual in excess of 4.*

CHAPTER 8

STEP VI: STATEMENT OF SOCIAL SECURITY NUMBER, STATEMENT OF INTENTION, AND STATEMENT OF FINANCIAL AFFAIRS

STATEMENT OF SOCIAL SECURITY (FORM 121)

Use this form to tell the court about any Social Security or Federal Identification numbers you have used. You are instructed not to file this form as part of the public case file. It must be submitted separately and must not be included in the court's public electronic records. Please consult local court procedures for submission requirements.

Unlike all other forms your full social security number is required on this form. To protect your privacy, the court will not make this form available to the public. You should not include a full Social Security Number or Individual Taxpayer Number on any other document filed with the court. The court will make only the last four digits of your numbers known to the public. However, the full numbers will be available to your creditors, the U.S. Trustee or bankruptcy administrator, and the trustee assigned to your case. An example of my "Statement of Social Security (Form 121)" can be located in this chapter.

STATEMENT OF INTENTION (FORM 108)

If you are an individual filing under Chapter 7, you must fill out the "Statement of Intention" if:
1) Creditors have claims secured by your property, or
2) You have leased personal property and the lease has not expired.

The Bankruptcy Code requires you to state your intentions about such claims and provides for early termination of the automatic stay as to personal property if the statement is not timely filed. The same early termination of the automatic stay applies to any unexpired lease of personal property unless you state that you intend to assume the unexpired lease if the trustee does not do so.

To help complete this form you will use information you have already provided on schedules D, C, and G.

Most inmates will not have debts secured by property. I had no secured property; therefore, no example is included. However, if needed the sample form is available in Chapter 10. You may also find more explanation on this form in your online legal law library under "Instructions – Bankruptcy Forms for Individuals."

STATEMENT OF FINANCIAL AFFAIRS (FORM 107)

Your "Statement of Financial Affairs" for Individuals filing for bankruptcy provides a summary of your financial history over certain periods of time before you file for bankruptcy. If you are an individual in a bankruptcy case, you must fill out this statement. 11 U.S.C. § 521(a) and Bankruptcy Rule 1007(b)(1).

If you are in business as a sole proprietor, partner, family farmer, or self-employed professional, you must provide the information about all of your business and personal financial activities. Although this statement may ask you questions that are similar to some questions on the schedules, you must fill out all of the forms completely to protect your legal rights. Please read each question carefully and pay particular attention to time periods or other specific details pertaining to each question. An example of my "Statement of Financial Affairs" can be located in this chapter.

Fill in this information to identify your case:

United States Bankruptcy Court for the:

Northern District of Texas (State)

Case number (if known) ____________

Official Form 121

Statement About Your Social Security Numbers

12/15

Use this form to tell the court about any Social Security or federal Individual Taxpayer Identification numbers you have used. Do not file this form as part of the public case file. This form must be submitted separately and must not be included in the court's public electronic records. Please consult local court procedures for submission requirements.

To protect your privacy, the court will not make this form available to the public. You should not include a full Social Security Number or Individual Taxpayer Number on any other document filed with the court. The court will make only the last four digits of your numbers known to the public. However, the full numbers will be available to your creditors, the U.S. Trustee or bankruptcy administrator, and the trustee assigned to your case.

Making a false statement, concealing property, or obtaining money or property by fraud in connection with a bankruptcy case can result in fines up to $250,000, or imprisonment for up to 20 years, or both. 18 U.S.C. §§ 152, 1341, 1519, and 3571.

Part 1: Tell the Court About Yourself and Your spouse If Your Spouse Is Filing With You

	For Debtor 1:	For Debtor 2 (Only If Spouse Is Filing):
1. Your name	William (First name)	____ (First name)
	John (Middle name)	____ (Middle name)
	Patterson (Last name)	____ (Last name)

Part 2: Tell the Court About all of Your Social Security or Federal Individual Taxpayer Identification Numbers

	For Debtor 1:	For Debtor 2:
2. All Social Security Numbers you have used	1 2 3 4 4 5 6 7 0	___ – __ – ____
	___ ___ ____	___ – __ – ____
	☐ You do not have a Social Security number.	☐ You do not have a Social Security number.
3. All federal Individual Taxpayer Identification Numbers (ITIN) you have used	9 __ – __ – ____	9 __ – __ – ____
	9 __ – __ – ____	9 __ – __ – ____
	☒ You do not have an ITIN.	☐ You do not have an ITIN.

Part 3: Sign Below

Debtor 1	Debtor 2
Under penalty of perjury, I declare that the information I have provided in this form is true and correct.	Under penalty of perjury, I declare that the information I have provided in this form is true and correct.
✗ ____________ Signature of Debtor 1	✗ ____________ Signature of Debtor 2
Date 10/18/2017 MM / DD / YYYY	Date ______ MM / DD / YYYY

Fill in this information to identify your case:

Debtor 1: William John Patterson
First Name / Middle Name / Last Name

Debtor 2
(Spouse, if filing) First Name / Middle Name / Last Name

United States Bankruptcy Court for the: Northern District of Texas

Case number (If known)

☐ Check if this is an amended filing

Official Form 107

Statement of Financial Affairs for Individuals Filing for Bankruptcy

04/16

Be as complete and accurate as possible. If two married people are filing together, both are equally responsible for supplying correct information. If more space is needed, attach a separate sheet to this form. On the top of any additional pages, write your name and case number (if known). Answer every question.

Part 1: Give Details About Your Marital Status and Where You Lived Before

1. What is your current marital status?

☐ Married
☒ Not married

2. During the last 3 years, have you lived anywhere other than where you live now?

☐ No
☒ Yes. List all of the places you lived in the last 3 years. Do not include where you live now.

Debtor 1:	Dates Debtor 1 lived there	Debtor 2:	Dates Debtor 2 lived there
F.C.I Texarkanna P.O. Box 7000 Number Street Texarkanna, TX 75505 City State ZIP Code	From 2014 To 2016	☐ Same as Debtor 1 Number Street City State ZIP Code	☐ Same as Debtor 1 From To
Number Street City State ZIP Code	From To	☐ Same as Debtor 1 Number Street City State ZIP Code	☐ Same as Debtor 1 From To

3. Within the last 8 years, did you ever live with a spouse or legal equivalent in a community property state or territory? (*Community property states and territories* include Arizona, California, Idaho, Louisiana, Nevada, New Mexico, Puerto Rico, Texas, Washington, and Wisconsin.)

☒ No
☐ Yes. Make sure you fill out *Schedule H: Your Codebtors* (Official Form 106H).

Part 2: Explain the Sources of Your Income

Debtor 1 William John Patterson — First Name / Middle Name / Last Name — Case number (if known) ______

4. **Did you have any income from employment or from operating a business during this year or the two previous calendar years?**
Fill in the total amount of income you received from all jobs and all businesses, including part-time activities.
If you are filing a joint case and you have income that you receive together, list it only once under Debtor 1.

☒ No
☐ Yes. Fill in the details.

	Debtor 1		Debtor 2	
	Sources of income Check all that apply.	**Gross income** (before deductions and exclusions)	**Sources of income** Check all that apply.	**Gross income** (before deductions and exclusions)
From January 1 of current year until the date you filed for bankruptcy:	☐ Wages, commissions, bonuses, tips ☐ Operating a business	$______	☐ Wages, commissions, bonuses, tips ☐ Operating a business	$______
For last calendar year: (January 1 to December 31, ______) YYYY	☐ Wages, commissions, bonuses, tips ☐ Operating a business	$______	☐ Wages, commissions, bonuses, tips ☐ Operating a business	$______
For the calendar year before that: (January 1 to December 31, ______) YYYY	☐ Wages, commissions, bonuses, tips ☐ Operating a business	$______	☐ Wages, commissions, bonuses, tips ☐ Operating a business	$______

5. **Did you receive any other income during this year or the two previous calendar years?**
Include income regardless of whether that income is taxable. Examples of *other income* are alimony; child support; Social Security, unemployment, and other public benefit payments; pensions; rental income; interest; dividends; money collected from lawsuits; royalties; and gambling and lottery winnings. If you are filing a joint case and you have income that you received together, list it only once under Debtor 1.

List each source and the gross income from each source separately. Do not include income that you listed in line 4.

☐ No
☒ Yes. Fill in the details.

	Debtor 1		Debtor 2	
	Sources of income Describe below.	**Gross income from each source** (before deductions and exclusions)	**Sources of income** Describe below.	**Gross income from each source** (before deductions and exclusions)
From January 1 of current year until the date you filed for bankruptcy:	FBOP RDAP	$ 40.00		$
	FBOP inmate pay	$ 63.00		$
	Wells Fargo	$ 1,026.00		$
For last calendar year: (January 1 to December 31, 2016) YYYY	Family gifts	$ 7,781.00		$
	FBOP RDAP	$ 80.00		$
		$		$
For the calendar year before that: (January 1 to December 31, 2015) YYYY	Family gifts	$ 1,875.00		$
		$		$
		$		$

Official Form 107 — Statement of Financial Affairs for Individuals Filing for Bankruptcy — page 2

Debtor 1 William John Patterson Case number (if known) ________________

First Name Middle Name Last Name

Part 3: List Certain Payments You Made Before You Filed for Bankruptcy

6. **Are either Debtor 1's or Debtor 2's debts primarily consumer debts?**

☐ No. **Neither Debtor 1 nor Debtor 2 has primarily consumer debts.** *Consumer debts* are defined in 11 U.S.C. § 101(8) as "incurred by an individual primarily for a personal, family, or household purpose."

During the 90 days before you filed for bankruptcy, did you pay any creditor a total of $6,425* or more?

☐ No. Go to line 7.

☐ Yes. List below each creditor to whom you paid a total of $6,425* or more in one or more payments and the total amount you paid that creditor. Do not include payments for domestic support obligations, such as child support and alimony. Also, do not include payments to an attorney for this bankruptcy case.

* Subject to adjustment on 4/01/19 and every 3 years after that for cases filed on or after the date of adjustment.

☒ Yes. **Debtor 1 or Debtor 2 or both have primarily consumer debts.**

During the 90 days before you filed for bankruptcy, did you pay any creditor a total of $600 or more?

☒ No. Go to line 7.

☐ Yes. List below each creditor to whom you paid a total of $600 or more and the total amount you paid that creditor. Do not include payments for domestic support obligations, such as child support and alimony. Also, do not include payments to an attorney for this bankruptcy case.

	Dates of payment	Total amount paid	Amount you still owe	Was this payment for...
Creditor's Name Number Street City State ZIP Code		$	$	☐ Mortgage ☐ Car ☐ Credit card ☐ Loan repayment ☐ Suppliers or vendors ☐ Other ____
Creditor's Name Number Street City State ZIP Code		$	$	☐ Mortgage ☐ Car ☐ Credit card ☐ Loan repayment ☐ Suppliers or vendors ☐ Other ____
Creditor's Name Number Street City State ZIP Code		$	$	☐ Mortgage ☐ Car ☐ Credit card ☐ Loan repayment ☐ Suppliers or vendors ☐ Other ____

Debtor 1 William John Patterson — Case number (if known) ________
First Name Middle Name Last Name

7. **Within 1 year before you filed for bankruptcy, did you make a payment on a debt you owed anyone who was an insider?**
Insiders include your relatives; any general partners; relatives of any general partners; partnerships of which you are a general partner; corporations of which you are an officer, director, person in control, or owner of 20% or more of their voting securities; and any managing agent, including one for a business you operate as a sole proprietor. 11 U.S.C. § 101. Include payments for domestic support obligations, such as child support and alimony.

- [X] No
- [ ] Yes. List all payments to an insider.

	Dates of payment	Total amount paid	Amount you still owe	Reason for this payment
Insider's Name Number Street City State ZIP Code		$	$	
Insider's Name Number Street City State ZIP Code		$	$	

8. **Within 1 year before you filed for bankruptcy, did you make any payments or transfer any property on account of a debt that benefited an insider?**
Include payments on debts guaranteed or cosigned by an insider.

- [X] No
- [ ] Yes. List all payments that benefited an insider.

	Dates of payment	Total amount paid	Amount you still owe	Reason for this payment Include creditor's name
Insider's Name Number Street City State ZIP Code		$	$	
Insider's Name Number Street City State ZIP Code		$	$	

Debtor 1 William John Patterson Case number (if known)______________
First Name Middle Name Last Name

Part 4: Identify Legal Actions, Repossessions, and Foreclosures

9. **Within 1 year before you filed for bankruptcy, were you a party in any lawsuit, court action, or administrative proceeding?**
List all such matters, including personal injury cases, small claims actions, divorces, collection suits, paternity actions, support or custody modifications, and contract disputes.

- [x] No
- [ ] Yes. Fill in the details.

	Nature of the case	Court or agency	Status of the case
Case title______________ ______________ Case number ______________		Court Name Number Street City State ZIP Code	☐ Pending ☐ On appeal ☐ Concluded
Case title______________ ______________ Case number ______________		Court Name Number Street City State ZIP Code	☐ Pending ☐ On appeal ☐ Concluded

10. **Within 1 year before you filed for bankruptcy, was any of your property repossessed, foreclosed, garnished, attached, seized, or levied?**
Check all that apply and fill in the details below.

- [x] No. Go to line 11.
- [ ] Yes. Fill in the information below.

	Describe the property	Date	Value of the property
Creditor's Name Number Street City State ZIP Code	 **Explain what happened** ☐ Property was repossessed. ☐ Property was foreclosed. ☐ Property was garnished. ☐ Property was attached, seized, or levied.	________	$__________
Creditor's Name Number Street City State ZIP Code	 **Explain what happened** ☐ Property was repossessed. ☐ Property was foreclosed. ☐ Property was garnished. ☐ Property was attached, seized, or levied.	________	$__________

Debtor 1 William John Patterson
First Name Middle Name Last Name

Case number (if known) ______

11. Within 90 days before you filed for bankruptcy, did any creditor, including a bank or financial institution, set off any amounts from your accounts or refuse to make a payment because you owed a debt?

X No
☐ Yes. Fill in the details.

	Describe the action the creditor took	Date action was taken	Amount
Creditor's Name Number Street City State ZIP Code	 Last 4 digits of account number: XXXX–__ __ __ __	______	$______

12. Within 1 year before you filed for bankruptcy, was any of your property in the possession of an assignee for the benefit of creditors, a court-appointed receiver, a custodian, or another official?

X No
☐ Yes

Part 5: List Certain Gifts and Contributions

13. Within 2 years before you filed for bankruptcy, did you give any gifts with a total value of more than $600 per person?

X No
☐ Yes. Fill in the details for each gift.

Gifts with a total value of more than $600 per person	Describe the gifts	Dates you gave the gifts	Value
Person to Whom You Gave the Gift Number Street City State ZIP Code Person's relationship to you ______		______ ______	$______ $______

Gifts with a total value of more than $600 per person	Describe the gifts	Dates you gave the gifts	Value
Person to Whom You Gave the Gift Number Street City State ZIP Code Person's relationship to you ______		______ ______	$______ $______

Official Form 107 Statement of Financial Affairs for Individuals Filing for Bankruptcy page 6

Debtor 1 William John Patterson Case number (if known)
First Name Middle Name Last Name

14. Within 2 years before you filed for bankruptcy, did you give any gifts or contributions with a total value of more than $600 to any charity?

☒ No
☐ Yes. Fill in the details for each gift or contribution.

Gifts or contributions to charities that total more than $600	Describe what you contributed	Date you contributed	Value
Charity's Name			$
			$
Number Street			
City State ZIP Code			

Part 6: List Certain Losses

15. Within 1 year before you filed for bankruptcy or since you filed for bankruptcy, did you lose anything because of theft, fire, other disaster, or gambling?

☒ No
☐ Yes. Fill in the details.

Describe the property you lost and how the loss occurred	Describe any insurance coverage for the loss Include the amount that insurance has paid. List pending insurance claims on line 33 of *Schedule A/B: Property.*	Date of your loss	Value of property lost
			$

Part 7: List Certain Payments or Transfers

16. Within 1 year before you filed for bankruptcy, did you or anyone else acting on your behalf pay or transfer any property to anyone you consulted about seeking bankruptcy or preparing a bankruptcy petition?
Include any attorneys, bankruptcy petition preparers, or credit counseling agencies for services required in your bankruptcy.

☒ No
☐ Yes. Fill in the details.

	Description and value of any property transferred	Date payment or transfer was made	Amount of payment
Person Who Was Paid			
Number Street			$
			$
City State ZIP Code			
Email or website address			
Person Who Made the Payment, if Not You			

Debtor 1 William John Patterson
First Name Middle Name Last Name
Case number (if known) ____________

	Description and value of any property transferred	Date payment or transfer was made	Amount of payment
Person Who Was Paid Number Street City State ZIP Code Email or website address Person Who Made the Payment, if Not You		______ ______	$______ $______

17. **Within 1 year before you filed for bankruptcy, did you or anyone else acting on your behalf pay or transfer any property to anyone who promised to help you deal with your creditors or to make payments to your creditors?**
Do not include any payment or transfer that you listed on line 16.

☒ No
☐ Yes. Fill in the details.

	Description and value of any property transferred	Date payment or transfer was made	Amount of payment
Person Who Was Paid Number Street City State ZIP Code		______ ______	$______ $______

18. **Within 2 years before you filed for bankruptcy, did you sell, trade, or otherwise transfer any property to anyone, other than property transferred in the ordinary course of your business or financial affairs?**
Include both outright transfers and transfers made as security (such as the granting of a security interest or mortgage on your property).
Do not include gifts and transfers that you have already listed on this statement.

☒ No
☐ Yes. Fill in the details.

	Description and value of property transferred	Describe any property or payments received or debts paid in exchange	Date transfer was made
Person Who Received Transfer Number Street City State ZIP Code Person's relationship to you ______			______
Person Who Received Transfer Number Street City State ZIP Code Person's relationship to you ______			______

Official Form 107 Statement of Financial Affairs for Individuals Filing for Bankruptcy page 8

Debtor 1 William John Patterson
First Name Middle Name Last Name

Case number (if known) ______

19. Within 10 years before you filed for bankruptcy, did you transfer any property to a self-settled trust or similar device of which you are a beneficiary? (These are often called *asset-protection devices.*)

☒ No
☐ Yes. Fill in the details.

	Description and value of the property transferred	Date transfer was made
Name of trust ______		______

Part 8: List Certain Financial Accounts, Instruments, Safe Deposit Boxes, and Storage Units

20. Within 1 year before you filed for bankruptcy, were any financial accounts or instruments held in your name, or for your benefit, closed, sold, moved, or transferred?
Include checking, savings, money market, or other financial accounts; certificates of deposit; shares in banks, credit unions, brokerage houses, pension funds, cooperatives, associations, and other financial institutions.

☒ No
☐ Yes. Fill in the details.

	Last 4 digits of account number	Type of account or instrument	Date account was closed, sold, moved, or transferred	Last balance before closing or transfer
Name of Financial Institution Number Street City State ZIP Code	XXXX–___ ___ ___ ___	☐ Checking ☐ Savings ☐ Money market ☐ Brokerage ☐ Other______	______	$______
Name of Financial Institution Number Street City State ZIP Code	XXXX–___ ___ ___ ___	☐ Checking ☐ Savings ☐ Money market ☐ Brokerage ☐ Other______	______	$______

21. Do you now have, or did you have within 1 year before you filed for bankruptcy, any safe deposit box or other depository for securities, cash, or other valuables?

☒ No
☐ Yes. Fill in the details.

	Who else had access to it?	Describe the contents	Do you still have it?
Name of Financial Institution Number Street City State ZIP Code	Name Number Street City State ZIP Code		☐ No ☐ Yes

Debtor 1 William John Patterson Case number (if known)

First Name Middle Name Last Name

22. Have you stored property in a storage unit or place other than your home within 1 year before you filed for bankruptcy?

☒ No

☐ Yes. Fill in the details.

	Who else has or had access to it?	Describe the contents	Do you still have it?
Name of Storage Facility Number Street City State ZIP Code	Name Number Street City State ZIP Code		☐ No ☐ Yes

Part 9: Identify Property You Hold or Control for Someone Else

23. Do you hold or control any property that someone else owns? Include any property you borrowed from, are storing for, or hold in trust for someone.

☒ No

☐ Yes. Fill in the details.

	Where is the property?	Describe the property	Value
Owner's Name Number Street City State ZIP Code	Number Street City State ZIP Code		$

Part 10: Give Details About Environmental Information

For the purpose of Part 10, the following definitions apply:

- *Environmental law* means any federal, state, or local statute or regulation concerning pollution, contamination, releases of hazardous or toxic substances, wastes, or material into the air, land, soil, surface water, groundwater, or other medium, including statutes or regulations controlling the cleanup of these substances, wastes, or material.
- *Site* means any location, facility, or property as defined under any environmental law, whether you now own, operate, or utilize it or used to own, operate, or utilize it, including disposal sites.
- *Hazardous material* means anything an environmental law defines as a hazardous waste, hazardous substance, toxic substance, hazardous material, pollutant, contaminant, or similar term.

Report all notices, releases, and proceedings that you know about, regardless of when they occurred.

24. Has any governmental unit notified you that you may be liable or potentially liable under or in violation of an environmental law?

☒ No

☐ Yes. Fill in the details.

	Governmental unit	Environmental law, if you know it	Date of notice
Name of site Number Street City State ZIP Code	Governmental unit Number Street City State ZIP Code		

Official Form 107 Statement of Financial Affairs for Individuals Filing for Bankruptcy page 10

Debtor 1 William John Patterson — Case number (if known) ____

25. Have you notified any governmental unit of any release of hazardous material?

- [x] No
- [ ] Yes. Fill in the details.

	Governmental unit	Environmental law, if you know it	Date of notice
Name of site	Governmental unit		
Number Street	Number Street		
	City State ZIP Code		
City State ZIP Code			

26. Have you been a party in any judicial or administrative proceeding under any environmental law? Include settlements and orders.

- [x] No
- [ ] Yes. Fill in the details.

	Court or agency	Nature of the case	Status of the case
Case title ____	Court Name		☐ Pending
	Number Street		☐ On appeal
Case number	City State ZIP Code		☐ Concluded

Part 11: Give Details About Your Business or Connections to Any Business

27. Within 4 years before you filed for bankruptcy, did you own a business or have any of the following connections to any business?

- [ ] A sole proprietor or self-employed in a trade, profession, or other activity, either full-time or part-time
- [ ] A member of a limited liability company (LLC) or limited liability partnership (LLP)
- [ ] A partner in a partnership
- [ ] An officer, director, or managing executive of a corporation
- [ ] An owner of at least 5% of the voting or equity securities of a corporation

- [x] No. None of the above applies. Go to Part 12.
- [ ] Yes. Check all that apply above and fill in the details below for each business.

	Describe the nature of the business	Employer Identification number Do not include Social Security number or ITIN.
Business Name		EIN: __ __ – __ __ __ __ __ __ __
Number Street	Name of accountant or bookkeeper	Dates business existed
City State ZIP Code		From ____ To ____

	Describe the nature of the business	Employer Identification number Do not include Social Security number or ITIN.
Business Name		EIN: __ __ – __ __ __ __ __ __ __
Number Street	Name of accountant or bookkeeper	Dates business existed
City State ZIP Code		From ____ To ____

Debtor 1 William John Patterson
First Name Middle Name Last Name

Case number (if known) ______

Business Name / Number Street / City State ZIP Code	Describe the nature of the business / Name of accountant or bookkeeper	Employer Identification number. Do not include Social Security number or ITIN. EIN: __ __ - __ __ __ __ __ __ __ / Dates business existed From ______ To ______

28. Within 2 years before you filed for bankruptcy, did you give a financial statement to anyone about your business? Include all financial institutions, creditors, or other parties.

☒ No
☐ Yes. Fill in the details below.

Name ______ Date issued MM / DD / YYYY

Number Street

City State ZIP Code

Part 12: Sign Below

I have read the answers on this *Statement of Financial Affairs* and any attachments, and I declare under penalty of perjury that the answers are true and correct. I understand that making a false statement, concealing property, or obtaining money or property by fraud in connection with a bankruptcy case can result in fines up to $250,000, or imprisonment for up to 20 years, or both. 18 U.S.C. §§ 152, 1341, 1519, and 3571.

✘ William John Patterson ✘ ______
Signature of Debtor 1 Signature of Debtor 2

William John Patterson

Date 10/18/2017 Date ______

Did you attach additional pages to *Your Statement of Financial Affairs for Individuals Filing for Bankruptcy* (Official Form 107)?

☒ No
☐ Yes

Did you pay or agree to pay someone who is not an attorney to help you fill out bankruptcy forms?

☒ No
☐ Yes. Name of person ______. Attach the *Bankruptcy Petition Preparer's Notice, Declaration, and Signature* (Official Form 119).

Official Form 107 Statement of Financial Affairs for Individuals Filing for Bankruptcy page 12

CHAPTER 9

STEP VII: FINANCIAL MANAGEMENT COURSE (POST PETITION), MEETING OF CREDITORS, AND DISCHARGE

PERSONAL FINANCIAL MANAGEMENT (POST PETITION)

The bankruptcy court will not grant a discharge until you have completed a post-petition instructional course concerning personal financial management. We discussed this previously in Chapter 4 of this book, and it is recommended that you utilize the same agency that provided you with the prepetition credit counseling. You will receive a workbook from the agency which requires you to read and answer the questions provided in the book. You may mail the answers and/or contact the agency via telephone to discuss your answers. Upon your satisfactory completion of the test, the agency will promptly mail your required certificate.

Upon receipt of your certificate, you must fill out a "Debtor's Certification of Completion of Postpetition Instructional Course Concerning Personal Financial Management (Form B423)." You will attach this form to your certificate and file them with the clerk. My example "Form B423" and my "Personal Management Course Certificate" can be located in the back of this chapter. Under rule 341 of the Bankruptcy Code, these forms must be received within 45 days of the first date set for the meeting of creditors.

BANKRUPTCY CASE NOTIFICATION, MEETING OF CREDITORS AND DATES

After your initial bankruptcy filing you will receive a "Form 309A" from the court. The form will also be sent to all other parties involved in your case. The form will provide your bankruptcy case number, date filed, trustee contact information, contact information for your clerk's office, meeting of creditors date, deadlines and other pertinent information. As an example, my "Form 309A" can be located at the end of this chapter.

PERSONAL APPEARANCE WAIVER

The Bankruptcy Code requires you to appear and submit to an examination under oath at the, meeting of creditors. The decision to waive your appearance is at the discretion of the U.S. trustee and only in limited circumstances. An effort must be made to appear but for those incarcerated this is not possible. An alternative to appearing in person will be to appear via telephone.

If incarcerated, I recommend that you immediately notify your counselor or other appropriate staff member upon receipt of your notice of meeting of creditors. Make any arrangements so that you will be available for the meeting of creditors via telephone. Also, make arrangements to complete your post-petition financial management course. Remember, it is due within 45 days of the meeting of the creditor's date. You will want to prepare a letter addressed to your assigned trustee. Explain that you are incarcerated and unable to attend in person. Request that your personal appearance be waived, and instead, respectfully request that you be allowed to attend telephonically or respond by written interrogatories as the trustee deems appropriate.

Be sure to provide to the trustee all pertinent information including – the institution and all staff contact information so that arrangements can be made on your behalf for you to have telephone access on the appointed date and time. My example letter to the trustee requesting a waiver can be located at the end of this chapter.

In my case, I notified my institution counselor prior to receiving the notice of the meeting of creditors. I did not want any surprises and found out she was soon leaving her position and would be out of her office for an extended period. This was important to know in preparing my letter. I had my rough draft waiver letter prepared so that when the "Form 309A" arrived, I could immediately send it out to the appointed trustee. On October 31, 2017 I mailed my letter requesting to be waived from personal appearance.

My meeting of creditors was scheduled for November 29, 2017. By November 16, 2017, I had not received any correspondence from the trustee's office. On that day I called his office and spoke with his staff. I wrote down the date and time called, staff spoken to as well as the specifics of our discussion. I recommend you do the same when making any outside contacts. It turned out the information I had written down would later be vital in my response to the court. I was assured by the trustee's secretary that she was familiar with my case, and it would be handled. From time to time, I checked with my case manager to see if she had received any calls or notifications from the court, and she had not.

On January 2, 2018, I received a much unexpected letter from the Bankruptcy Court – An "Order to Show Cause Why Case Should Not Be Dismissed with Prejudice." A copy of this order is included at the end of this chapter. It stated that I not only failed to appear for the initial meeting, but that I failed to appear for a rescheduled second meeting of which I was not made aware of by the trustee's office. I had 21 days to respond in order to avoid my case from being dismissed. I responded by filing a motion to the court with an explanation with all the specifics that had transpired. Within days of the court's receipt, my case manager called me in notifying me of a new meeting of the creditor's date. An example of my response motion to the court can be located at the end of this chapter.

MEETING OF CREDITORS

The meeting of creditors is a formal proceeding. At the designated time I joined my case manager and unit secretary who is a notary. When the trustee called, the secretary swore me in under oath and notarized a document as testament to my presence and oath. The trustee will ask you a number of questions concerning your financial situation. Some of the questions presented to me were, for example: “Do you have any outside bank accounts?” “Do you own any real estate?” “Do your parents own any real estate that you might inherit upon their death?” “Are your schedules true and accurate?” and so forth. The creditors most likely will not attend. None were present during mine. The meeting usually takes less than an hour; in my case, it took no more than ten minutes.

DISCHARGE

A discharge is usually granted promptly after the time expires for filing a complaint to discharge or a motion to dismiss your case. Either of these must occur within 60 days following the first date set in regards to your meeting of creditors. Generally a discharge occurs approximately four months from the initial bankruptcy filing date. In my case, my discharge was granted the following day after my meeting of creditors. An example of my discharge order can be located in the back of this chapter. Once a discharge is granted by the court the clerk will promptly send you and your creditors a copy of the discharge order.

Although the process may seem daunting at times, if you follow the instructions provided for each step along the way, you will find yourself that much closer to securing your own financial freedom and a second chance at personal success. Good Luck!

Fill in this information to identify the case:

Debtor 1 William John Patterson
First Name Middle Name Last Name

Debtor 2
(Spouse, if filing) First Name Middle Name Last Name

United States Bankruptcy Court for the Northern District of Texas

Case number 17-33972
(If known)

Official Form 423

Certification About a Financial Management Course

12/15

If you are an individual, you must take an approved course about personal financial management if:

- **you filed for bankruptcy under chapter 7 or 13, or**
- **you filed for bankruptcy under chapter 11 and § 1141 (d)(3) applies.**

In a joint case, each debtor must take the course. 11 U.S.C. §§ 727(a)(11) and 1328(g).

After you finish the course, the provider will give you a certificate. The provider may notify the court that you have completed the course. If the provider does notify the court, you need not file this form. If the provider does not notify the court, then Debtor 1 and Debtor 2 must each file this form with the certificate number before your debts will be discharged.

- If you filed under chapter 7 and you need to file this form, file it within 60 days after the first date set for the meeting of creditors under § 341 of the Bankruptcy Code.
- If you filed under chapter 11 or 13 and you need to file this form, file it before you make the last payment that your plan requires or before you file a motion for a discharge under § 1141(d)(5)(B) or § 1328(b) of the Bankruptcy Code. Fed. R. Bankr. P. 1007(c).

In some cases, the court can waive the requirement to take the financial management course. To have the requirement waived, you must file a motion with the court and obtain a court order.

Part 1: Tell the Court About the Required Course

You must check one:

☒ **I completed an approved course in personal financial management:**

Date I took the course 12/04/2017
MM / DD / YYYY

Name of approved provider Stand Sure Informations Services, Inc.

Certificate number 01201-TXN-DE-030256533

☐ **I am not required to complete a course in personal financial management because the court has granted my motion for a waiver of the requirement based on** *(check one)*:

☐ **Incapacity.** I have a mental illness or a mental deficiency that makes me incapable of realizing or making rational decisions about finances.

☐ **Disability.** My physical disability causes me to be unable to complete a course in personal financial management in person, by phone, or through the internet, even after I reasonably tried to do so.

☐ **Active duty.** I am currently on active military duty in a military combat zone.

☐ **Residence.** I live in a district in which the United States trustee (or bankruptcy administrator) has determined that the approved instructional courses cannot adequately meet my needs.

Part 2: Sign Here

I certify that the information I have provided is true and correct.

William John Patterson — Signature of debtor named on certificate

William John Patterson — Printed name of debtor

Date 12/04/2017
MM / DD / YYYY

Official Form 423 **Certification About a Financial Management Course**

Certificate Number: 01201-TXN-DE-030256533

Bankruptcy Case Number: 17-33972

01201-TXN-DE-030256533

CERTIFICATE OF DEBTOR EDUCATION

I CERTIFY that on December 4, 2017, at 11:06 o'clock AM CST, William J. Patterson completed a course on personal financial management given by telephone by Stand Sure Information Services, Inc. , a provider approved pursuant to 11 U.S.C. § 111 to provide an instructional course concerning personal financial management in the Northern District of Texas.

Date: December 4, 2017

By: /s/Carol McWaters

Name: Carol McWaters

Title: Debtor Education Specialist

Case 17-33972-bjh7 Doc 4 Filed 10/23/17 Entered 10/23/17 15:52:26 Page 1 of 2

Information to identify the case:

Debtor 1	**William John Patterson** First Name Middle Name Last Name	Social Security number or ITIN	**xxx-xx-0300**
		EIN	__-_______
Debtor 2 (Spouse, if filing)	First Name Middle Name Last Name	Social Security number or ITIN	____
		EIN	__-_______
United States Bankruptcy Court	**Northern District of Texas**	Date case filed for chapter **7**	**10/23/17**
Case number:	**17-33972-bjh7**		

Official Form 309A (For Individuals or Joint Debtors)

Notice of Chapter 7 Bankruptcy Case -- No Proof of Claim Deadline 12/15

For the debtors listed above, a case has been filed under chapter 7 of the Bankruptcy Code. An order for relief has been entered.

This notice has important information about the case for creditors, debtors, and trustees, including information about the meeting of creditors and deadlines. Read both pages carefully.

The filing of the case imposed an automatic stay against most collection activities. This means that creditors generally may not take action to collect debts from the debtors or the debtors' property. For example, while the stay is in effect, creditors cannot sue, garnish wages, assert a deficiency, repossess property, or otherwise try to collect from the debtors. Creditors cannot demand repayment from debtors by mail, phone, or otherwise. Creditors who violate the stay can be required to pay actual and punitive damages and attorney's fees. Under certain circumstances, the stay may be limited to 30 days or not exist at all, although debtors can ask the court to extend or impose a stay.

The debtors are seeking a discharge. Creditors who assert that the debtors are not entitled to a discharge of any debts or who want to have a particular debt excepted from discharge may be required to file a complaint in the bankruptcy clerk's office within the deadlines specified in this notice. (See line 9 for more information.)

To protect your rights, consult an attorney. All documents filed in the case may be inspected at the bankruptcy clerk's office at the address listed below or through PACER (Public Access to Court Electronic Records at www.pacer.gov).

The staff of the bankruptcy clerk's office cannot give legal advice.

To help creditors correctly identify debtors, debtors submit full Social Security or Individual Taxpayer Identification Numbers, which may appear on a version of this notice. However, the full numbers must not appear on any document filed with the court.

Do not file this notice with any proof of claim or other filing in the case. Do not include more than the last four digits of a Social Security or Individual Taxpayer Identification Number in any document, including attachments, that you file with the court.

		About Debtor 1:	**About Debtor 2:**
1.	**Debtor's full name**	William John Patterson	
2.	**All other names used in the last 8 years**		
3.	**Address**	P.O. Box 9000 Seagoville, TX 75159	
4.	**Debtor's attorney** Name and address	William John Patterson P.O. Box 9000 Seagoville, TX 75159	Contact phone: __________ Email: **None**
5.	**Bankruptcy trustee** Name and address	Daniel J. Sherman 509 N. Montclair Dallas, TX 75208	Contact phone: (214)942-5502 Email: djsherman@syllp.com

For more information, see page 2 >

6. Bankruptcy clerk's office Documents in this case may be filed at this address. You may inspect all records filed in this case at this office or online at www.pacer.gov.	1100 Commerce Street Room 1254 Dallas, TX 75242	Office Hours: Mon.-Fri. 8:30-4:30 Contact Phone: 214-753-2000
7. Meeting of creditors Debtors must attend the meeting to be questioned under oath. In a joint case, both spouses must attend. Creditors may attend, but are not required to do so.	**November 29, 2017 at 09:50 AM** The meeting may be continued or adjourned to a later date. If so, the date will be on the court docket.	Location: **Office of the U.S. Trustee, 1100 Commerce St., Rm 524, Dallas, TX 75242**
8. Presumption of abuse If the presumption of abuse arises, you may have the right to file a motion to dismiss the case under 11 U.S.C. § 707(b). Debtors may rebut the presumption by showing special circumstances.	Insufficient information has been filed to date to permit the clerk to make any determination concerning the presumption of abuse. If more complete information, when filed, shows that the presumption has arisen, creditors will be notified.	
9. Deadlines The bankruptcy clerk's office must receive these documents and any required filing fee by the following deadlines.	**File by the deadline to object to discharge or to challenge whether certain debts are dischargeable:** **You must file a complaint:** • if you assert that the debtor is not entitled to receive a discharge of any debts under any of the subdivisions of 11 U.S.C. § 727(a)(2) through (7), or • if you want to have a debt excepted from discharge under 11 U.S.C § 523(a)(2), (4), or (6). **You must file a motion:** • if you assert that the discharge should be denied under § 727(a)(8) or (9).	**Filing deadline: 1/29/18**
	Deadline to object to exemptions: The law permits debtors to keep certain property as exempt. If you believe that the law does not authorize an exemption claimed, you may file an objection.	**Filing deadline:** 30 days after the *conclusion* of the meeting of creditors
10. Proof of claim Please do not file a proof of claim unless you receive a notice to do so.	No property appears to be available to pay creditors. Therefore, please do not file a proof of claim now. If it later appears that assets are available to pay creditors, the clerk will send you another notice telling you that you may file a proof of claim and stating the deadline.	
11. Creditors with a foreign address	If you are a creditor receiving a notice mailed to a foreign address, you may file a motion asking the court to extend the deadlines in this notice. Consult an attorney familiar with United States bankruptcy law if you have any questions about your rights in this case.	
12. Exempt property	The law allows debtors to keep certain property as exempt. Fully exempt property will not be sold and distributed to creditors. Debtors must file a list of property claimed as exempt. You may inspect that list at the bankruptcy clerk's office or online at www.pacer.gov. If you believe that the law does not authorize an exemption that the debtors claim, you may file an objection. The bankruptcy clerk's office must receive the objection by the deadline to object to exemptions in line 9.	

Daniel Sherman, Esq.
U.S. Bankruptcy Trustee
509 N. Montclair
Dallas, TX 75208

October 31, 2017

Re: Request for waiver of personal appearance at Creditor's meeting
William John Patterson, Case No. 17-33972-bjh7
DATE 11/29/2017 TIME 9:50 a.m.

Dear Mr. Sherman:

I am the debtor who has filed pro se in the above Chapter 7 bankruptcy case. I am currently incarcerated and thus unable to physically attend the above referenced meeting of creditors in this matter.

I have complted the pre-counseling course and will soon have complted the post-counseling course.

Under the circumstances, I respectfully request to be permitted to attend the meeting of creditors telephonically and/or by written interrogatories, as you may deem appropriate. Arrangements for my appearance by telephone can be made by calling my counselor, Ms. Goins at (972) 287-4000. She can coordinate a date and time that would allow me to participate..

In light of my circumstances, I ask you to please waive my personal appearance and allow me to attend the meeting by one of the methods stated above. Thank you for your time and consideration in this matter.

Repectfully,

William John Patterson

William John Patterson

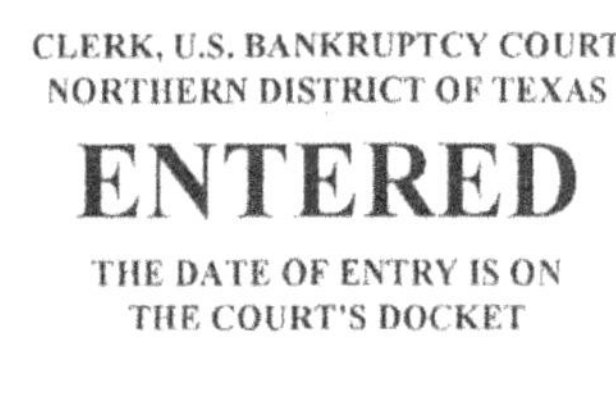

The following constitutes the ruling of the court and has the force and effect therein described.

Signed December 26, 2017

Harlin DeWayne Hale
United States Bankruptcy Judge

BTXN 165 (rev. 10/04)

UNITED STATES BANKRUPTCY COURT
NORTHERN DISTRICT OF TEXAS

In Re:	§	
William John Patterson	§	Case No.: 17–33972–bjh7
	§	Chapter No.: 7
Debtor(s)	§	

ORDER TO SHOW CAUSE WHY CASE SHOULD NOT BE DISMISSED WITH PREJUDICE

The debtor(s) failed to appear at the initially scheduled meeting of creditors. The Chapter 7 trustee continued the meeting of creditors to a new date/time. The debtor(s) failed to appear at the continued meeting of creditors. Based on the debtor(s) failure to appear at the continued meeting of creditors (second no show),

IT IS ORDERED that the debtor(s) show cause, by written statement filed within 21 days of entry of this order, why the case should not be dismissed with prejudice to filing another case under the Bankruptcy Code for 180 days. Failure to file a timely response will result in the automatic dismissal of the case. If a response is timely filed, the court will consider the matter on the pleadings unless the court directs that a hearing be set.

End of Order # #

UNITED STATES BANKRUPTCY COURT
NORTHERN DISTRICT OF TEXAS

In Re:	)	
William John Patterson	)	Case No.: 17-33972-bjh7
	)	Chapter No.: 7
Debtor	)	

<u>RESPONSE TO ORDER TO SHOW CAUSE WHY CASE SHOULD NOT BE DISMISSED WITH PREJUDICE</u>

I, William John Patterson, the debtor in this Chapter 7 case, state the following in response to the Court's Order to Show Cause Why Case Should Not Be Dismissed With Prejudice ("the Order"):

1. I filed this case on October 23, 2017 and received a written notice of a Creditor's meeting set by the Court and Chapter 7 trustee for November 29, 2017 within a few days of the Court's acceptance of my filing.

2. Due to my incarceration and inability to physically attend the scheduled Creditor's meeting in person, I wrote to the Chapter 7 trustee, Daniel Sherman on October 31, 2017 notifying him of my circumstances and requesting permission to attend the the meeting of crditors telephonically and/or by written interrogatories. A copy of my letter to Trustee Sherman is attached hereto.

3. I did not receive any response to my letter from Trustee Sherman , so I telephoned his office on November 16, 2017 to confirm his receipt of my October 31 letter and to inquire about the status of the creditors meeting. Mr. Sherman was not available , but I spoke to his assistant Ms. Adrian, who told me that the Trustee was familiar with my case and requests and would work out something to accomodate me. I provided Ms. Adrian with the names of some alternative BOP staff personnel

who could be available to receive a telephone call for any re-scheduled creditor's meeting, coordinate a meeting date and time with the Trustee, and act as notary to swear me in at any creditor's meeting. Ms. Adrian assured me on the telphone that arrangements for a new crditors meeting time would be taken care of, but I never received anything from the Court or Chapter 7 trustee setting a new hearing date/time.

4. The Order/correctly states that I failed to appear at the initially scheduled meeting of creditors. I took all reasonable steps to participate by alternative means before the scheduled date and time and was assured by the Chapter 7 trustee's office that I would be accomodated. I was never notified of any continuance of the creditors meeting "to a new date/time" as the Order states. I have no idea when the continued date and time was, but can only presume it was sometime between November 29 and the December 26 Order. It is inaccurate and unfair to characterize me as a "second no show," under all the circumstances. I remain ready and willing to participate in any creditors meeting by telphone at a convenient time to the Chapter 7 trustee when BOP staff can also be available for a call. I also remain willing and ready to answer written interrogatories in lieu of a creditors meeting.

5. Any of the following BOP personnel can coordinate my attendance at a telephonic creditors meeting and are available by telphone at (972) 287-4000 during regular business hours: (a) Ms. Evans, Inmate Case Manager; (b) Mr. Johnson, Unit 54 Housing Manager; and (c) Mr. Donald Albert, Assistant Warden.

6. I believe there has been a breakdown in communication between the Chapter 7 Trustee's office and BOP personnel who can coordinate and secure my attendace at a creditors meeting. In particular, Ms. Goins (whom I identified to the Trustee in my October 31 letter) has been re-assigned to other duties in the F.C.I. Seagoville facility. Ms. Evans my case manager was out of the office for much of the month of December. As an inmate, I cannot control BOP staff nor their scheduling efforts with the Chapter 7 trustee's office.

7. This Chapter 7 bankruptcy is very important to me as I am trying to get my financial affairs in order before my anticipated release in late 2018 or early 2019. I have no assets and simply need my debts discharged to make a fresh start.

I respectfully request that the Court enter orders: (A) allowing this case to proceed and excusing my attandance at any previously scheduled meeting of creditors; and (B) directing the Chapter 7 trustee to accept my written interrogatory answers in lieu of my appearance and testimony at a meeting of creditors. Alternatively, I ask the Court to compel the Chapter 7 trustee to secure my attendance by teleconference coordinated through the BOP personnel identified in Paragraph 5 above, including a directive to each of them to make me available.

Respectfully submitted,

Dated: January 4, 2018

William John Patterson

William John Patterson, Pro Se

William J. Patterson

Information to identify the case:

Debtor 1	William John Patterson First Name Middle Name Last Name	Social Security number or ITIN	xxx-xx-0300
		EIN	_ _-_ _ _ _ _ _ _
Debtor 2 (Spouse, if filing)	First Name Middle Name Last Name	Social Security number or ITIN	_ _ _ _
		EIN	_ _-_ _ _ _ _ _ _
United States Bankruptcy Court	Northern District of Texas		
Case number:	17-33972-bjh7		

Order of Discharge

12/15

IT IS ORDERED: A discharge under 11 U.S.C. § 727 is granted to:

William John Patterson

2/15/18

By the court: Barbara J. Houser
United States Bankruptcy Judge

Explanation of Bankruptcy Discharge in a Chapter 7 Case

This order does not close or dismiss the case, and it does not determine how much money, if any, the trustee will pay creditors.

Creditors cannot collect discharged debts

This order means that no one may make any attempt to collect a discharged debt from the debtors personally. For example, creditors cannot sue, garnish wages, assert a deficiency, or otherwise try to collect from the debtors personally on discharged debts. Creditors cannot contact the debtors by mail, phone, or otherwise in any attempt to collect the debt personally. Creditors who violate this order can be required to pay debtors damages and attorney's fees.

However, a creditor with a lien may enforce a claim against the debtors' property subject to that lien unless the lien was avoided or eliminated. For example, a creditor may have the right to foreclose a home mortgage or repossess an automobile.

This order does not prevent debtors from paying any debt voluntarily or from paying reaffirmed debts according to the reaffirmation agreement. 11 U.S.C. § 524(c), (f).

Most debts are discharged

Most debts are covered by the discharge, but not all. Generally, a discharge removes the debtors' personal liability for debts owed before the debtors' bankruptcy case was filed.

Also, if this case began under a different chapter of the Bankruptcy Code and was later converted to chapter 7, debts owed before the conversion are discharged.

In a case involving community property: Special rules protect certain community property owned by the debtor's spouse, even if that spouse did not file a bankruptcy case.

For more information, see page 2 >

BANKRUPTCY FORMS

Fill in this information to identify your case:

United States Bankruptcy Court for the:

__________ District of __________

Case number *(If known)*: ____________________

Chapter you are filing under:
- ❑ Chapter 7
- ❑ Chapter 11
- ❑ Chapter 12
- ❑ Chapter 13

❑ Check if this is an amended filing

Official Form 101

Voluntary Petition for Individuals Filing for Bankruptcy

12/17

The bankruptcy forms use *you* and *Debtor 1* to refer to a debtor filing alone. A married couple may file a bankruptcy case together—called a *joint case*—and in joint cases, these forms use *you* to ask for information from both debtors. For example, if a form asks, "Do you own a car," the answer would be *yes* if either debtor owns a car. When information is needed about the spouses separately, the form uses *Debtor 1* and *Debtor 2* to distinguish between them. In joint cases, one of the spouses must report information as *Debtor 1* and the other as *Debtor 2*. The same person must be *Debtor 1* in all of the forms.

Be as complete and accurate as possible. If two married people are filing together, both are equally responsible for supplying correct information. If more space is needed, attach a separate sheet to this form. On the top of any additional pages, write your name and case number (if known). Answer every question.

Part 1: Identify Yourself

	About Debtor 1:	About Debtor 2 (Spouse Only in a Joint Case):
1. **Your full name** Write the name that is on your government-issued picture identification (for example, your driver's license or passport). Bring your picture identification to your meeting with the trustee.	____________________ First name ____________________ Middle name ____________________ Last name __________ Suffix (Sr., Jr., II, III)	____________________ First name ____________________ Middle name ____________________ Last name __________ Suffix (Sr., Jr., II, III)
2. **All other names you have used in the last 8 years** Include your married or maiden names.	____________________ First name ____________________ Middle name ____________________ Last name ____________________ First name ____________________ Middle name ____________________ Last name	____________________ First name ____________________ Middle name ____________________ Last name ____________________ First name ____________________ Middle name ____________________ Last name
3. **Only the last 4 digits of your Social Security number or federal Individual Taxpayer Identification number** (ITIN)	XXX – XX – ___ ___ ___ ___ OR 9 XX – XX – ___ ___ ___ ___	XXX – XX – ___ ___ ___ ___ OR 9 XX – XX – ___ ___ ___ ___

Debtor 1 ______________________ First Name Middle Name Last Name   Case number *(if known)* ______________________

	About Debtor 1:	About Debtor 2 (Spouse Only in a Joint Case):
4. Any business names and Employer Identification Numbers (EIN) you have used in the last 8 years Include trade names and *doing business as* names	❑ I have not used any business names or EINs. ______________________ Business name ______________________ Business name __ __ - __ __ __ __ __ __ __ EIN __ __ - __ __ __ __ __ __ __ EIN	❑ I have not used any business names or EINs. ______________________ Business name ______________________ Business name __ __ - __ __ __ __ __ __ __ EIN __ __ - __ __ __ __ __ __ __ EIN
5. Where you live	______________________ Number Street ______________________ ______________________ City State ZIP Code ______________________ County **If your mailing address is different from the one above, fill it in here.** Note that the court will send any notices to you at this mailing address. ______________________ Number Street ______________________ P.O. Box ______________________ City State ZIP Code	**If Debtor 2 lives at a different address:** ______________________ Number Street ______________________ ______________________ City State ZIP Code ______________________ County **If Debtor 2's mailing address is different from yours, fill it in here.** Note that the court will send any notices to this mailing address. ______________________ Number Street ______________________ P.O. Box ______________________ City State ZIP Code
6. Why you are choosing *this district* to file for bankruptcy	*Check one:* ❑ Over the last 180 days before filing this petition, I have lived in this district longer than in any other district. ❑ I have another reason. Explain. (See 28 U.S.C. § 1408.) ______________________ ______________________ ______________________ ______________________	*Check one:* ❑ Over the last 180 days before filing this petition, I have lived in this district longer than in any other district. ❑ I have another reason. Explain. (See 28 U.S.C. § 1408.) ______________________ ______________________ ______________________ ______________________

William J. Patterson

Debtor 1 ______________________ First Name Middle Name Last Name Case number (if known)______________________

Part 2: Tell the Court About Your Bankruptcy Case

7. The chapter of the Bankruptcy Code you are choosing to file under

Check one. (For a brief description of each, see *Notice Required by 11 U.S.C. § 342(b) for Individuals Filing for Bankruptcy* (Form 2010)). Also, go to the top of page 1 and check the appropriate box.

- ☐ Chapter 7
- ☐ Chapter 11
- ☐ Chapter 12
- ☐ Chapter 13

8. How you will pay the fee

☐ **I will pay the entire fee when I file my petition.** Please check with the clerk's office in your local court for more details about how you may pay. Typically, if you are paying the fee yourself, you may pay with cash, cashier's check, or money order. If your attorney is submitting your payment on your behalf, your attorney may pay with a credit card or check with a pre-printed address.

☐ **I need to pay the fee in installments.** If you choose this option, sign and attach the *Application for Individuals to Pay The Filing Fee in Installments* (Official Form 103A).

☐ **I request that my fee be waived** (You may request this option only if you are filing for Chapter 7. By law, a judge may, but is not required to, waive your fee, and may do so only if your income is less than 150% of the official poverty line that applies to your family size and you are unable to pay the fee in installments). If you choose this option, you must fill out the *Application to Have the Chapter 7 Filing Fee Waived* (Official Form 103B) and file it with your petition.

9. Have you filed for bankruptcy within the last 8 years?

☐ No

☐ Yes. District ______________ When ________ MM / DD / YYYY Case number ______________

District ______________ When ________ MM / DD / YYYY Case number ______________

District ______________ When ________ MM / DD / YYYY Case number ______________

10. Are any bankruptcy cases pending or being filed by a spouse who is not filing this case with you, or by a business partner, or by an affiliate?

☐ No

☐ Yes. Debtor ______________ Relationship to you ______________

District ______________ When ________ MM / DD / YYYY Case number, if known______________

Debtor ______________ Relationship to you ______________

District ______________ When ________ MM / DD / YYYY Case number, if known______________

11. Do you rent your residence?

☐ No. Go to line 12.

☐ Yes. Has your landlord obtained an eviction judgment against you?

- ☐ No. Go to line 12.
- ☐ Yes. Fill out *Initial Statement About an Eviction Judgment Against You* (Form 101A) and file it as part of this bankruptcy petition.

Debtor 1 ______________________________ Case number *(if known)* ______________________________
First Name Middle Name Last Name

Part 3: Report About Any Businesses You Own as a Sole Proprietor

12. **Are you a sole proprietor of any full- or part-time business?**

A sole proprietorship is a business you operate as an individual, and is not a separate legal entity such as a corporation, partnership, or LLC.

If you have more than one sole proprietorship, use a separate sheet and attach it to this petition.

❑ No. Go to Part 4.

❑ Yes. Name and location of business

____
Name of business, if any

____
Number Street

____

______________________________ ______ ______________
City State ZIP Code

Check the appropriate box to describe your business:

❑ Health Care Business (as defined in 11 U.S.C. § 101(27A))

❑ Single Asset Real Estate (as defined in 11 U.S.C. § 101(51B))

❑ Stockbroker (as defined in 11 U.S.C. § 101(53A))

❑ Commodity Broker (as defined in 11 U.S.C. § 101(6))

❑ None of the above

13. **Are you filing under Chapter 11 of the Bankruptcy Code and are you a *small business debtor*?**

For a definition of *small business debtor*, see 11 U.S.C. § 101(51D).

If you are filing under Chapter 11, the court must know whether you are a small business debtor so that it can set appropriate deadlines. If you indicate that you are a small business debtor, you must attach your most recent balance sheet, statement of operations, cash-flow statement, and federal income tax return or if any of these documents do not exist, follow the procedure in 11 U.S.C. § 1116(1)(B).

❑ No. I am not filing under Chapter 11.

❑ No. I am filing under Chapter 11, but I am NOT a small business debtor according to the definition in the Bankruptcy Code.

❑ Yes. I am filing under Chapter 11 and I am a small business debtor according to the definition in the Bankruptcy Code.

Part 4: Report if You Own or Have Any Hazardous Property or Any Property That Needs Immediate Attention

14. **Do you own or have any property that poses or is alleged to pose a threat of imminent and identifiable hazard to public health or safety? Or do you own any property that needs immediate attention?**

For example, do you own perishable goods, or livestock that must be fed, or a building that needs urgent repairs?

❑ No

❑ Yes. What is the hazard? ______________________________

____

If immediate attention is needed, why is it needed? ______________________________

____

Where is the property? ______________________________
Number Street

____

______________________________ ______ ______________
City State ZIP Code

William J. Patterson

Debtor 1 ______________________________ Case number (if known) ______________
First Name Middle Name Last Name

Part 5: Explain Your Efforts to Receive a Briefing About Credit Counseling

15. Tell the court whether you have received a briefing about credit counseling.

The law requires that you receive a briefing about credit counseling before you file for bankruptcy. You must truthfully check one of the following choices. If you cannot do so, you are not eligible to file.

If you file anyway, the court can dismiss your case, you will lose whatever filing fee you paid, and your creditors can begin collection activities again.

About Debtor 1:

You must check one:

- ❑ **I received a briefing from an approved credit counseling agency within the 180 days before I filed this bankruptcy petition, and I received a certificate of completion.**

  Attach a copy of the certificate and the payment plan, if any, that you developed with the agency.

- ❑ **I received a briefing from an approved credit counseling agency within the 180 days before I filed this bankruptcy petition, but I do not have a certificate of completion.**

  Within 14 days after you file this bankruptcy petition, you MUST file a copy of the certificate and payment plan, if any.

- ❑ **I certify that I asked for credit counseling services from an approved agency, but was unable to obtain those services during the 7 days after I made my request, and exigent circumstances merit a 30-day temporary waiver of the requirement.**

  To ask for a 30-day temporary waiver of the requirement, attach a separate sheet explaining what efforts you made to obtain the briefing, why you were unable to obtain it before you filed for bankruptcy, and what exigent circumstances required you to file this case.

  Your case may be dismissed if the court is dissatisfied with your reasons for not receiving a briefing before you filed for bankruptcy.

  If the court is satisfied with your reasons, you must still receive a briefing within 30 days after you file. You must file a certificate from the approved agency, along with a copy of the payment plan you developed, if any. If you do not do so, your case may be dismissed.

  Any extension of the 30-day deadline is granted only for cause and is limited to a maximum of 15 days.

- ❑ **I am not required to receive a briefing about credit counseling because of:**

  - ❑ **Incapacity.** I have a mental illness or a mental deficiency that makes me incapable of realizing or making rational decisions about finances.
  - ❑ **Disability.** My physical disability causes me to be unable to participate in a briefing in person, by phone, or through the internet, even after I reasonably tried to do so.
  - ❑ **Active duty.** I am currently on active military duty in a military combat zone.

  If you believe you are not required to receive a briefing about credit counseling, you must file a motion for waiver of credit counseling with the court.

About Debtor 2 (Spouse Only in a Joint Case):

You must check one:

- ❑ **I received a briefing from an approved credit counseling agency within the 180 days before I filed this bankruptcy petition, and I received a certificate of completion.**

  Attach a copy of the certificate and the payment plan, if any, that you developed with the agency.

- ❑ **I received a briefing from an approved credit counseling agency within the 180 days before I filed this bankruptcy petition, but I do not have a certificate of completion.**

  Within 14 days after you file this bankruptcy petition, you MUST file a copy of the certificate and payment plan, if any.

- ❑ **I certify that I asked for credit counseling services from an approved agency, but was unable to obtain those services during the 7 days after I made my request, and exigent circumstances merit a 30-day temporary waiver of the requirement.**

  To ask for a 30-day temporary waiver of the requirement, attach a separate sheet explaining what efforts you made to obtain the briefing, why you were unable to obtain it before you filed for bankruptcy, and what exigent circumstances required you to file this case.

  Your case may be dismissed if the court is dissatisfied with your reasons for not receiving a briefing before you filed for bankruptcy.

  If the court is satisfied with your reasons, you must still receive a briefing within 30 days after you file. You must file a certificate from the approved agency, along with a copy of the payment plan you developed, if any. If you do not do so, your case may be dismissed.

  Any extension of the 30-day deadline is granted only for cause and is limited to a maximum of 15 days.

- ❑ **I am not required to receive a briefing about credit counseling because of:**

  - ❑ **Incapacity.** I have a mental illness or a mental deficiency that makes me incapable of realizing or making rational decisions about finances.
  - ❑ **Disability.** My physical disability causes me to be unable to participate in a briefing in person, by phone, or through the internet, even after I reasonably tried to do so.
  - ❑ **Active duty.** I am currently on active military duty in a military combat zone.

  If you believe you are not required to receive a briefing about credit counseling, you must file a motion for waiver of credit counseling with the court.

Debtor 1 ______________________________ First Name Middle Name Last Name   Case number (if known) ______________________

Part 6: Answer These Questions for Reporting Purposes

16. What kind of debts do you have?

16a. **Are your debts primarily consumer debts?** *Consumer debts* are defined in 11 U.S.C. § 101(8) as "incurred by an individual primarily for a personal, family, or household purpose."

- ❑ No. Go to line 16b.
- ❑ Yes. Go to line 17.

16b. **Are your debts primarily business debts?** *Business debts* are debts that you incurred to obtain money for a business or investment or through the operation of the business or investment.

- ❑ No. Go to line 16c.
- ❑ Yes. Go to line 17.

16c. State the type of debts you owe that are not consumer debts or business debts.

____

17. Are you filing under Chapter 7?

Do you estimate that after any exempt property is excluded and administrative expenses are paid that funds will be available for distribution to unsecured creditors?

- ❑ No. I am not filing under Chapter 7. Go to line 18.
- ❑ Yes. I am filing under Chapter 7. Do you estimate that after any exempt property is excluded and administrative expenses are paid that funds will be available to distribute to unsecured creditors?
  - ❑ No
  - ❑ Yes

18. How many creditors do you estimate that you owe?

❑ 1-49	❑ 1,000-5,000	❑ 25,001-50,000
❑ 50-99	❑ 5,001-10,000	❑ 50,001-100,000
❑ 100-199	❑ 10,001-25,000	❑ More than 100,000
❑ 200-999		

19. How much do you estimate your assets to be worth?

❑ $0-$50,000	❑ $1,000,001-$10 million	❑ $500,000,001-$1 billion
❑ $50,001-$100,000	❑ $10,000,001-$50 million	❑ $1,000,000,001-$10 billion
❑ $100,001-$500,000	❑ $50,000,001-$100 million	❑ $10,000,000,001-$50 billion
❑ $500,001-$1 million	❑ $100,000,001-$500 million	❑ More than $50 billion

20. How much do you estimate your liabilities to be?

❑ $0-$50,000	❑ $1,000,001-$10 million	❑ $500,000,001-$1 billion
❑ $50,001-$100,000	❑ $10,000,001-$50 million	❑ $1,000,000,001-$10 billion
❑ $100,001-$500,000	❑ $50,000,001-$100 million	❑ $10,000,000,001-$50 billion
❑ $500,001-$1 million	❑ $100,000,001-$500 million	❑ More than $50 billion

Part 7: Sign Below

For you

I have examined this petition, and I declare under penalty of perjury that the information provided is true and correct.

If I have chosen to file under Chapter 7, I am aware that I may proceed, if eligible, under Chapter 7, 11,12, or 13 of title 11, United States Code. I understand the relief available under each chapter, and I choose to proceed under Chapter 7.

If no attorney represents me and I did not pay or agree to pay someone who is not an attorney to help me fill out this document, I have obtained and read the notice required by 11 U.S.C. § 342(b).

I request relief in accordance with the chapter of title 11, United States Code, specified in this petition.

I understand making a false statement, concealing property, or obtaining money or property by fraud in connection with a bankruptcy case can result in fines up to $250,000, or imprisonment for up to 20 years, or both. 18 U.S.C. §§ 152, 1341, 1519, and 3571.

✘ ______________________________   ✘ ______________________________
Signature of Debtor 1   Signature of Debtor 2

Executed on ____________ MM / DD / YYYY   Executed on ____________ MM / DD / YYYY

Debtor 1 ______________________ Case number (if known)______________
First Name Middle Name Last Name

For your attorney, if you are represented by one

If you are not represented by an attorney, you do not need to file this page.

I, the attorney for the debtor(s) named in this petition, declare that I have informed the debtor(s) about eligibility to proceed under Chapter 7, 11, 12, or 13 of title 11, United States Code, and have explained the relief available under each chapter for which the person is eligible. I also certify that I have delivered to the debtor(s) the notice required by 11 U.S.C. § 342(b) and, in a case in which § 707(b)(4)(D) applies, certify that I have no knowledge after an inquiry that the information in the schedules filed with the petition is incorrect.

✗ ______________________ Date ______________
Signature of Attorney for Debtor MM / DD / YYYY

____
Printed name

____
Firm name

____
Number Street

____

____
City State ZIP Code

Contact phone ______________ Email address ______________

______________________ ________
Bar number State

Debtor 1 ______________________________ Case number *(if known)*______________________
First Name Middle Name Last Name

For you if you are filing this bankruptcy without an attorney

If you are represented by an attorney, you do not need to file this page.

The law allows you, as an individual, to represent yourself in bankruptcy court, but **you should understand that many people find it extremely difficult to represent themselves successfully. Because bankruptcy has long-term financial and legal consequences, you are strongly urged to hire a qualified attorney.**

To be successful, you must correctly file and handle your bankruptcy case. The rules are very technical, and a mistake or inaction may affect your rights. For example, your case may be dismissed because you did not file a required document, pay a fee on time, attend a meeting or hearing, or cooperate with the court, case trustee, U.S. trustee, bankruptcy administrator, or audit firm if your case is selected for audit. If that happens, you could lose your right to file another case, or you may lose protections, including the benefit of the automatic stay.

You must list all your property and debts in the schedules that you are required to file with the court. Even if you plan to pay a particular debt outside of your bankruptcy, you must list that debt in your schedules. If you do not list a debt, the debt may not be discharged. If you do not list property or properly claim it as exempt, you may not be able to keep the property. The judge can also deny you a discharge of all your debts if you do something dishonest in your bankruptcy case, such as destroying or hiding property, falsifying records, or lying. Individual bankruptcy cases are randomly audited to determine if debtors have been accurate, truthful, and complete. **Bankruptcy fraud is a serious crime; you could be fined and imprisoned.**

If you decide to file without an attorney, the court expects you to follow the rules as if you had hired an attorney. The court will not treat you differently because you are filing for yourself. To be successful, you must be familiar with the United States Bankruptcy Code, the Federal Rules of Bankruptcy Procedure, and the local rules of the court in which your case is filed. You must also be familiar with any state exemption laws that apply.

Are you aware that filing for bankruptcy is a serious action with long-term financial and legal consequences?

- ☐ No
- ☐ Yes

Are you aware that bankruptcy fraud is a serious crime and that if your bankruptcy forms are inaccurate or incomplete, you could be fined or imprisoned?

- ☐ No
- ☐ Yes

Did you pay or agree to pay someone who is not an attorney to help you fill out your bankruptcy forms?

- ☐ No
- ☐ Yes. Name of Person______________________________
  Attach *Bankruptcy Petition Preparer's Notice, Declaration, and Signature* (Official Form 119).

By signing here, I acknowledge that I understand the risks involved in filing without an attorney. I have read and understood this notice, and I am aware that filing a bankruptcy case without an attorney may cause me to lose my rights or property if I do not properly handle the case.

✘ ______________________	✘ ______________________
Signature of Debtor 1	Signature of Debtor 2
Date ________ MM / DD / YYYY	Date ________ MM / DD / YYYY
Contact phone ________	Contact phone ________
Cell phone ________	Cell phone ________
Email address ________	Email address ________

Fill in this information to identify your case:

Debtor 1 ______________________________
First Name Middle Name Last Name

Debtor 2 ______________________________
(Spouse, if filing) First Name Middle Name Last Name

United States Bankruptcy Court for the: __________ District of __________

Case number ______________________________
(If known)

☐ Check if this is an amended filing

Official Form 103A

Application for Individuals to Pay the Filing Fee in Installments

12/15

Be as complete and accurate as possible. If two married people are filing together, both are equally responsible for supplying correct information.

Part 1: Specify Your Proposed Payment Timetable

1. **Which chapter of the Bankruptcy Code are you choosing to file under?**

   ☐ Chapter 7
   ☐ Chapter 11
   ☐ Chapter 12
   ☐ Chapter 13

2. **You may apply to pay the filing fee in up to four installments. Fill in the amounts you propose to pay and the dates you plan to pay them. Be sure all dates are business days. Then add the payments you propose to pay.**

   You must propose to pay the entire fee no later than 120 days after you file this bankruptcy case. If the court approves your application, the court will set your final payment timetable.

You propose to pay...		
$__________	☐ With the filing of the petition ☐ On or before this date........	MM / DD / YYYY
$__________	On or before this date...........	MM / DD / YYYY
$__________	On or before this date...........	MM / DD / YYYY
+ $__________	On or before this date...........	MM / DD / YYYY
Total $__________	◄ Your total must equal the entire fee for the chapter you checked in line 1.	

Part 2: Sign Below

By signing here, you state that you are unable to pay the full filing fee at once, that you want to pay the fee in installments, and that you understand that:

- You must pay your entire filing fee before you make any more payments or transfer any more property to an attorney, bankruptcy petition preparer, or anyone else for services in connection with your bankruptcy case.
- You must pay the entire fee no later than 120 days after you first file for bankruptcy, unless the court later extends your deadline. Your debts will not be discharged until your entire fee is paid.
- If you do not make any payment when it is due, your bankruptcy case may be dismissed, and your rights in other bankruptcy proceedings may be affected.

✗ ______________________	✗ ______________________	✗ ______________________
Signature of Debtor 1	Signature of Debtor 2	Your attorney's name and signature, if you used one
Date ________ MM / DD / YYYY	Date ________ MM / DD / YYYY	Date ________ MM / DD / YYYY

Fill in this information to identify the case:

Debtor 1 ____
First Name Middle Name Last Name

Debtor 2 ____
(Spouse, if filing) First Name Middle Name Last Name

United States Bankruptcy Court for the: ____________________ District of

Case number ____________________
(If known)

Chapter filing under:

- ❑ Chapter 7
- ❑ Chapter 11
- ❑ Chapter 12
- ❑ Chapter 13

Order Approving Payment of Filing Fee in Installments

After considering the *Application for Individuals to Pay the Filing Fee in Installments* (Official Form 103A), the court orders that:

[ ] The debtor(s) may pay the filing fee in installments on the terms proposed in the application.

[ ] The debtor(s) must pay the filing fee according to the following terms:

	You must pay...	On or before this date...
	$__________	__________ Month / day / year
	$__________	__________ Month / day / year
	$__________	__________ Month / day / year
+	$__________	__________ Month / day / year
Total	$__________	

Until the filing fee is paid in full, the debtor(s) must not make any additional payment or transfer any additional property to an attorney or to anyone else for services in connection with this case.

__________ Month / day / year **By the court:** ______________________________ United States Bankruptcy Judge

Fill in this information to identify your case:

Debtor 1 ________________________________
First Name Middle Name Last Name

Debtor 2 ________________________________
(Spouse, if filing) First Name Middle Name Last Name

United States Bankruptcy Court for the: __________ District of __________

Case number ________________________
(If known)

☐ Check if this is an amended filing

Official Form 103B

Application to Have the Chapter 7 Filing Fee Waived

12/15

Be as complete and accurate as possible. If two married people are filing together, both are equally responsible for supplying correct information. If more space is needed, attach a separate sheet to this form. On the top of any additional pages, write your name and case number (if known).

Part 1: Tell the Court About Your Family and Your Family's Income

1. **What is the size of your family?**
   Your family includes you, your spouse, and any dependents listed on *Schedule J: Your Expenses* (Official Form 106J).

   Check all that apply:
   ☐ You
   ☐ Your spouse
   ☐ Your dependents ________ How many dependents? ________ Total number of people

2. **Fill in your family's average monthly income.**
   Include your spouse's income if your spouse is living with you, even if your spouse is not filing.
   Do not include your spouse's income if you are separated and your spouse is not filing with you.

   Add your income and your spouse's income. Include the value (if known) of any non-cash governmental assistance that you receive, such as food stamps (benefits under the Supplemental Nutrition Assistance Program) or housing subsidies.

   If you have already filled out *Schedule I: Your Income*, see line 10 of that schedule.

		That person's average monthly net income (take-home pay)
You		$________
Your spouse	+	$________
Subtotal		$________
Subtract any non-cash governmental assistance that you included above.	−	$________
Your family's average monthly net income — Total		$________

3. **Do you receive non-cash governmental assistance?**
   ☐ No
   ☐ Yes. Describe.......... **Type of assistance** ________

4. **Do you expect your family's average monthly net income to increase or decrease by more than 10% during the next 6 months?**
   ☐ No
   ☐ Yes. Explain. ________

5. **Tell the court why you are unable to pay the filing fee in installments within 120 days.** If you have some additional circumstances that cause you to not be able to pay your filing fee in installments, explain them. ________

Debtor 1 ______________________________ Case number (if known) ______________________
First Name Middle Name Last Name

Part 2: Tell the Court About Your Monthly Expenses

6. **Estimate your average monthly expenses.**
   Include amounts paid by any government assistance that you reported on line 2. $____________

   If you have already filled out *Schedule J, Your Expenses,* copy line 22 from that form.

7. **Do these expenses cover anyone who is not included in your family as reported in line 1?**
   ☐ No
   ☐ Yes. Identify who........

8. **Does anyone other than you regularly pay any of these expenses?**
   If you have already filled out *Schedule I: Your Income*, copy the total from line 11.
   ☐ No
   ☐ Yes. How much do you regularly receive as contributions? $________ monthly

9. **Do you expect your average monthly expenses to increase or decrease by more than 10% during the next 6 months?**
   ☐ No
   ☐ Yes. Explain ....

Part 3: Tell the Court About Your Property

If you have already filled out *Schedule A/B: Property (Official Form 106A/B)* attach copies to this application and go to Part 4.

10. **How much cash do you have?**
    Examples: Money you have in your wallet, in your home, and on hand when you file this application
    Cash: $____________

11. **Bank accounts and other deposits of money?**
    Examples: Checking, savings, money market, or other financial accounts; certificates of deposit; shares in banks, credit unions, brokerage houses, and other similar institutions. If you have more than one account with the same institution, list each. Do not include 401(k) and IRA accounts.

	Institution name:	Amount:
Checking account:	____________	$________
Savings account:	____________	$________
Other financial accounts:	____________	$________
Other financial accounts:	____________	$________

12. **Your home?** (if you own it outright or are purchasing it)
    Examples: House, condominium, manufactured home, or mobile home

    ______________________________ Current value: $________
    Number Street
    ______________________________ Amount you owe on mortgage and liens: $________
    City State ZIP Code

13. **Other real estate?**

    ______________________________ Current value: $________
    Number Street
    ______________________________ Amount you owe on mortgage and liens: $________
    City State ZIP Code

14. **The vehicles you own?**
    Examples: Cars, vans, trucks, sports utility vehicles, motorcycles, tractors, boats

    Make: ____________
    Model: ____________ Current value: $________
    Year: ____________
    Mileage ____________ Amount you owe on liens: $________

    Make: ____________
    Model: ____________ Current value: $________
    Year: ____________
    Mileage ____________ Amount you owe on liens: $________

Debtor 1 ______________________________ Case number (if known) ____________
First Name Middle Name Last Name

15. Other assets?

Do not include household items and clothing.

Describe the other assets:

Current value: $________

Amount you owe on liens: $________

16. Money or property due you?

Examples: Tax refunds, past due or lump sum alimony, spousal support, child support, maintenance, divorce or property settlements, Social Security benefits, workers' compensation, personal injury recovery

Who owes you the money or property?

How much is owed?

$________

$________

Do you believe you will likely receive payment in the next 180 days?

☐ No

☐ Yes. Explain:

Part 4: Answer These Additional Questions

17. Have you paid anyone for services for this case, including filling out this application, the bankruptcy filing package, or the schedules?

☐ No

☐ Yes. **Whom did you pay?** *Check all that apply:*

☐ An attorney

☐ A bankruptcy petition preparer, paralegal, or typing service

☐ Someone else ________

How much did you pay?

$________

18. Have you promised to pay or do you expect to pay someone for services for your bankruptcy case?

☐ No

☐ Yes. **Whom do you expect to pay?** *Check all that apply:*

☐ An attorney

☐ A bankruptcy petition preparer, paralegal, or typing service

☐ Someone else ________

How much do you expect to pay?

$________

19. Has anyone paid someone on your behalf for services for this case?

☐ No

☐ Yes. **Who was paid on your behalf?** *Check all that apply:*

☐ An attorney

☐ A bankruptcy petition preparer, paralegal, or typing service

☐ Someone else ________

Who paid? *Check all that apply:*

☐ Parent

☐ Brother or sister

☐ Friend

☐ Pastor or clergy

☐ Someone else ________

How much did someone else pay?

$________

20. Have you filed for bankruptcy within the last 8 years?

☐ No

☐ Yes. District ________ When ________ Case number ________
MM/ DD/ YYYY

District ________ When ________ Case number ________
MM/ DD/ YYYY

District ________ When ________ Case number ________
MM/ DD/ YYYY

Part 5: Sign Below

By signing here under penalty of perjury, I declare that I cannot afford to pay the filing fee either in full or in installments. I also declare that the information I provided in this application is true and correct.

✘ ______________________________
Signature of Debtor 1

Date ________
MM / DD / YYYY

✘ ______________________________
Signature of Debtor 2

Date ________
MM / DD / YYYY

Debtor 1 ______________________________ Case number (if known) ____________________
First Name Middle Name Last Name

15. Other assets?

Do not include household items and clothing.

Describe the other assets:

Current value: $__________

Amount you owe on liens: $__________

16. Money or property due you?

Examples: Tax refunds, past due or lump sum alimony, spousal support, child support, maintenance, divorce or property settlements, Social Security benefits, workers' compensation, personal injury recovery

Who owes you the money or property?

____

____

How much is owed?

$__________

$__________

Do you believe you will likely receive payment in the next 180 days?

☐ No

☐ Yes. Explain:

Part 4: Answer These Additional Questions

17. Have you paid anyone for services for this case, including filling out this application, the bankruptcy filing package, or the schedules?

☐ No

☐ Yes. **Whom did you pay?** *Check all that apply:*

☐ An attorney

☐ A bankruptcy petition preparer, paralegal, or typing service

☐ Someone else __________

How much did you pay?

$__________

18. Have you promised to pay or do you expect to pay someone for services for your bankruptcy case?

☐ No

☐ Yes. **Whom do you expect to pay?** *Check all that apply:*

☐ An attorney

☐ A bankruptcy petition preparer, paralegal, or typing service

☐ Someone else __________

How much do you expect to pay?

$__________

19. Has anyone paid someone on your behalf for services for this case?

☐ No

☐ Yes. **Who was paid on your behalf?** *Check all that apply:*

☐ An attorney

☐ A bankruptcy petition preparer, paralegal, or typing service

☐ Someone else __________

Who paid? *Check all that apply:*

☐ Parent

☐ Brother or sister

☐ Friend

☐ Pastor or clergy

☐ Someone else __________

How much did someone else pay?

$__________

20. Have you filed for bankruptcy within the last 8 years?

☐ No

☐ Yes. District __________ When __________ (MM/ DD/ YYYY) Case number __________

District __________ When __________ (MM/ DD/ YYYY) Case number __________

District __________ When __________ (MM/ DD/ YYYY) Case number __________

Part 5: Sign Below

By signing here under penalty of perjury, I declare that I cannot afford to pay the filing fee either in full or in installments. I also declare that the information I provided in this application is true and correct.

✗ ______________________________
Signature of Debtor 1

Date __________
MM / DD / YYYY

✗ ______________________________
Signature of Debtor 2

Date __________
MM / DD / YYYY

Fill in this information to identify the case:			
Debtor 1	First Name	Middle Name	Last Name
Debtor 2 (Spouse, if filing)	First Name	Middle Name	Last Name
United States Bankruptcy Court for the:	District of		
Case number (If known)			

Order on the Application to Have the Chapter 7 Filing Fee Waived

After considering the debtor's *Application to Have the Chapter 7 Filing Fee Waived* (Official Form 103B), the court orders that the application is:

[ ] **Granted.** However, the court may order the debtor to pay the fee in the future if developments in administering the bankruptcy case show that the waiver was unwarranted.

[ ] **Denied.** The debtor must pay the filing fee according to the following terms:

	You must pay…	On or before this date…
	$________	Month / day / year
	$________	Month / day / year
	$________	Month / day / year
+	$________	Month / day / year
Total		

If the debtor would like to propose a different payment timetable, the debtor must file a motion promptly with a payment proposal. The debtor may use *Application for Individuals to Pay the Filing Fee in Installments* (Official Form 103A) for this purpose. The court will consider it.

The debtor must pay the entire filing fee before making any more payments or transferring any more property to an attorney, bankruptcy petition preparer, or anyone else in connection with the bankruptcy case. The debtor must also pay the entire filing fee to receive a discharge. If the debtor does not make any payment when it is due, the bankruptcy case may be dismissed and the debtor's rights in future bankruptcy cases may be affected.

[ ] **Scheduled for hearing.**

A hearing to consider the debtor's application will be held

on __________ at _______ AM / PM at ____________________.
Month / day / year — Address of courthouse

If the debtor does not appear at this hearing, the court may deny the application.

__________ **By the court:** ____________________
Month / day / year — United States Bankruptcy Judge

Fill in this information to identify your case and this filing:

Debtor 1 ______ First Name ______ Middle Name ______ Last Name

Debtor 2 (Spouse, if filing) ______ First Name ______ Middle Name ______ Last Name

United States Bankruptcy Court for the: ______ District of ______

Case number ______

☐ Check if this is an amended filing

Official Form 106A/B

Schedule A/B: Property

12/15

In each category, separately list and describe items. List an asset only once. If an asset fits in more than one category, list the asset in the category where you think it fits best. Be as complete and accurate as possible. If two married people are filing together, both are equally responsible for supplying correct information. If more space is needed, attach a separate sheet to this form. On the top of any additional pages, write your name and case number (if known). Answer every question.

Part 1: Describe Each Residence, Building, Land, or Other Real Estate You Own or Have an Interest In

1. **Do you own or have any legal or equitable interest in any residence, building, land, or similar property?**

☐ No. Go to Part 2.

☐ Yes. Where is the property?

1.1. ______ Street address, if available, or other description

______

______ City State ZIP Code

______ County

What is the property? Check all that apply.

☐ Single-family home
☐ Duplex or multi-unit building
☐ Condominium or cooperative
☐ Manufactured or mobile home
☐ Land
☐ Investment property
☐ Timeshare
☐ Other ______

Who has an interest in the property? Check one.

☐ Debtor 1 only
☐ Debtor 2 only
☐ Debtor 1 and Debtor 2 only
☐ At least one of the debtors and another

Do not deduct secured claims or exemptions. Put the amount of any secured claims on *Schedule D: Creditors Who Have Claims Secured by Property.*

Current value of the entire property? $______

Current value of the portion you own? $______

Describe the nature of your ownership interest (such as fee simple, tenancy by the entireties, or a life estate), if known.

______

☐ **Check if this is community property** (see instructions)

Other information you wish to add about this item, such as local property identification number: ______

If you own or have more than one, list here:

1.2. ______ Street address, if available, or other description

______

______ City State ZIP Code

______ County

What is the property? Check all that apply.

☐ Single-family home
☐ Duplex or multi-unit building
☐ Condominium or cooperative
☐ Manufactured or mobile home
☐ Land
☐ Investment property
☐ Timeshare
☐ Other ______

Who has an interest in the property? Check one.

☐ Debtor 1 only
☐ Debtor 2 only
☐ Debtor 1 and Debtor 2 only
☐ At least one of the debtors and another

Do not deduct secured claims or exemptions. Put the amount of any secured claims on *Schedule D: Creditors Who Have Claims Secured by Property.*

Current value of the entire property? $______

Current value of the portion you own? $______

Describe the nature of your ownership interest (such as fee simple, tenancy by the entireties, or a life estate), if known.

______

☐ **Check if this is community property** (see instructions)

Other information you wish to add about this item, such as local property identification number: ______

William J. Patterson

Debtor 1 ______________________________ Case number (if known) ______________
First Name Middle Name Last Name

1.3. ______________________________
Street address, if available, or other description

____

____
City State ZIP Code

____
County

What is the property? Check all that apply.

- ❑ Single-family home
- ❑ Duplex or multi-unit building
- ❑ Condominium or cooperative
- ❑ Manufactured or mobile home
- ❑ Land
- ❑ Investment property
- ❑ Timeshare
- ❑ Other ______________

Who has an interest in the property? Check one.

- ❑ Debtor 1 only
- ❑ Debtor 2 only
- ❑ Debtor 1 and Debtor 2 only
- ❑ At least one of the debtors and another

Other information you wish to add about this item, such as local property identification number: ______________

Do not deduct secured claims or exemptions. Put the amount of any secured claims on *Schedule D: Creditors Who Have Claims Secured by Property.*

Current value of the entire property?	**Current value of the portion you own?**
$________	$________

Describe the nature of your ownership interest (such as fee simple, tenancy by the entireties, or a life estate), if known.

____

❑ **Check if this is community property** (see instructions)

2. **Add the dollar value of the portion you own for all of your entries from Part 1, including any entries for pages you have attached for Part 1. Write that number here.** .... ➔ $________

Part 2: Describe Your Vehicles

Do you own, lease, or have legal or equitable interest in any vehicles, whether they are registered or not? Include any vehicles you own that someone else drives. If you lease a vehicle, also report it on *Schedule G: Executory Contracts and Unexpired Leases.*

3. **Cars, vans, trucks, tractors, sport utility vehicles, motorcycles**

- ❑ No
- ❑ Yes

3.1. Make: ________
Model: ________
Year: ________
Approximate mileage: ________
Other information:

Who has an interest in the property? Check one.

- ❑ Debtor 1 only
- ❑ Debtor 2 only
- ❑ Debtor 1 and Debtor 2 only
- ❑ At least one of the debtors and another

❑ **Check if this is community property** (see instructions)

Do not deduct secured claims or exemptions. Put the amount of any secured claims on *Schedule D: Creditors Who Have Claims Secured by Property.*

Current value of the entire property?	**Current value of the portion you own?**
$________	$________

If you own or have more than one, describe here:

3.2. Make: ________
Model: ________
Year: ________
Approximate mileage: ________
Other information:

Who has an interest in the property? Check one.

- ❑ Debtor 1 only
- ❑ Debtor 2 only
- ❑ Debtor 1 and Debtor 2 only
- ❑ At least one of the debtors and another

❑ **Check if this is community property** (see instructions)

Do not deduct secured claims or exemptions. Put the amount of any secured claims on *Schedule D: Creditors Who Have Claims Secured by Property.*

Current value of the entire property?	**Current value of the portion you own?**
$________	$________

Debtor 1 ______________________________ Case number (if known)______________________
First Name Middle Name Last Name

3.3. Make: __________
Model: __________
Year: __________
Approximate mileage: __________
Other information: [ ]

Who has an interest in the property? Check one.
❑ Debtor 1 only
❑ Debtor 2 only
❑ Debtor 1 and Debtor 2 only
❑ At least one of the debtors and another

❑ **Check if this is community property** (see instructions)

Do not deduct secured claims or exemptions. Put the amount of any secured claims on *Schedule D: Creditors Who Have Claims Secured by Property.*

Current value of the entire property? $__________
Current value of the portion you own? $__________

3.4. Make: __________
Model: __________
Year: __________
Approximate mileage: __________
Other information: [ ]

Who has an interest in the property? Check one.
❑ Debtor 1 only
❑ Debtor 2 only
❑ Debtor 1 and Debtor 2 only
❑ At least one of the debtors and another

❑ **Check if this is community property** (see instructions)

Do not deduct secured claims or exemptions. Put the amount of any secured claims on *Schedule D: Creditors Who Have Claims Secured by Property.*

Current value of the entire property? $__________
Current value of the portion you own? $__________

4. **Watercraft, aircraft, motor homes, ATVs and other recreational vehicles, other vehicles, and accessories**
Examples: Boats, trailers, motors, personal watercraft, fishing vessels, snowmobiles, motorcycle accessories
❑ No
❑ Yes

4.1. Make: __________
Model: __________
Year: __________
Other information: [ ]

Who has an interest in the property? Check one.
❑ Debtor 1 only
❑ Debtor 2 only
❑ Debtor 1 and Debtor 2 only
❑ At least one of the debtors and another

❑ **Check if this is community property** (see instructions)

Do not deduct secured claims or exemptions. Put the amount of any secured claims on *Schedule D: Creditors Who Have Claims Secured by Property.*

Current value of the entire property? $__________
Current value of the portion you own? $__________

If you own or have more than one, list here:

4.2. Make: __________
Model: __________
Year: __________
Other information: [ ]

Who has an interest in the property? Check one.
❑ Debtor 1 only
❑ Debtor 2 only
❑ Debtor 1 and Debtor 2 only
❑ At least one of the debtors and another

❑ **Check if this is community property** (see instructions)

Do not deduct secured claims or exemptions. Put the amount of any secured claims on *Schedule D: Creditors Who Have Claims Secured by Property.*

Current value of the entire property? $__________
Current value of the portion you own? $__________

5. **Add the dollar value of the portion you own for all of your entries from Part 2, including any entries for pages you have attached for Part 2. Write that number here** .... → $__________

Debtor 1 ______________________________ Case number *(if known)*______________________
First Name Middle Name Last Name

Part 3: Describe Your Personal and Household Items

Do you own or have any legal or equitable interest in any of the following items?

Current value of the portion you own?
Do not deduct secured claims or exemptions.

6. **Household goods and furnishings**
Examples: Major appliances, furniture, linens, china, kitchenware
☐ No
☐ Yes. Describe......... $________

7. **Electronics**
Examples: Televisions and radios; audio, video, stereo, and digital equipment; computers, printers, scanners; music collections; electronic devices including cell phones, cameras, media players, games
☐ No
☐ Yes. Describe......... $________

8. **Collectibles of value**
Examples: Antiques and figurines; paintings, prints, or other artwork; books, pictures, or other art objects; stamp, coin, or baseball card collections; other collections, memorabilia, collectibles
☐ No
☐ Yes. Describe......... $________

9. **Equipment for sports and hobbies**
Examples: Sports, photographic, exercise, and other hobby equipment; bicycles, pool tables, golf clubs, skis; canoes and kayaks; carpentry tools; musical instruments
☐ No
☐ Yes. Describe......... $________

10. **Firearms**
Examples: Pistols, rifles, shotguns, ammunition, and related equipment
☐ No
☐ Yes. Describe......... $________

11. **Clothes**
Examples: Everyday clothes, furs, leather coats, designer wear, shoes, accessories
☐ No
☐ Yes. Describe......... $________

12. **Jewelry**
Examples: Everyday jewelry, costume jewelry, engagement rings, wedding rings, heirloom jewelry, watches, gems, gold, silver
☐ No
☐ Yes. Describe......... $________

13. **Non-farm animals**
Examples: Dogs, cats, birds, horses
☐ No
☐ Yes. Describe......... $________

14. **Any other personal and household items you did not already list, including any health aids you did not list**
☐ No
☐ Yes. Give specific information. .... $________

15. **Add the dollar value of all of your entries from Part 3, including any entries for pages you have attached for Part 3. Write that number here** .... → $________

Debtor 1 ______________________________ Case number *(if known)* ______________________________
First Name Middle Name Last Name

Part 4: Describe Your Financial Assets

Do you own or have any legal or equitable interest in any of the following?

Current value of the portion you own?
Do not deduct secured claims or exemptions.

16. **Cash**

Examples: Money you have in your wallet, in your home, in a safe deposit box, and on hand when you file your petition

❑ No
❑ Yes .... Cash: .... $__________

17. **Deposits of money**

Examples: Checking, savings, or other financial accounts; certificates of deposit; shares in credit unions, brokerage houses, and other similar institutions. If you have multiple accounts with the same institution, list each.

❑ No
❑ Yes .... Institution name:

17.1. Checking account: __________ $__________
17.2. Checking account: __________ $__________
17.3. Savings account: __________ $__________
17.4. Savings account: __________ $__________
17.5. Certificates of deposit: __________ $__________
17.6. Other financial account: __________ $__________
17.7. Other financial account: __________ $__________
17.8. Other financial account: __________ $__________
17.9. Other financial account: __________ $__________

18. **Bonds, mutual funds, or publicly traded stocks**

Examples: Bond funds, investment accounts with brokerage firms, money market accounts

❑ No
❑ Yes .... Institution or issuer name:

__________ $__________
__________ $__________
__________ $__________

19. **Non-publicly traded stock and interests in incorporated and unincorporated businesses, including an interest in an LLC, partnership, and joint venture**

❑ No
❑ Yes. Give specific information about them..........

Name of entity:	% of ownership:	
__________	0% %	$__________
__________	0% %	$__________
__________	0% %	$__________

William J. Patterson

20. **Government and corporate bonds and other negotiable and non-negotiable instruments**

Negotiable instruments include personal checks, cashiers' checks, promissory notes, and money orders.
Non-negotiable instruments are those you cannot transfer to someone by signing or delivering them.

❑ No

❑ Yes. Give specific information about them.................... Issuer name:

______________________________ $__________

______________________________ $__________

______________________________ $__________

21. **Retirement or pension accounts**

Examples: Interests in IRA, ERISA, Keogh, 401(k), 403(b), thrift savings accounts, or other pension or profit-sharing plans

❑ No

❑ Yes. List each account separately.

Type of account:	Institution name:	
401(k) or similar plan:	______________________________	$__________
Pension plan:	______________________________	$__________
IRA:	______________________________	$__________
Retirement account:	______________________________	$__________
Keogh:	______________________________	$__________
Additional account:	______________________________	$__________
Additional account:	______________________________	$__________

22. **Security deposits and prepayments**

Your share of all unused deposits you have made so that you may continue service or use from a company

Examples: Agreements with landlords, prepaid rent, public utilities (electric, gas, water), telecommunications companies, or others

❑ No

❑ Yes......................

	Institution name or individual:	
Electric:	______________________________	$__________
Gas:	______________________________	$__________
Heating oil:	______________________________	$__________
Security deposit on rental unit:	______________________________	$__________
Prepaid rent:	______________________________	$__________
Telephone:	______________________________	$__________
Water:	______________________________	$__________
Rented furniture:	______________________________	$__________
Other:	______________________________	$__________

23. **Annuities** (A contract for a periodic payment of money to you, either for life or for a number of years)

❑ No

❑ Yes...................... Issuer name and description:

______________________________ $__________

______________________________ $__________

______________________________ $__________

Debtor 1 ______________________________ Case number (if known)______________________
First Name Middle Name Last Name

24. **Interests in an education IRA, in an account in a qualified ABLE program, or under a qualified state tuition program.**
26 U.S.C. §§ 530(b)(1), 529A(b), and 529(b)(1).

❑ No
❑ Yes .... Institution name and description. Separately file the records of any interests.11 U.S.C. § 521(c):

______________________________ $__________
______________________________ $__________
______________________________ $__________

25. **Trusts, equitable or future interests in property (other than anything listed in line 1), and rights or powers exercisable for your benefit**

❑ No
❑ Yes. Give specific information about them.... $__________

26. **Patents, copyrights, trademarks, trade secrets, and other intellectual property**
Examples: Internet domain names, websites, proceeds from royalties and licensing agreements

❑ No
❑ Yes. Give specific information about them.... $__________

27. **Licenses, franchises, and other general intangibles**
Examples: Building permits, exclusive licenses, cooperative association holdings, liquor licenses, professional licenses

❑ No
❑ Yes. Give specific information about them.... $__________

Money or property owed to you?

Current value of the portion you own?
Do not deduct secured claims or exemptions.

28. **Tax refunds owed to you**

❑ No
❑ Yes. Give specific information about them, including whether you already filed the returns and the tax years. ....

Federal: $__________
State: $__________
Local: $__________

29. **Family support**
Examples: Past due or lump sum alimony, spousal support, child support, maintenance, divorce settlement, property settlement

❑ No
❑ Yes. Give specific information.............

Alimony: $__________
Maintenance: $__________
Support: $__________
Divorce settlement: $__________
Property settlement: $__________

30. **Other amounts someone owes you**
Examples: Unpaid wages, disability insurance payments, disability benefits, sick pay, vacation pay, workers' compensation, Social Security benefits; unpaid loans you made to someone else

❑ No
❑ Yes. Give specific information.............. $__________

William J. Patterson

31. **Interests in insurance policies**
Examples: Health, disability, or life insurance; health savings account (HSA); credit, homeowner's, or renter's insurance

☐ No
☐ Yes. Name the insurance company of each policy and list its value. ...

Company name:	Beneficiary:	Surrender or refund value:
		$
		$
		$

32. **Any interest in property that is due you from someone who has died**
If you are the beneficiary of a living trust, expect proceeds from a life insurance policy, or are currently entitled to receive property because someone has died.

☐ No
☐ Yes. Give specific information. .... $______

33. **Claims against third parties, whether or not you have filed a lawsuit or made a demand for payment**
Examples: Accidents, employment disputes, insurance claims, or rights to sue

☐ No
☐ Yes. Describe each claim. .... $______

34. **Other contingent and unliquidated claims of every nature, including counterclaims of the debtor and rights to set off claims**

☐ No
☐ Yes. Describe each claim. .... $______

35. **Any financial assets you did not already list**

☐ No
☐ Yes. Give specific information. .... $______

36. **Add the dollar value of all of your entries from Part 4, including any entries for pages you have attached for Part 4. Write that number here** .... → $______

Part 5: Describe Any Business-Related Property You Own or Have an Interest In. List any real estate in Part 1.

37. **Do you own or have any legal or equitable interest in any business-related property?**

☐ No. Go to Part 6.
☐ Yes. Go to line 38.

Current value of the portion you own?
Do not deduct secured claims or exemptions.

38. **Accounts receivable or commissions you already earned**

☐ No
☐ Yes. Describe...... $______

39. **Office equipment, furnishings, and supplies**
Examples: Business-related computers, software, modems, printers, copiers, fax machines, rugs, telephones, desks, chairs, electronic devices

☐ No
☐ Yes. Describe...... $______

Debtor 1 ______________________ Case number *(if known)*______________
First Name Middle Name Last Name

40. **Machinery, fixtures, equipment, supplies you use in business, and tools of your trade**

❑ No
❑ Yes. Describe....... $______

41. **Inventory**
❑ No
❑ Yes. Describe....... $______

42. **Interests in partnerships or joint ventures**
❑ No
❑ Yes. Describe....... Name of entity: % of ownership:
______ ____% $______
______ ____% $______
______ ____% $______

43. **Customer lists, mailing lists, or other compilations**
❑ No
❑ Yes. **Do your lists include personally identifiable information** (as defined in 11 U.S.C. § 101(41A))?
❑ No
❑ Yes. Describe........ $______

44. **Any business-related property you did not already list**
❑ No
❑ Yes. Give specific information ....
______ $______
______ $______
______ $______
______ $______
______ $______
______ $______

45. **Add the dollar value of all of your entries from Part 5, including any entries for pages you have attached for Part 5. Write that number here** .... ➔ $______

Part 6: Describe Any Farm- and Commercial Fishing-Related Property You Own or Have an Interest In.
If you own or have an interest in farmland, list it in Part 1.

46. **Do you own or have any legal or equitable interest in any farm- or commercial fishing-related property?**
❑ No. Go to Part 7.
❑ Yes. Go to line 47.

Current value of the portion you own?
Do not deduct secured claims or exemptions.

47. **Farm animals**
Examples: Livestock, poultry, farm-raised fish
❑ No
❑ Yes........................ $______

Debtor 1 ______________________________ Case number (if known) ______________
First Name Middle Name Last Name

48. **Crops—either growing or harvested**

- ❑ No
- ❑ Yes. Give specific information .... $________

49. **Farm and fishing equipment, implements, machinery, fixtures, and tools of trade**

- ❑ No
- ❑ Yes .... $________

50. **Farm and fishing supplies, chemicals, and feed**

- ❑ No
- ❑ Yes .... $________

51. **Any farm- and commercial fishing-related property you did not already list**

- ❑ No
- ❑ Yes. Give specific information .... $________

52. **Add the dollar value of all of your entries from Part 6, including any entries for pages you have attached for Part 6. Write that number here** .... ➔ $________

Part 7: Describe All Property You Own or Have an Interest in That You Did Not List Above

53. **Do you have other property of any kind you did not already list?**
Examples: Season tickets, country club membership

- ❑ No
- ❑ Yes. Give specific information .... $________ $________ $________

54. **Add the dollar value of all of your entries from Part 7. Write that number here** .... ➔ $________

Part 8: List the Totals of Each Part of this Form

55. **Part 1: Total real estate, line 2** .... ➔ $________

56. **Part 2: Total vehicles, line 5** $________

57. **Part 3: Total personal and household items, line 15** $________

58. **Part 4: Total financial assets, line 36** $________

59. **Part 5: Total business-related property, line 45** $________

60. **Part 6: Total farm- and fishing-related property, line 52** $________

61. **Part 7: Total other property not listed, line 54** + $________

62. **Total personal property.** Add lines 56 through 61. .... $________ Copy personal property total ➔ + $________

63. **Total of all property on Schedule A/B.** Add line 55 + line 62. .... $________

Fill in this information to identify your case:

Debtor 1 ______________________________
First Name Middle Name Last Name

Debtor 2 ______________________________
(Spouse, if filing) First Name Middle Name Last Name

United States Bankruptcy Court for the: __________ District of __________

Case number ______________________________
(If known)

❑ Check if this is an amended filing

Official Form 106C

Schedule C: The Property You Claim as Exempt

04/16

Be as complete and accurate as possible. If two married people are filing together, both are equally responsible for supplying correct information. Using the property you listed on *Schedule A/B: Property* (Official Form 106A/B) as your source, list the property that you claim as exempt. If more space is needed, fill out and attach to this page as many copies of *Part 2: Additional Page* as necessary. On the top of any additional pages, write your name and case number (if known).

For each item of property you claim as exempt, you must specify the amount of the exemption you claim. One way of doing so is to state a specific dollar amount as exempt. Alternatively, you may claim the full fair market value of the property being exempted up to the amount of any applicable statutory limit. Some exemptions—such as those for health aids, rights to receive certain benefits, and tax-exempt retirement funds—may be unlimited in dollar amount. However, if you claim an exemption of 100% of fair market value under a law that limits the exemption to a particular dollar amount and the value of the property is determined to exceed that amount, your exemption would be limited to the applicable statutory amount.

Part 1: Identify the Property You Claim as Exempt

1. **Which set of exemptions are you claiming?** *Check one only, even if your spouse is filing with you.*
   - ❑ You are claiming state and federal nonbankruptcy exemptions. 11 U.S.C. § 522(b)(3)
   - ❑ You are claiming federal exemptions. 11 U.S.C. § 522(b)(2)

2. **For any property you list on *Schedule A/B* that you claim as exempt, fill in the information below.**

Brief description of the property and line on *Schedule A/B* that lists this property	Current value of the portion you own Copy the value from *Schedule A/B*	Amount of the exemption you claim *Check only one box for each exemption.*	Specific laws that allow exemption
Brief description: ________ Line from *Schedule A/B*: ____	$________	❑ $________ ❑ 100% of fair market value, up to any applicable statutory limit	________
Brief description: ________ Line from *Schedule A/B*: ____	$________	❑ $________ ❑ 100% of fair market value, up to any applicable statutory limit	________
Brief description: ________ Line from *Schedule A/B*: ____	$________	❑ $________ ❑ 100% of fair market value, up to any applicable statutory limit	________

3. **Are you claiming a homestead exemption of more than $160,375?**
   (Subject to adjustment on 4/01/19 and every 3 years after that for cases filed on or after the date of adjustment.)
   - ❑ No
   - ❑ Yes. Did you acquire the property covered by the exemption within 1,215 days before you filed this case?
     - ❑ No
     - ❑ Yes

Official Form 106C **Schedule C: The Property You Claim as Exempt** page 1 of __

William J. Patterson

Debtor 1 ______________________________ Case number (if known)______________
First Name Middle Name Last Name

Part 2: Additional Page

Brief description of the property and line on *Schedule A/B* that lists this property	Current value of the portion you own Copy the value from *Schedule A/B*	Amount of the exemption you claim *Check only one box for each exemption*	Specific laws that allow exemption
Brief description: ________ Line from *Schedule A/B*: ____	$________	❑ $ ________ ❑ 100% of fair market value, up to any applicable statutory limit	________
Brief description: ________ Line from *Schedule A/B*: ____	$________	❑ $ ________ ❑ 100% of fair market value, up to any applicable statutory limit	________
Brief description: ________ Line from *Schedule A/B*: ____	$________	❑ $ ________ ❑ 100% of fair market value, up to any applicable statutory limit	________
Brief description: ________ Line from *Schedule A/B*: ____	$________	❑ $ ________ ❑ 100% of fair market value, up to any applicable statutory limit	________
Brief description: ________ Line from *Schedule A/B*: ____	$________	❑ $ ________ ❑ 100% of fair market value, up to any applicable statutory limit	________
Brief description: ________ Line from *Schedule A/B*: ____	$________	❑ $ ________ ❑ 100% of fair market value, up to any applicable statutory limit	________
Brief description: ________ Line from *Schedule A/B*: ____	$________	❑ $ ________ ❑ 100% of fair market value, up to any applicable statutory limit	________
Brief description: ________ Line from *Schedule A/B*: ____	$________	❑ $ ________ ❑ 100% of fair market value, up to any applicable statutory limit	________
Brief description: ________ Line from *Schedule A/B*: ____	$________	❑ $ ________ ❑ 100% of fair market value, up to any applicable statutory limit	________
Brief description: ________ Line from *Schedule A/B*: ____	$________	❑ $ ________ ❑ 100% of fair market value, up to any applicable statutory limit	________
Brief description: ________ Line from *Schedule A/B*: ____	$________	❑ $ ________ ❑ 100% of fair market value, up to any applicable statutory limit	________
Brief description: ________ Line from *Schedule A/B*: ____	$________	❑ $ ________ ❑ 100% of fair market value, up to any applicable statutory limit	________

Fill in this information to identify your case:

Debtor 1 ______________________________
First Name Middle Name Last Name

Debtor 2 ______________________________
(Spouse, if filing) First Name Middle Name Last Name

United States Bankruptcy Court for the: __________ District of __________

Case number ______________________________
(If known)

☐ Check if this is an amended filing

Official Form 106D

Schedule D: Creditors Who Have Claims Secured by Property

12/15

Be as complete and accurate as possible. If two married people are filing together, both are equally responsible for supplying correct information. If more space is needed, copy the Additional Page, fill it out, number the entries, and attach it to this form. On the top of any additional pages, write your name and case number (if known).

1. **Do any creditors have claims secured by your property?**
   - ☐ No. Check this box and submit this form to the court with your other schedules. You have nothing else to report on this form.
   - ☐ Yes. Fill in all of the information below.

Part 1: List All Secured Claims

2. **List all secured claims.** If a creditor has more than one secured claim, list the creditor separately for each claim. If more than one creditor has a particular claim, list the other creditors in Part 2. As much as possible, list the claims in alphabetical order according to the creditor's name.

Column A **Amount of claim** Do not deduct the value of collateral. | *Column B* **Value of collateral that supports this claim** | *Column C* **Unsecured portion** If any

2.1 ______________________________
Creditor's Name

____
Number Street

____

____
City State ZIP Code

Who owes the debt? Check one.
- ☐ Debtor 1 only
- ☐ Debtor 2 only
- ☐ Debtor 1 and Debtor 2 only
- ☐ At least one of the debtors and another

☐ **Check if this claim relates to a community debt**

Date debt was incurred __________

Describe the property that secures the claim: $__________ $__________ $__________

As of the date you file, the claim is: Check all that apply
- ☐ Contingent
- ☐ Unliquidated
- ☐ Disputed

Nature of lien. Check all that apply.
- ☐ An agreement you made (such as mortgage or secured car loan)
- ☐ Statutory lien (such as tax lien, mechanic's lien)
- ☐ Judgment lien from a lawsuit
- ☐ Other (including a right to offset) __________

Last 4 digits of account number ___ ___ ___ ___

2.2 ______________________________
Creditor's Name

____
Number Street

____

____
City State ZIP Code

Who owes the debt? Check one.
- ☐ Debtor 1 only
- ☐ Debtor 2 only
- ☐ Debtor 1 and Debtor 2 only
- ☐ At least one of the debtors and another

☐ **Check if this claim relates to a community debt**

Date debt was incurred __________

Describe the property that secures the claim: $__________ $__________ $__________

As of the date you file, the claim is: Check all that apply
- ☐ Contingent
- ☐ Unliquidated
- ☐ Disputed

Nature of lien. Check all that apply.
- ☐ An agreement you made (such as mortgage or secured car loan)
- ☐ Statutory lien (such as tax lien, mechanic's lien)
- ☐ Judgment lien from a lawsuit
- ☐ Other (including a right to offset) __________

Last 4 digits of account number ___ ___ ___ ___

Add the dollar value of your entries in Column A on this page. Write that number here: $__________

William J. Patterson

Debtor 1 ______________________________ Case number (if known)______________________
First Name Middle Name Last Name

Part 1: **Additional Page**

After listing any entries on this page, number them beginning with 2.3, followed by 2.4, and so forth.

		Column A **Amount of claim** Do not deduct the value of collateral.	*Column B* **Value of collateral that supports this claim**	*Column C* **Unsecured portion** If any
☐ ______________________ Creditor's Name ______________________ Number Street ______________________ ______________________ City State ZIP Code **Who owes the debt?** Check one. ☐ Debtor 1 only ☐ Debtor 2 only ☐ Debtor 1 and Debtor 2 only ☐ At least one of the debtors and another ☐ **Check if this claim relates to a community debt** **Date debt was incurred** ________	**Describe the property that secures the claim:** **As of the date you file, the claim is:** Check all that apply. ☐ Contingent ☐ Unliquidated ☐ Disputed **Nature of lien.** Check all that apply. ☐ An agreement you made (such as mortgage or secured car loan) ☐ Statutory lien (such as tax lien, mechanic's lien) ☐ Judgment lien from a lawsuit ☐ Other (including a right to offset) ________ **Last 4 digits of account number** __ __ __ __	$________	$________	$________
☐ ______________________ Creditor's Name ______________________ Number Street ______________________ ______________________ City State ZIP Code **Who owes the debt?** Check one. ☐ Debtor 1 only ☐ Debtor 2 only ☐ Debtor 1 and Debtor 2 only ☐ At least one of the debtors and another ☐ **Check if this claim relates to a community debt** **Date debt was incurred** ________	**Describe the property that secures the claim:** **As of the date you file, the claim is:** Check all that apply. ☐ Contingent ☐ Unliquidated ☐ Disputed **Nature of lien.** Check all that apply. ☐ An agreement you made (such as mortgage or secured car loan) ☐ Statutory lien (such as tax lien, mechanic's lien) ☐ Judgment lien from a lawsuit ☐ Other (including a right to offset) ________ **Last 4 digits of account number** __ __ __ __	$________	$________	$________
☐ ______________________ Creditor's Name ______________________ Number Street ______________________ ______________________ City State ZIP Code **Who owes the debt?** Check one. ☐ Debtor 1 only ☐ Debtor 2 only ☐ Debtor 1 and Debtor 2 only ☐ At least one of the debtors and another ☐ **Check if this claim relates to a community debt** **Date debt was incurred** ________	**Describe the property that secures the claim:** **As of the date you file, the claim is:** Check all that apply. ☐ Contingent ☐ Unliquidated ☐ Disputed **Nature of lien.** Check all that apply. ☐ An agreement you made (such as mortgage or secured car loan) ☐ Statutory lien (such as tax lien, mechanic's lien) ☐ Judgment lien from a lawsuit ☐ Other (including a right to offset) ________ **Last 4 digits of account number** __ __ __ __	$________	$________	$________

Add the dollar value of your entries in Column A on this page. Write that number here: $________

If this is the last page of your form, add the dollar value totals from all pages. Write that number here: $________

Debtor 1 ______________________________ Case number *(if known)* ______________________
First Name Middle Name Last Name

Part 2: List Others to Be Notified for a Debt That You Already Listed

Use this page only if you have others to be notified about your bankruptcy for a debt that you already listed in Part 1. For example, if a collection agency is trying to collect from you for a debt you owe to someone else, list the creditor in Part 1, and then list the collection agency here. Similarly, if you have more than one creditor for any of the debts that you listed in Part 1, list the additional creditors here. If you do not have additional persons to be notified for any debts in Part 1, do not fill out or submit this page.

☐ Name | **On which line in Part 1 did you enter the creditor?** ____
Last 4 digits of account number ___ ___ ___ ___
Number Street
City State ZIP Code

☐ Name | **On which line in Part 1 did you enter the creditor?** ____
Last 4 digits of account number ___ ___ ___ ___
Number Street
City State ZIP Code

☐ Name | **On which line in Part 1 did you enter the creditor?** ____
Last 4 digits of account number ___ ___ ___ ___
Number Street
City State ZIP Code

☐ Name | **On which line in Part 1 did you enter the creditor?** ____
Last 4 digits of account number ___ ___ ___ ___
Number Street
City State ZIP Code

☐ Name | **On which line in Part 1 did you enter the creditor?** ____
Last 4 digits of account number ___ ___ ___ ___
Number Street
City State ZIP Code

☐ Name | **On which line in Part 1 did you enter the creditor?** ____
Last 4 digits of account number ___ ___ ___ ___
Number Street
City State ZIP Code

Official Form 106D Part 2 of **Schedule D: Creditors Who Have Claims Secured by Property** page ___ of ___

Fill in this information to identify your case:

Debtor 1 ______________________________
First Name Middle Name Last Name

Debtor 2 ______________________________
(Spouse, if filing) First Name Middle Name Last Name

United States Bankruptcy Court for the: ________ District of ________

Case number ______________________________
(If known)

☐ Check if this is an amended filing

Official Form 106E/F

Schedule E/F: Creditors Who Have Unsecured Claims

12/15

Be as complete and accurate as possible. Use Part 1 for creditors with PRIORITY claims and Part 2 for creditors with NONPRIORITY claims. List the other party to any executory contracts or unexpired leases that could result in a claim. Also list executory contracts on *Schedule A/B: Property* (Official Form 106A/B) and on *Schedule G: Executory Contracts and Unexpired Leases* (Official Form 106G). Do not include any creditors with partially secured claims that are listed in *Schedule D: Creditors Who Have Claims Secured by Property*. If more space is needed, copy the Part you need, fill it out, number the entries in the boxes on the left. Attach the Continuation Page to this page. On the top of any additional pages, write your name and case number (if known).

Part 1: List All of Your PRIORITY Unsecured Claims

1. **Do any creditors have priority unsecured claims against you?**
   ☐ No. Go to Part 2.
   ☐ Yes.

2. **List all of your priority unsecured claims.** If a creditor has more than one priority unsecured claim, list the creditor separately for each claim. For each claim listed, identify what type of claim it is. If a claim has both priority and nonpriority amounts, list that claim here and show both priority and nonpriority amounts. As much as possible, list the claims in alphabetical order according to the creditor's name. If you have more than two priority unsecured claims, fill out the Continuation Page of Part 1. If more than one creditor holds a particular claim, list the other creditors in Part 3.

   (For an explanation of each type of claim, see the instructions for this form in the instruction booklet.)

Total claim | **Priority amount** | **Nonpriority amount**

2.1 ______________________________
Priority Creditor's Name

Last 4 digits of account number __ __ __ __ $________ $________ $________

When was the debt incurred? ________

____
Number Street

____

____
City State ZIP Code

As of the date you file, the claim is: Check all that apply
☐ Contingent
☐ Unliquidated
☐ Disputed

Who incurred the debt? Check one.
☐ Debtor 1 only
☐ Debtor 2 only
☐ Debtor 1 and Debtor 2 only
☐ At least one of the debtors and another
☐ **Check if this claim is for a community debt**

Type of PRIORITY unsecured claim:
☐ Domestic support obligations
☐ Taxes and certain other debts you owe the government
☐ Claims for death or personal injury while you were intoxicated
☐ Other. Specify ________________

Is the claim subject to offset?
☐ No
☐ Yes

2.2 ______________________________
Priority Creditor's Name

Last 4 digits of account number __ __ __ __ $________ $________ $________

When was the debt incurred? ________

____
Number Street

____

____
City State ZIP Code

As of the date you file, the claim is: Check all that apply
☐ Contingent
☐ Unliquidated
☐ Disputed

Who incurred the debt? Check one.
☐ Debtor 1 only
☐ Debtor 2 only
☐ Debtor 1 and Debtor 2 only
☐ At least one of the debtors and another
☐ **Check if this claim is for a community debt**

Type of PRIORITY unsecured claim:
☐ Domestic support obligations
☐ Taxes and certain other debts you owe the government
☐ Claims for death or personal injury while you were intoxicated
☐ Other. Specify ________________

Is the claim subject to offset?
☐ No
☐ Yes

Debtor 1 ______________________________ Case number (if known) ______________________
First Name Middle Name Last Name

Part 1: Your PRIORITY Unsecured Claims – Continuation Page

After listing any entries on this page, number them beginning with 2.3, followed by 2.4, and so forth. | **Total claim** | **Priority amount** | **Nonpriority amount**

☐ ______________________________
Priority Creditor's Name
____
Number Street
____
____
City State ZIP Code

Who incurred the debt? Check one.

- ☐ Debtor 1 only
- ☐ Debtor 2 only
- ☐ Debtor 1 and Debtor 2 only
- ☐ At least one of the debtors and another

☐ **Check if this claim is for a community debt**

Is the claim subject to offset?

- ☐ No
- ☐ Yes

Last 4 digits of account number ___ ___ ___ ___ $________ $________ $________

When was the debt incurred? ________

As of the date you file, the claim is: Check all that apply.

- ☐ Contingent
- ☐ Unliquidated
- ☐ Disputed

Type of PRIORITY unsecured claim:

- ☐ Domestic support obligations
- ☐ Taxes and certain other debts you owe the government
- ☐ Claims for death or personal injury while you were intoxicated
- ☐ Other. Specify ______________________

☐ ______________________________
Priority Creditor's Name
____
Number Street
____
____
City State ZIP Code

Who incurred the debt? Check one.

- ☐ Debtor 1 only
- ☐ Debtor 2 only
- ☐ Debtor 1 and Debtor 2 only
- ☐ At least one of the debtors and another

☐ **Check if this claim is for a community debt**

Is the claim subject to offset?

- ☐ No
- ☐ Yes

Last 4 digits of account number ___ ___ ___ ___ $________ $________ $________

When was the debt incurred? ________

As of the date you file, the claim is: Check all that apply.

- ☐ Contingent
- ☐ Unliquidated
- ☐ Disputed

Type of PRIORITY unsecured claim:

- ☐ Domestic support obligations
- ☐ Taxes and certain other debts you owe the government
- ☐ Claims for death or personal injury while you were intoxicated
- ☐ Other. Specify ______________________

☐ ______________________________
Priority Creditor's Name
____
Number Street
____
____
City State ZIP Code

Who incurred the debt? Check one.

- ☐ Debtor 1 only
- ☐ Debtor 2 only
- ☐ Debtor 1 and Debtor 2 only
- ☐ At least one of the debtors and another

☐ **Check if this claim is for a community debt**

Is the claim subject to offset?

- ☐ No
- ☐ Yes

Last 4 digits of account number ___ ___ ___ ___ $________ $________ $________

When was the debt incurred? ________

As of the date you file, the claim is: Check all that apply.

- ☐ Contingent
- ☐ Unliquidated
- ☐ Disputed

Type of PRIORITY unsecured claim:

- ☐ Domestic support obligations
- ☐ Taxes and certain other debts you owe the government
- ☐ Claims for death or personal injury while you were intoxicated
- ☐ Other. Specify ______________________

William J. Patterson

Debtor 1 ____________________ Case number (if known)____________________
First Name Middle Name Last Name

Part 2: List All of Your NONPRIORITY Unsecured Claims

3. **Do any creditors have nonpriority unsecured claims against you?**
   - ❑ No. You have nothing to report in this part. Submit this form to the court with your other schedules.
   - ❑ Yes

4. **List all of your nonpriority unsecured claims in the alphabetical order of the creditor who holds each claim.** If a creditor has more than one nonpriority unsecured claim, list the creditor separately for each claim. For each claim listed, identify what type of claim it is. Do not list claims already included in Part 1. If more than one creditor holds a particular claim, list the other creditors in Part 3.If you have more than three nonpriority unsecured claims fill out the Continuation Page of Part 2.

Total claim

4.1 ____________________
Nonpriority Creditor's Name
____
Number Street
____
City State ZIP Code

Last 4 digits of account number __ __ __ __ $__________

When was the debt incurred? ________

As of the date you file, the claim is: Check all that apply.
- ❑ Contingent
- ❑ Unliquidated
- ❑ Disputed

Who incurred the debt? Check one.
- ❑ Debtor 1 only
- ❑ Debtor 2 only
- ❑ Debtor 1 and Debtor 2 only
- ❑ At least one of the debtors and another

❑ **Check if this claim is for a community debt**

Is the claim subject to offset?
- ❑ No
- ❑ Yes

Type of NONPRIORITY unsecured claim:
- ❑ Student loans
- ❑ Obligations arising out of a separation agreement or divorce that you did not report as priority claims
- ❑ Debts to pension or profit-sharing plans, and other similar debts
- ❑ Other. Specify ____________________

4.2 ____________________
Nonpriority Creditor's Name
____
Number Street
____
City State ZIP Code

Last 4 digits of account number __ __ __ __ $__________

When was the debt incurred? ________

As of the date you file, the claim is: Check all that apply.
- ❑ Contingent
- ❑ Unliquidated
- ❑ Disputed

Who incurred the debt? Check one.
- ❑ Debtor 1 only
- ❑ Debtor 2 only
- ❑ Debtor 1 and Debtor 2 only
- ❑ At least one of the debtors and another

❑ **Check if this claim is for a community debt**

Is the claim subject to offset?
- ❑ No
- ❑ Yes

Type of NONPRIORITY unsecured claim:
- ❑ Student loans
- ❑ Obligations arising out of a separation agreement or divorce that you did not report as priority claims
- ❑ Debts to pension or profit-sharing plans, and other similar debts
- ❑ Other. Specify ____________________

4.3 ____________________
Nonpriority Creditor's Name
____
Number Street
____
City State ZIP Code

Last 4 digits of account number __ __ __ __ $__________

When was the debt incurred? ________

As of the date you file, the claim is: Check all that apply
- ❑ Contingent
- ❑ Unliquidated
- ❑ Disputed

Who incurred the debt? Check one.
- ❑ Debtor 1 only
- ❑ Debtor 2 only
- ❑ Debtor 1 and Debtor 2 only
- ❑ At least one of the debtors and another

❑ **Check if this claim is for a community debt**

Is the claim subject to offset?
- ❑ No
- ❑ Yes

Type of NONPRIORITY unsecured claim:
- ❑ Student loans
- ❑ Obligations arising out of a separation agreement or divorce that you did not report as priority claims
- ❑ Debts to pension or profit-sharing plans, and other similar debts
- ❑ Other. Specify ____________________

Debtor 1 ______________________________ Case number (if known)______________________________
First Name Middle Name Last Name

Part 2: Your NONPRIORITY Unsecured Claims – Continuation Page

After listing any entries on this page, number them beginning with 4.4, followed by 4.5, and so forth. **Total claim**

☐

____
Nonpriority Creditor's Name
____
Number Street
____
City State ZIP Code

Who incurred the debt? Check one.

- ❑ Debtor 1 only
- ❑ Debtor 2 only
- ❑ Debtor 1 and Debtor 2 only
- ❑ At least one of the debtors and another

❑ **Check if this claim is for a community debt**

Is the claim subject to offset?

- ❑ No
- ❑ Yes

Last 4 digits of account number ___ ___ ___ ___ $__________

When was the debt incurred? __________

As of the date you file, the claim is: Check all that apply.

- ❑ Contingent
- ❑ Unliquidated
- ❑ Disputed

Type of **NONPRIORITY** unsecured claim:

- ❑ Student loans
- ❑ Obligations arising out of a separation agreement or divorce that you did not report as priority claims
- ❑ Debts to pension or profit-sharing plans, and other similar debts
- ❑ Other. Specify______________________

☐

____
Nonpriority Creditor's Name
____
Number Street
____
City State ZIP Code

Who incurred the debt? Check one.

- ❑ Debtor 1 only
- ❑ Debtor 2 only
- ❑ Debtor 1 and Debtor 2 only
- ❑ At least one of the debtors and another

❑ **Check if this claim is for a community debt**

Is the claim subject to offset?

- ❑ No
- ❑ Yes

Last 4 digits of account number ___ ___ ___ ___ $__________

When was the debt incurred? __________

As of the date you file, the claim is: Check all that apply.

- ❑ Contingent
- ❑ Unliquidated
- ❑ Disputed

Type of **NONPRIORITY** unsecured claim:

- ❑ Student loans
- ❑ Obligations arising out of a separation agreement or divorce that you did not report as priority claims
- ❑ Debts to pension or profit-sharing plans, and other similar debts
- ❑ Other. Specify______________________

☐

____
Nonpriority Creditor's Name
____
Number Street
____
City State ZIP Code

Who incurred the debt? Check one.

- ❑ Debtor 1 only
- ❑ Debtor 2 only
- ❑ Debtor 1 and Debtor 2 only
- ❑ At least one of the debtors and another

❑ **Check if this claim is for a community debt**

Is the claim subject to offset?

- ❑ No
- ❑ Yes

Last 4 digits of account number ___ ___ ___ ___ $__________

When was the debt incurred? __________

As of the date you file, the claim is: Check all that apply.

- ❑ Contingent
- ❑ Unliquidated
- ❑ Disputed

Type of **NONPRIORITY** unsecured claim:

- ❑ Student loans
- ❑ Obligations arising out of a separation agreement or divorce that you did not report as priority claims
- ❑ Debts to pension or profit-sharing plans, and other similar debts
- ❑ Other. Specify______________________

William J. Patterson

Debtor 1 ______________________________ Case number (if known)______________________
First Name Middle Name Last Name

Part 3: List Others to Be Notified About a Debt That You Already Listed

5. **Use this page only if you have others to be notified about your bankruptcy, for a debt that you already listed in Parts 1 or 2. For example, if a collection agency is trying to collect from you for a debt you owe to someone else, list the original creditor in Parts 1 or 2, then list the collection agency here.** Similarly, if you have more than one creditor for any of the debts that you listed in Parts 1 or 2, list the additional creditors here. **If you do not have additional persons to be notified for any debts in Parts 1 or 2, do not fill out or submit this page.**

Name Number Street City State ZIP Code	**On which entry in Part 1 or Part 2 did you list the original creditor?** Line _____ of *(Check one)*: ❑ Part 1: Creditors with Priority Unsecured Claims ❑ Part 2: Creditors with Nonpriority Unsecured Claims **Last 4 digits of account number** ___ ___ ___ ___
Name Number Street City State ZIP Code	**On which entry in Part 1 or Part 2 did you list the original creditor?** Line _____ of *(Check one)*: ❑ Part 1: Creditors with Priority Unsecured Claims ❑ Part 2: Creditors with Nonpriority Unsecured Claims **Last 4 digits of account number** ___ ___ ___ ___
Name Number Street City State ZIP Code	**On which entry in Part 1 or Part 2 did you list the original creditor?** Line _____ of *(Check one)*: ❑ Part 1: Creditors with Priority Unsecured Claims ❑ Part 2: Creditors with Nonpriority Unsecured Claims **Last 4 digits of account number** ___ ___ ___ ___
Name Number Street City State ZIP Code	**On which entry in Part 1 or Part 2 did you list the original creditor?** Line _____ of *(Check one)*: ❑ Part 1: Creditors with Priority Unsecured Claims ❑ Part 2: Creditors with Nonpriority Unsecured Claims **Last 4 digits of account number** ___ ___ ___ ___
Name Number Street City State ZIP Code	**On which entry in Part 1 or Part 2 did you list the original creditor?** Line _____ of *(Check one)*: ❑ Part 1: Creditors with Priority Unsecured Claims ❑ Part 2: Creditors with Nonpriority Unsecured Claims **Last 4 digits of account number** ___ ___ ___ ___
Name Number Street City State ZIP Code	**On which entry in Part 1 or Part 2 did you list the original creditor?** Line _____ of *(Check one)*: ❑ Part 1: Creditors with Priority Unsecured Claims ❑ Part 2: Creditors with Nonpriority Unsecured Claims **Last 4 digits of account number** ___ ___ ___ ___
Name Number Street City State ZIP Code	**On which entry in Part 1 or Part 2 did you list the original creditor?** Line _____ of *(Check one)*: ❑ Part 1: Creditors with Priority Unsecured Claims ❑ Part 2: Creditors with Nonpriority Unsecured Claims **Last 4 digits of account number** ___ ___ ___ ___

Debtor 1 ______________________ Case number (if known)______________________
First Name Middle Name Last Name

Part 4: Add the Amounts for Each Type of Unsecured Claim

6. **Total the amounts of certain types of unsecured claims. This information is for statistical reporting purposes only. 28 U.S.C. § 159. Add the amounts for each type of unsecured claim.**

			Total claim
Total claims from Part 1	6a. **Domestic support obligations**	6a.	$________
	6b. **Taxes and certain other debts you owe the government**	6b.	$________
	6c. **Claims for death or personal injury while you were intoxicated**	6c.	$________
	6d. **Other.** Add all other priority unsecured claims. Write that amount here.	6d.	+ $________
	6e. **Total.** Add lines 6a through 6d.	6e.	$________

			Total claim
Total claims from Part 2	6f. **Student loans**	6f.	$________
	6g. **Obligations arising out of a separation agreement or divorce that you did not report as priority claims**	6g.	$________
	6h. **Debts to pension or profit-sharing plans, and other similar debts**	6h.	$________
	6i. **Other.** Add all other nonpriority unsecured claims. Write that amount here.	6i.	+ $________
	6j. **Total.** Add lines 6f through 6i.	6j.	$________

Fill in this information to identify your case:

Debtor ______ First Name Middle Name Last Name

Debtor 2 (Spouse if filing) ______ First Name Middle Name Last Name

United States Bankruptcy Court for the: __________ District of __________

Case number (If known) ______________________

☐ Check if this is an amended filing

Official Form 106G

Schedule G: Executory Contracts and Unexpired Leases

12/15

Be as complete and accurate as possible. If two married people are filing together, both are equally responsible for supplying correct information. If more space is needed, copy the additional page, fill it out, number the entries, and attach it to this page. On the top of any additional pages, write your name and case number (if known).

1. **Do you have any executory contracts or unexpired leases?**
   ☐ No. Check this box and file this form with the court with your other schedules. You have nothing else to report on this form.
   ☐ Yes. Fill in all of the information below even if the contracts or leases are listed on *Schedule A/B: Property* (Official Form 106A/B).

2. **List separately each person or company with whom you have the contract or lease. Then state what each contract or lease is for (for example, rent, vehicle lease, cell phone).** See the instructions for this form in the instruction booklet for more examples of executory contracts and unexpired leases.

	Person or company with whom you have the contract or lease	State what the contract or lease is for
2.1	Name Number Street City State ZIP Code	
2.2	Name Number Street City State ZIP Code	
2.3	Name Number Street City State ZIP Code	
2.4	Name Number Street City State ZIP Code	
2.5	Name Number Street City State ZIP Code	

Debtor 1 ______________________________ Case number *(if known)* ______________________
First Name Middle Name Last Name

Additional Page if You Have More Contracts or Leases

Person or company with whom you have the contract or lease	What the contract or lease is for
2.2 ______ Name ______ Number Street ______ City State ZIP Code	
2._ ______ Name ______ Number Street ______ City State ZIP Code	
2._ ______ Name ______ Number Street ______ City State ZIP Code	
2._ ______ Name ______ Number Street ______ City State ZIP Code	
2._ ______ Name ______ Number Street ______ City State ZIP Code	
2._ ______ Name ______ Number Street ______ City State ZIP Code	
2._ ______ Name ______ Number Street ______ City State ZIP Code	
2._ ______ Name ______ Number Street ______ City State ZIP Code	

Fill in this information to identify your case:

Debtor 1 ______________________________
First Name Middle Name Last Name

Debtor 2 ______________________________
(Spouse, if filing) First Name Middle Name Last Name

United States Bankruptcy Court for the: __________ District of __________

Case number ______________________________
(If known)

❑ Check if this is an amended filing

Official Form 106H

Schedule H: Your Codebtors

12/15

Codebtors are people or entities who are also liable for any debts you may have. Be as complete and accurate as possible. If two married people are filing together, both are equally responsible for supplying correct information. If more space is needed, copy the Additional Page, fill it out, and number the entries in the boxes on the left. Attach the Additional Page to this page. On the top of any Additional Pages, write your name and case number (if known). Answer every question.

1. **Do you have any codebtors?** (If you are filing a joint case, do not list either spouse as a codebtor.)
   - ❑ No
   - ❑ Yes

2. **Within the last 8 years, have you lived in a community property state or territory?** (*Community property states and territories* include Arizona, California, Idaho, Louisiana, Nevada, New Mexico, Puerto Rico, Texas, Washington, and Wisconsin.)
   - ❑ No. Go to line 3.
   - ❑ Yes. Did your spouse, former spouse, or legal equivalent live with you at the time?
     - ❑ No
     - ❑ Yes. In which community state or territory did you live? ______________. Fill in the name and current address of that person.

   ____
   Name of your spouse, former spouse, or legal equivalent

   ____
   Number Street

   ____
   City State ZIP Code

3. **In Column 1, list all of your codebtors. Do not include your spouse as a codebtor if your spouse is filing with you. List the person shown in line 2 again as a codebtor only if that person is a guarantor or cosigner. Make sure you have listed the creditor on *Schedule D* (Official Form 106D), *Schedule E/F* (Official Form 106E/F), or *Schedule G* (Official Form 106G). Use *Schedule D, Schedule E/F, or Schedule G* to fill out Column 2.**

	Column 1: **Your codebtor**	*Column 2:* **The creditor to whom you owe the debt** Check all schedules that apply:
3.1	______________________________ Name ______________________________ Number Street ______________________________ City State ZIP Code	❑ Schedule D, line ______ ❑ Schedule E/F, line ______ ❑ Schedule G, line ______
3.2	______________________________ Name ______________________________ Number Street ______________________________ City State ZIP Code	❑ Schedule D, line ______ ❑ Schedule E/F, line ______ ❑ Schedule G, line ______
3.3	______________________________ Name ______________________________ Number Street ______________________________ City State ZIP Code	❑ Schedule D, line ______ ❑ Schedule E/F, line ______ ❑ Schedule G, line ______

Debtor 1 ______________________________ Case number (if known) ______________________
First Name Middle Name Last Name

Additional Page to List More Codebtors

Column 1: Your codebtor	*Column 2:* The creditor to whom you owe the debt Check all schedules that apply:
3._ Name Number Street City State ZIP Code	❑ Schedule D, line _____ ❑ Schedule E/F, line _____ ❑ Schedule G, line _____
3._ Name Number Street City State ZIP Code	❑ Schedule D, line _____ ❑ Schedule E/F, line _____ ❑ Schedule G, line _____
3._ Name Number Street City State ZIP Code	❑ Schedule D, line _____ ❑ Schedule E/F, line _____ ❑ Schedule G, line _____
3._ Name Number Street City State ZIP Code	❑ Schedule D, line _____ ❑ Schedule E/F, line _____ ❑ Schedule G, line _____
3._ Name Number Street City State ZIP Code	❑ Schedule D, line _____ ❑ Schedule E/F, line _____ ❑ Schedule G, line _____
3._ Name Number Street City State ZIP Code	❑ Schedule D, line _____ ❑ Schedule E/F, line _____ ❑ Schedule G, line _____
3._ Name Number Street City State ZIP Code	❑ Schedule D, line _____ ❑ Schedule E/F, line _____ ❑ Schedule G, line _____
3._ Name Number Street City State ZIP Code	❑ Schedule D, line _____ ❑ Schedule E/F, line _____ ❑ Schedule G, line _____

Official Form 106H **Schedule H: Your Codebtors** page ___ of ___

Fill in this information to identify your case:

Debtor 1 ______________________________
First Name Middle Name Last Name

Debtor 2 ______________________________
(Spouse, if filing) First Name Middle Name Last Name

United States Bankruptcy Court for the: __________ District of __________

Case number ______________________________
(If known)

Check if this is:

- ☐ An amended filing
- ☐ A supplement showing postpetition chapter 13 income as of the following date:

____
MM / DD / YYYY

Official Form 106I

Schedule I: Your Income

12/15

Be as complete and accurate as possible. If two married people are filing together (Debtor 1 and Debtor 2), both are equally responsible for supplying correct information. If you are married and not filing jointly, and your spouse is living with you, include information about your spouse. If you are separated and your spouse is not filing with you, do not include information about your spouse. If more space is needed, attach a separate sheet to this form. On the top of any additional pages, write your name and case number (if known). Answer every question.

Part 1: Describe Employment

1. **Fill in your employment information.**

If you have more than one job, attach a separate page with information about additional employers.

Include part-time, seasonal, or self-employed work.

Occupation may include student or homemaker, if it applies.

	Debtor 1	Debtor 2 or non-filing spouse
Employment status	☐ Employed ☐ Not employed	☐ Employed ☐ Not employed
Occupation	______________	______________
Employer's name	______________	______________
Employer's address	______________ Number Street ______________ ______________ ______________ City State ZIP Code	______________ Number Street ______________ ______________ ______________ City State ZIP Code
How long employed there?	________	________

Part 2: Give Details About Monthly Income

Estimate monthly income as of the date you file this form. If you have nothing to report for any line, write $0 in the space. Include your non-filing spouse unless you are separated.

If you or your non-filing spouse have more than one employer, combine the information for all employers for that person on the lines below. If you need more space, attach a separate sheet to this form.

		For Debtor 1	For Debtor 2 or non-filing spouse
2. **List monthly gross wages, salary, and commissions** (before all payroll deductions). If not paid monthly, calculate what the monthly wage would be.	2.	$________	$________
3. **Estimate and list monthly overtime pay.**	3.	+ $________	+ $________
4. **Calculate gross income.** Add line 2 + line 3.	4.	$________	$________

Debtor 1 ______________________________ Case number (if known) ______________________________
First Name Middle Name Last Name

		For Debtor 1	For Debtor 2 or non-filing spouse
Copy line 4 here .... →	4.	$________	$________
5. **List all payroll deductions:**			
5a. **Tax, Medicare, and Social Security deductions**	5a.	$________	$________
5b. **Mandatory contributions for retirement plans**	5b.	$________	$________
5c. **Voluntary contributions for retirement plans**	5c.	$________	$________
5d. **Required repayments of retirement fund loans**	5d.	$________	$________
5e. **Insurance**	5e.	$________	$________
5f. **Domestic support obligations**	5f.	$________	$________
5g. **Union dues**	5g.	$________	$________
5h. **Other deductions.** Specify: ________________	5h.	+ $________	+ $________
6. **Add the payroll deductions**. Add lines 5a + 5b + 5c + 5d + 5e +5f + 5g + 5h.	6.	$________	$________
7. **Calculate total monthly take-home pay.** Subtract line 6 from line 4.	7.	$________	$________
8. **List all other income regularly received:**			
8a. **Net income from rental property and from operating a business, profession, or farm** Attach a statement for each property and business showing gross receipts, ordinary and necessary business expenses, and the total monthly net income.	8a.	$________	$________
8b. **Interest and dividends**	8b.	$________	$________
8c. **Family support payments that you, a non-filing spouse, or a dependent regularly receive** Include alimony, spousal support, child support, maintenance, divorce settlement, and property settlement.	8c.	$________	$________
8d. **Unemployment compensation**	8d.	$________	$________
8e. **Social Security**	8e.	$________	$________
8f. **Other government assistance that you regularly receive** Include cash assistance and the value (if known) of any non-cash assistance that you receive, such as food stamps (benefits under the Supplemental Nutrition Assistance Program) or housing subsidies. Specify: ________________	8f.	$________	$________
8g. **Pension or retirement income**	8g.	$________	$________
8h. **Other monthly income.** Specify: ________________	8h.	+ $________	+ $________
9. **Add all other income**. Add lines 8a + 8b + 8c + 8d + 8e + 8f +8g + 8h.	9.	$________	$________

10. **Calculate monthly income.** Add line 7 + line 9. Add the entries in line 10 for Debtor 1 and Debtor 2 or non-filing spouse.	10.	$________	+	$________	=	$________

11. **State all other regular contributions to the expenses that you list in *Schedule J.***
Include contributions from an unmarried partner, members of your household, your dependents, your roommates, and other friends or relatives.
Do not include any amounts already included in lines 2-10 or amounts that are not available to pay expenses listed in *Schedule J*.
Specify: ______________________________ 11. + $________

12. **Add the amount in the last column of line 10 to the amount in line 11.** The result is the combined monthly income.
Write that amount on the *Summary of Your Assets and Liabilities and Certain Statistical Information*, if it applies 12. $________
Combined monthly income

13. **Do you expect an increase or decrease within the year after you file this form?**
- ☐ No.
- ☐ Yes. Explain: ______________________________

Official Form 106I **Schedule I: Your Income** page **2**

William J. Patterson

Fill in this information to identify your case:

Debtor 1 ______________________________
First Name Middle Name Last Name

Debtor 2 ______________________________
(Spouse, if filing) First Name Middle Name Last Name

United States Bankruptcy Court for the: __________ District of __________

Case number ______________________________
(If known)

Check if this is:

❑ An amended filing

❑ A supplement showing postpetition chapter 13 expenses as of the following date:

____
MM / DD / YYYY

Official Form 106J

Schedule J: Your Expenses

12/15

Be as complete and accurate as possible. If two married people are filing together, both are equally responsible for supplying correct information. If more space is needed, attach another sheet to this form. On the top of any additional pages, write your name and case number (if known). Answer every question.

Part 1: Describe Your Household

1. **Is this a joint case?**

❑ No. Go to line 2.
❑ Yes. **Does Debtor 2 live in a separate household?**

❑ No
❑ Yes. Debtor 2 must file Official Form 106J-2, *Expenses for Separate Household of Debtor 2.*

2. **Do you have dependents?**

Do not list Debtor 1 and Debtor 2.

Do not state the dependents' names.

❑ No
❑ Yes. Fill out this information for each dependent..........................

Dependent's relationship to Debtor 1 or Debtor 2	Dependent's age	Does dependent live with you?
____________	______	❑ No ❑ Yes
____________	______	❑ No ❑ Yes
____________	______	❑ No ❑ Yes
____________	______	❑ No ❑ Yes
____________	______	❑ No ❑ Yes

3. **Do your expenses include expenses of people other than yourself and your dependents?**

❑ No
❑ Yes

Part 2: Estimate Your Ongoing Monthly Expenses

Estimate your expenses as of your bankruptcy filing date unless you are using this form as a supplement in a Chapter 13 case to report expenses as of a date after the bankruptcy is filed. If this is a supplemental *Schedule J*, check the box at the top of the form and fill in the applicable date.

Include expenses paid for with non-cash government assistance if you know the value of such assistance and have included it on *Schedule I: Your Income* (Official Form 106I.)

		Your expenses
4. **The rental or home ownership expenses for your residence.** Include first mortgage payments and any rent for the ground or lot.	4	$__________
If not included in line 4:		
4a. Real estate taxes	4a.	$__________
4b. Property, homeowner's, or renter's insurance	4b.	$__________
4c. Home maintenance, repair, and upkeep expenses	4c.	$__________
4d. Homeowner's association or condominium dues	4d.	$__________

Debtor 1 ______________________ Case number *(if known)*______________________
First Name Middle Name Last Name

		Your expenses
5. **Additional mortgage payments for your residence**, such as home equity loans	5.	$________
6. **Utilities:**		
6a. Electricity, heat, natural gas	6a.	$________
6b. Water, sewer, garbage collection	6b.	$________
6c. Telephone, cell phone, Internet, satellite, and cable services	6c.	$________
6d. Other. Specify: ________	6d.	$________
7. **Food and housekeeping supplies**	7.	$________
8. **Childcare and children's education costs**	8.	$________
9. **Clothing, laundry, and dry cleaning**	9.	$________
10. **Personal care products and services**	10.	$________
11. **Medical and dental expenses**	11.	$________
12. **Transportation.** Include gas, maintenance, bus or train fare. Do not include car payments.	12.	$________
13. **Entertainment, clubs, recreation, newspapers, magazines, and books**	13.	$________
14. **Charitable contributions and religious donations**	14.	$________
15. **Insurance.** Do not include insurance deducted from your pay or included in lines 4 or 20.		
15a. Life insurance	15a.	$________
15b. Health insurance	15b.	$________
15c. Vehicle insurance	15c.	$________
15d. Other insurance. Specify: ________	15d.	$________
16. **Taxes.** Do not include taxes deducted from your pay or included in lines 4 or 20. Specify: ________	16.	$________
17. **Installment or lease payments:**		
17a. Car payments for Vehicle 1	17a.	$________
17b. Car payments for Vehicle 2	17b.	$________
17c. Other. Specify: ________	17c.	$________
17d. Other. Specify: ________	17d.	$________
18. **Your payments of alimony, maintenance, and support that you did not report as deducted from your pay on line 5, *Schedule I, Your Income* (Official Form 106I).**	18.	$________
19. **Other payments you make to support others who do not live with you.** Specify: ________	19.	$________
20. **Other real property expenses not included in lines 4 or 5 of this form or on *Schedule I: Your Income*.**		
20a. Mortgages on other property	20a.	$________
20b. Real estate taxes	20b.	$________
20c. Property, homeowner's, or renter's insurance	20c.	$________
20d. Maintenance, repair, and upkeep expenses	20d.	$________
20e. Homeowner's association or condominium dues	20e.	$________

William J. Patterson

Debtor 1 ______________________________ Case number (if known)______________________
First Name Middle Name Last Name

21. **Other**. Specify: ______________________________ 21. +$__________

22. **Calculate your monthly expenses.**

22a. Add lines **4** through 21. 22a. $__________

22b. Copy line 22 (monthly expenses for Debtor 2), if any, from Official Form 106J-2 22b. $__________

22c. Add line 22a and 22b. The result is your monthly expenses. 22c. $__________

23. **Calculate your monthly net income.**

23a. Copy line 12 (*your combined monthly income*) from *Schedule I*. 23a. $__________

23b. Copy your monthly expenses from line 22c above. 23b. – $__________

23c. Subtract your monthly expenses from your monthly income.
The result is your *monthly net income*. 23c. $__________

24. **Do you expect an increase or decrease in your expenses within the year after you file this form?**

For example, do you expect to finish paying for your car loan within the year or do you expect your mortgage payment to increase or decrease because of a modification to the terms of your mortgage?

❑ No.

❑ Yes. Explain here:

Fill in this information to identify your case:
Debtor 1 ______ First Name / Middle Name / Last Name
Debtor 2 (Spouse, if filing) ______ First Name / Middle Name / Last Name
United States Bankruptcy Court for the: ______ District of ______
Case number (If known) ______

Check if this is:

- ❑ An amended filing
- ❑ A supplement showing postpetition chapter 13 expenses as of the following date:

______
MM / DD / YYYY

Official Form 106J-2

Schedule J-2: Expenses for Separate Household of Debtor 2 12/15

Use this form for Debtor 2's separate household expenses ONLY IF Debtor 1 and Debtor 2 maintain separate households. ***If Debtor 1 and Debtor 2 have one or more dependents in common, list the dependents on both Schedule J and this form. Answer the questions on this form only with respect to expenses for Debtor 2 that are not reported on Schedule J.*** **Be as complete and accurate as possible. If more space is needed, attach another sheet to this form. On the top of any additional pages, write your name and case number (if known). Answer every question.**

Part 1: Describe Your Household

1. **Do you and Debtor 1 maintain separate households?**

   ❑ No. Do not complete this form.
   ❑ Yes

2. **Do you have dependents?**

   Do not list Debtor 1 but list all other dependents of Debtor 2 regardless of whether listed as a dependent of Debtor 1 on Schedule J.

   Do not state the dependents' names.

   ❑ No
   ❑ Yes. Fill out this information for each dependent.........................

Dependent's relationship to Debtor 2:	Dependent's age	Does dependent live with you?
______	______	❑ No ❑ Yes
______	______	❑ No ❑ Yes
______	______	❑ No ❑ Yes
______	______	❑ No ❑ Yes
______	______	❑ No ❑ Yes

3. **Do your expenses include expenses of people other than yourself, your dependents, and Debtor 1?**

   ❑ No
   ❑ Yes

Part 2: Estimate Your Ongoing Monthly Expenses

Estimate your expenses as of your bankruptcy filing date unless you are using this form as a supplement in a Chapter 13 case to report expenses as of a date after the bankruptcy is filed.

Include expenses paid for with non-cash government assistance if you know the value of such assistance and have included it on ***Schedule I: Your Income*** **(Official Form 106I.)**

		Your expenses
4. **The rental or home ownership expenses for your residence.** Include first mortgage payments and any rent for the ground or lot.	4.	$______
If not included in line 4:		
4a. Real estate taxes	4a.	$______
4b. Property, homeowner's, or renter's insurance	4b.	$______
4c. Home maintenance, repair, and upkeep expenses	4c.	$______
4d. Homeowner's association or condominium dues	4d.	$______

William J. Patterson

Debtor 1 ______________________________ Case number (if known) ______________________
First Name Middle Name Last Name

		Your expenses
5. **Additional mortgage payments for your residence**, such as home equity loans	5.	$
6. **Utilities:**		
6a. Electricity, heat, natural gas	6a.	$
6b. Water, sewer, garbage collection	6b.	$
6c. Telephone, cell phone, Internet, satellite, and cable services	6c.	$
6d. Other. Specify: ____________	6d.	$
7. **Food and housekeeping supplies**	7.	$
8. **Childcare and children's education costs**	8.	$
9. **Clothing, laundry, and dry cleaning**	9.	$
10. **Personal care products and services**	10.	$
11. **Medical and dental expenses**	11.	$
12. **Transportation.** Include gas, maintenance, bus or train fare. Do not include car payments.	12.	$
13. **Entertainment, clubs, recreation, newspapers, magazines, and books**	13.	$
14. **Charitable contributions and religious donations**	14.	$
15. **Insurance.** Do not include insurance deducted from your pay or included in lines 4 or 20.		
15a. Life insurance	15a.	$
15b. Health insurance	15b.	$
15c. Vehicle insurance	15c.	$
15d. Other insurance. Specify: ____________	15d.	$
16. **Taxes.** Do not include taxes deducted from your pay or included in lines 4 or 20. Specify: ____________	16.	$
17. **Installment or lease payments:**		
17a. Car payments for Vehicle 1	17a.	$
17b. Car payments for Vehicle 2	17b.	$
17c. Other. Specify: ____________	17c.	$
17d. Other. Specify: ____________	17d.	$
18. **Your payments of alimony, maintenance, and support that you did not report as deducted from your pay on line 5, *Schedule I, Your Income*** (Official Form 106I).	18.	$
19. **Other payments you make to support others who do not live with you.** Specify: ____________	19.	$
20. **Other real property expenses not included in lines 4 or 5 of this form or on *Schedule I: Your Income*.**		
20a. Mortgages on other property	20a.	$
20b. Real estate taxes	20b.	$
20c. Property, homeowner's, or renter's insurance	20c.	$
20d. Maintenance, repair, and upkeep expenses	20d.	$
20e. Homeowner's association or condominium dues	20e.	$

Debtor 1 ______________________________ Case number (if known) ______________________
First Name Middle Name Last Name

21. **Other**. Specify: ______________________________ 21. +$__________

22. **Your monthly expenses.** Add lines 5 through 21.
The result is the monthly expenses of Debtor 2. Copy the result to line 22b of Schedule J to calculate the total expenses for Debtor 1 and Debtor 2. 22. $__________

23. Line not used on this form.

24. **Do you expect an increase or decrease in your expenses within the year after you file this form?**

For example, do you expect to finish paying for your car loan within the year or do you expect your mortgage payment to increase or decrease because of a modification to the terms of your mortgage?

- ☐ No.
- ☐ Yes. Explain here:

Fill in this information to identify your case:

Debtor 1 ______________________________________
First Name Middle Name Last Name

Debtor 2 ______________________________________
(Spouse, if filing) First Name Middle Name Last Name

United States Bankruptcy Court for the: __________ District of __________

Case number ______________________________
(If known)

☐ Check if this is an amended filing

Official Form 106Sum

Summary of Your Assets and Liabilities and Certain Statistical Information

12/15

Be as complete and accurate as possible. If two married people are filing together, both are equally responsible for supplying correct information. Fill out all of your schedules first; then complete the information on this form. If you are filing amended schedules after you file your original forms, you must fill out a new *Summary* and check the box at the top of this page.

Part 1: Summarize Your Assets

	Your assets Value of what you own
1. *Schedule A/B: Property* (Official Form 106A/B)	
1a. Copy line 55, Total real estate, from *Schedule A/B*	$ ________
1b. Copy line 62, Total personal property, from *Schedule A/B*	$ ________
1c. Copy line 63, Total of all property on *Schedule A/B*	$ ________

Part 2: Summarize Your Liabilities

	Your liabilities Amount you owe
2. *Schedule D: Creditors Who Have Claims Secured by Property* (Official Form 106D)	
2a. Copy the total you listed in Column A, *Amount of claim*, at the bottom of the last page of Part 1 of *Schedule D*	$ ________
3. *Schedule E/F: Creditors Who Have Unsecured Claims* (Official Form 106E/F)	
3a. Copy the total claims from Part 1 (priority unsecured claims) from line 6e of *Schedule E/F*	$ ________
3b. Copy the total claims from Part 2 (nonpriority unsecured claims) from line 6j of *Schedule E/F*	+ $ ________
Your total liabilities	$ ________

Part 3: Summarize Your Income and Expenses

4. *Schedule I: Your Income* (Official Form 106I)	
Copy your combined monthly income from line 12 of *Schedule I*	$ ________
5. *Schedule J: Your Expenses* (Official Form 106J)	
Copy your monthly expenses from line 22c of *Schedule J*	$ ________

Debtor 1 ______________________________ Case number *(if known)* ______________________
First Name Middle Name Last Name

Part 4: Answer These Questions for Administrative and Statistical Records

6. **Are you filing for bankruptcy under Chapters 7, 11, or 13?**

   ☐ No. You have nothing to report on this part of the form. Check this box and submit this form to the court with your other schedules.
   ☐ Yes

7. **What kind of debt do you have?**

   ☐ **Your debts are primarily consumer debts.** *Consumer debts* are those "incurred by an individual primarily for a personal, family, or household purpose." 11 U.S.C. § 101(8). Fill out lines 8-9g for statistical purposes. 28 U.S.C. § 159.

   ☐ **Your debts are not primarily consumer debts**. You have nothing to report on this part of the form. Check this box and submit this form to the court with your other schedules.

8. **From the *Statement of Your Current Monthly Income*:** Copy your total current monthly income from Official Form 122A-1 Line 11; **OR**, Form 122B Line 11; **OR**, Form 122C-1 Line 14. $________

9. **Copy the following special categories of claims from Part 4, line 6 of *Schedule E/F*:**

	Total claim
From Part 4 on *Schedule E/F*, copy the following:	
9a. Domestic support obligations (Copy line 6a.)	$________
9b. Taxes and certain other debts you owe the government. (Copy line 6b.)	$________
9c. Claims for death or personal injury while you were intoxicated. (Copy line 6c.)	$________
9d. Student loans. (Copy line 6f.)	$________
9e. Obligations arising out of a separation agreement or divorce that you did not report as priority claims. (Copy line 6g.)	$________
9f. Debts to pension or profit-sharing plans, and other similar debts. (Copy line 6h.)	+ $________
9g. **Total.** Add lines 9a through 9f.	$________

Fill in this information to identify your case:

Debtor 1 ______________________________________
First Name Middle Name Last Name

Debtor 2 ______________________________________
(Spouse, if filing) First Name Middle Name Last Name

United States Bankruptcy Court for the: __________ District of __________

Case number ______________________________
(If known)

☐ Check if this is an amended filing

Official Form 106Dec

Declaration About an Individual Debtor's Schedules

12/15

If two married people are filing together, both are equally responsible for supplying correct information.

You must file this form whenever you file bankruptcy schedules or amended schedules. Making a false statement, concealing property, or obtaining money or property by fraud in connection with a bankruptcy case can result in fines up to $250,000, or imprisonment for up to 20 years, or both. 18 U.S.C. §§ 152, 1341, 1519, and 3571.

Sign Below

Did you pay or agree to pay someone who is NOT an attorney to help you fill out bankruptcy forms?

☐ No

☐ Yes. Name of person ______________________________ Attach *Bankruptcy Petition Preparer's Notice, Declaration, and Signature* (Official Form 119).

Under penalty of perjury, I declare that I have read the summary and schedules filed with this declaration and that they are true and correct.

✗ ______________________________ ✗ ______________________________
Signature of Debtor 1 Signature of Debtor 2

Date ______________ Date ______________
MM / DD / YYYY MM / DD / YYYY

Fill in this information to identify your case:

Debtor 1 ______________________________
First Name Middle Name Last Name

Debtor 2 ______________________________
(Spouse, if filing) First Name Middle Name Last Name

United States Bankruptcy Court for the: __________ District of __________

Case number ______________________________
(If known)

☐ Check if this is an amended filing

Official Form 107

Statement of Financial Affairs for Individuals Filing for Bankruptcy

04/16

Be as complete and accurate as possible. If two married people are filing together, both are equally responsible for supplying correct information. If more space is needed, attach a separate sheet to this form. On the top of any additional pages, write your name and case number (if known). Answer every question.

Part 1: Give Details About Your Marital Status and Where You Lived Before

1. **What is your current marital status?**

☐ Married
☐ Not married

2. **During the last 3 years, have you lived anywhere other than where you live now?**

☐ No
☐ Yes. List all of the places you lived in the last 3 years. Do not include where you live now.

Debtor 1:	Dates Debtor 1 lived there	Debtor 2:	Dates Debtor 2 lived there
		☐ Same as Debtor 1	☐ Same as Debtor 1
Number Street ______ City State ZIP Code	From ____ To ____	Number Street ______ City State ZIP Code	From ____ To ____
		☐ Same as Debtor 1	☐ Same as Debtor 1
Number Street ______ City State ZIP Code	From ____ To ____	Number Street ______ City State ZIP Code	From ____ To ____

3. **Within the last 8 years, did you ever live with a spouse or legal equivalent in a community property state or territory?** (*Community property states and territories* include Arizona, California, Idaho, Louisiana, Nevada, New Mexico, Puerto Rico, Texas, Washington, and Wisconsin.)

☐ No
☐ Yes. Make sure you fill out *Schedule H: Your Codebtors* (Official Form 106H).

Part 2: Explain the Sources of Your Income

William J. Patterson

Debtor 1 ______________________________ Case number (if known)______________________
First Name Middle Name Last Name

4. **Did you have any income from employment or from operating a business during this year or the two previous calendar years?**
Fill in the total amount of income you received from all jobs and all businesses, including part-time activities.
If you are filing a joint case and you have income that you receive together, list it only once under Debtor 1.

- ❑ No
- ❑ Yes. Fill in the details.

	Debtor 1		**Debtor 2**	
	Sources of income Check all that apply.	**Gross income** (before deductions and exclusions)	**Sources of income** Check all that apply.	**Gross income** (before deductions and exclusions)
From January 1 of current year until the date you filed for bankruptcy:	❑ Wages, commissions, bonuses, tips ❑ Operating a business	$__________	❑ Wages, commissions, bonuses, tips ❑ Operating a business	$__________
For last calendar year: (January 1 to December 31, ________) YYYY	❑ Wages, commissions, bonuses, tips ❑ Operating a business	$__________	❑ Wages, commissions, bonuses, tips ❑ Operating a business	$__________
For the calendar year before that: (January 1 to December 31, ________) YYYY	❑ Wages, commissions, bonuses, tips ❑ Operating a business	$__________	❑ Wages, commissions, bonuses, tips ❑ Operating a business	$__________

5. **Did you receive any other income during this year or the two previous calendar years?**
Include income regardless of whether that income is taxable. Examples of *other income* are alimony; child support; Social Security, unemployment, and other public benefit payments; pensions; rental income; interest; dividends; money collected from lawsuits; royalties; and gambling and lottery winnings. If you are filing a joint case and you have income that you received together, list it only once under Debtor 1.

List each source and the gross income from each source separately. Do not include income that you listed in line 4.

- ❑ No
- ❑ Yes. Fill in the details.

	Debtor 1		**Debtor 2**	
	Sources of income Describe below.	**Gross income from each source** (before deductions and exclusions)	**Sources of income** Describe below.	**Gross income from each source** (before deductions and exclusions)
From January 1 of current year until the date you filed for bankruptcy:	__________	$__________	__________	$__________
	__________	$__________	__________	$__________
	__________	$__________	__________	$__________
For last calendar year: (January 1 to December 31, ______) YYYY	__________	$__________	__________	$__________
	__________	$__________	__________	$__________
	__________	$__________	__________	$__________
For the calendar year before that: (January 1 to December 31, ______) YYYY	__________	$__________	__________	$__________
	__________	$__________	__________	$__________
	__________	$__________	__________	$__________

Debtor 1 ______________________________ Case number (if known)______________________
First Name Middle Name Last Name

Part 3: List Certain Payments You Made Before You Filed for Bankruptcy

6. Are either Debtor 1's or Debtor 2's debts primarily consumer debts?

☐ No. **Neither Debtor 1 nor Debtor 2 has primarily consumer debts.** *Consumer debts* are defined in 11 U.S.C. § 101(8) as "incurred by an individual primarily for a personal, family, or household purpose."

During the 90 days before you filed for bankruptcy, did you pay any creditor a total of $6,425* or more?

☐ No. Go to line 7.

☐ Yes. List below each creditor to whom you paid a total of $6,425* or more in one or more payments and the total amount you paid that creditor. Do not include payments for domestic support obligations, such as child support and alimony. Also, do not include payments to an attorney for this bankruptcy case.

* Subject to adjustment on 4/01/19 and every 3 years after that for cases filed on or after the date of adjustment.

☐ Yes. **Debtor 1 or Debtor 2 or both have primarily consumer debts.**

During the 90 days before you filed for bankruptcy, did you pay any creditor a total of $600 or more?

☐ No. Go to line 7.

☐ Yes. List below each creditor to whom you paid a total of $600 or more and the total amount you paid that creditor. Do not include payments for domestic support obligations, such as child support and alimony. Also, do not include payments to an attorney for this bankruptcy case.

	Dates of payment	Total amount paid	Amount you still owe	Was this payment for...
______ Creditor's Name ______ Number Street ______ ______ City State ZIP Code	______ ______ ______	$______	$______	☐ Mortgage ☐ Car ☐ Credit card ☐ Loan repayment ☐ Suppliers or vendors ☐ Other ______
______ Creditor's Name ______ Number Street ______ ______ City State ZIP Code	______ ______ ______	$______	$______	☐ Mortgage ☐ Car ☐ Credit card ☐ Loan repayment ☐ Suppliers or vendors ☐ Other ______
______ Creditor's Name ______ Number Street ______ ______ City State ZIP Code	______ ______ ______	$______	$______	☐ Mortgage ☐ Car ☐ Credit card ☐ Loan repayment ☐ Suppliers or vendors ☐ Other ______

Debtor 1 ______ First Name Middle Name Last Name   Case number (if known) ______

7. **Within 1 year before you filed for bankruptcy, did you make a payment on a debt you owed anyone who was an insider?**
Insiders include your relatives; any general partners; relatives of any general partners; partnerships of which you are a general partner; corporations of which you are an officer, director, person in control, or owner of 20% or more of their voting securities; and any managing agent, including one for a business you operate as a sole proprietor. 11 U.S.C. § 101. Include payments for domestic support obligations, such as child support and alimony.

❑ No
❑ Yes. List all payments to an insider.

	Dates of payment	Total amount paid	Amount you still owe	Reason for this payment
Insider's Name		$	$	
Number Street				
City State ZIP Code				
Insider's Name		$	$	
Number Street				
City State ZIP Code				

8. **Within 1 year before you filed for bankruptcy, did you make any payments or transfer any property on account of a debt that benefited an insider?**
Include payments on debts guaranteed or cosigned by an insider.

❑ No
❑ Yes. List all payments that benefited an insider.

	Dates of payment	Total amount paid	Amount you still owe	Reason for this payment Include creditor's name
Insider's Name		$	$	
Number Street				
City State ZIP Code				
Insider's Name		$	$	
Number Street				
City State ZIP Code				

Debtor 1 ______________________________ Case number (if known)______________________
First Name Middle Name Last Name

Part 4: Identify Legal Actions, Repossessions, and Foreclosures

9. **Within 1 year before you filed for bankruptcy, were you a party in any lawsuit, court action, or administrative proceeding?**
List all such matters, including personal injury cases, small claims actions, divorces, collection suits, paternity actions, support or custody modifications, and contract disputes.

❑ No
❑ Yes. Fill in the details.

	Nature of the case	Court or agency	Status of the case
Case title______________ ______________ Case number ______________		______________ Court Name ______________ Number Street ______________ City State ZIP Code	❑ Pending ❑ On appeal ❑ Concluded
Case title______________ ______________ Case number ______________		______________ Court Name ______________ Number Street ______________ City State ZIP Code	❑ Pending ❑ On appeal ❑ Concluded

10. **Within 1 year before you filed for bankruptcy, was any of your property repossessed, foreclosed, garnished, attached, seized, or levied?**
Check all that apply and fill in the details below.

❑ No. Go to line 11.
❑ Yes. Fill in the information below.

	Describe the property	Date	Value of the property
______________ Creditor's Name ______________ Number Street ______________ ______________ City State ZIP Code	 **Explain what happened** ❑ Property was repossessed. ❑ Property was foreclosed. ❑ Property was garnished. ❑ Property was attached, seized, or levied.	________	$__________
______________ Creditor's Name ______________ Number Street ______________ ______________ City State ZIP Code	 **Explain what happened** ❑ Property was repossessed. ❑ Property was foreclosed. ❑ Property was garnished. ❑ Property was attached, seized, or levied.	________	$__________

Debtor 1 ______________________________ Case number (if known) ______________
First Name Middle Name Last Name

11. Within 90 days before you filed for bankruptcy, did any creditor, including a bank or financial institution, set off any amounts from your accounts or refuse to make a payment because you owed a debt?

- ❑ No
- ❑ Yes. Fill in the details.

	Describe the action the creditor took	**Date action was taken**	**Amount**
______________ Creditor's Name			
______________ Number Street		________	$________
______________			
______________ City State ZIP Code	Last 4 digits of account number: XXXX–___ ___ ___ ___		

12. Within 1 year before you filed for bankruptcy, was any of your property in the possession of an assignee for the benefit of creditors, a court-appointed receiver, a custodian, or another official?

- ❑ No
- ❑ Yes

Part 5: List Certain Gifts and Contributions

13. Within 2 years before you filed for bankruptcy, did you give any gifts with a total value of more than $600 per person?

- ❑ No
- ❑ Yes. Fill in the details for each gift.

Gifts with a total value of more than $600 per person	**Describe the gifts**	**Dates you gave the gifts**	**Value**
______________ Person to Whom You Gave the Gift		________	$________
______________		________	$________
______________ Number Street			
______________ City State ZIP Code			
Person's relationship to you ________			

Gifts with a total value of more than $600 per person	**Describe the gifts**	**Dates you gave the gifts**	**Value**
______________ Person to Whom You Gave the Gift		________	$________
______________		________	$________
______________ Number Street			
______________ City State ZIP Code			
Person's relationship to you ________			

Debtor 1 ______________________________ Case number (if known) ______________________
First Name Middle Name Last Name

14. Within 2 years before you filed for bankruptcy, did you give any gifts or contributions with a total value of more than $600 to any charity?

❑ No
❑ Yes. Fill in the details for each gift or contribution.

Gifts or contributions to charities that total more than $600	Describe what you contributed	Date you contributed	Value
______ Charity's Name ______ ______ Number Street ______ City State ZIP Code		______ ______	$______ $______

Part 6: List Certain Losses

15. Within 1 year before you filed for bankruptcy or since you filed for bankruptcy, did you lose anything because of theft, fire, other disaster, or gambling?

❑ No
❑ Yes. Fill in the details.

Describe the property you lost and how the loss occurred	Describe any insurance coverage for the loss Include the amount that insurance has paid. List pending insurance claims on line 33 of *Schedule A/B: Property*.	Date of your loss	Value of property lost
		______	$______

Part 7: List Certain Payments or Transfers

16. Within 1 year before you filed for bankruptcy, did you or anyone else acting on your behalf pay or transfer any property to anyone you consulted about seeking bankruptcy or preparing a bankruptcy petition?
Include any attorneys, bankruptcy petition preparers, or credit counseling agencies for services required in your bankruptcy.

❑ No
❑ Yes. Fill in the details.

	Description and value of any property transferred	Date payment or transfer was made	Amount of payment
______ Person Who Was Paid ______ Number Street ______ ______ City State ZIP Code ______ Email or website address ______ Person Who Made the Payment, if Not You		______ ______	$______ $______

Debtor 1 ______________________________ Case number (if known)____________________
First Name Middle Name Last Name

	Description and value of any property transferred	Date payment or transfer was made	Amount of payment
Person Who Was Paid		______	$________
Number Street		______	$________
City State ZIP Code			
Email or website address			
Person Who Made the Payment, if Not You			

17. **Within 1 year before you filed for bankruptcy, did you or anyone else acting on your behalf pay or transfer any property to anyone who promised to help you deal with your creditors or to make payments to your creditors?**
Do not include any payment or transfer that you listed on line 16.

- ☐ No
- ☐ Yes. Fill in the details.

	Description and value of any property transferred	Date payment or transfer was made	Amount of payment
Person Who Was Paid		______	$________
Number Street		______	$________
City State ZIP Code			

18. **Within 2 years before you filed for bankruptcy, did you sell, trade, or otherwise transfer any property to anyone, other than property transferred in the ordinary course of your business or financial affairs?**
Include both outright transfers and transfers made as security (such as the granting of a security interest or mortgage on your property).
Do not include gifts and transfers that you have already listed on this statement.

- ☐ No
- ☐ Yes. Fill in the details.

	Description and value of property transferred	Describe any property or payments received or debts paid in exchange	Date transfer was made
Person Who Received Transfer			______
Number Street			
City State ZIP Code			
Person's relationship to you ________			
Person Who Received Transfer			______
Number Street			
City State ZIP Code			
Person's relationship to you ________			

Debtor 1 ______________________________ Case number *(if known)*______________________
First Name Middle Name Last Name

19. **Within 10 years before you filed for bankruptcy, did you transfer any property to a self-settled trust or similar device of which you are a beneficiary?** (These are often called *asset-protection devices.*)

- ❑ No
- ❑ Yes. Fill in the details.

	Description and value of the property transferred	Date transfer was made
Name of trust ______________		________

Part 8: List Certain Financial Accounts, Instruments, Safe Deposit Boxes, and Storage Units

20. **Within 1 year before you filed for bankruptcy, were any financial accounts or instruments held in your name, or for your benefit, closed, sold, moved, or transferred?**
Include checking, savings, money market, or other financial accounts; certificates of deposit; shares in banks, credit unions, brokerage houses, pension funds, cooperatives, associations, and other financial institutions.

- ❑ **No**
- ❑ **Yes. Fill in the details.**

	Last 4 digits of account number	Type of account or instrument	Date account was closed, sold, moved, or transferred	Last balance before closing or transfer
Name of Financial Institution Number Street City State ZIP Code	XXXX–__ __ __ __	❑ Checking ❑ Savings ❑ Money market ❑ Brokerage ❑ Other________	________	$________
Name of Financial Institution Number Street City State ZIP Code	XXXX–__ __ __ __	❑ Checking ❑ Savings ❑ Money market ❑ Brokerage ❑ Other________	________	$________

21. **Do you now have, or did you have within 1 year before you filed for bankruptcy, any safe deposit box or other depository for securities, cash, or other valuables?**

- ❑ **No**
- ❑ **Yes. Fill in the details.**

	Who else had access to it?	Describe the contents	Do you still have it?
Name of Financial Institution Number Street City State ZIP Code	Name Number Street City State ZIP Code		❑ No ❑ Yes

22. Have you stored property in a storage unit or place other than your home within 1 year before you filed for bankruptcy?

- ☐ No
- ☐ Yes. Fill in the details.

	Who else has or had access to it?	Describe the contents	Do you still have it?
Name of Storage Facility	Name		☐ No ☐ Yes
Number Street	Number Street		
	City State ZIP Code		
City State ZIP Code			

Part 9: Identify Property You Hold or Control for Someone Else

23. Do you hold or control any property that someone else owns? Include any property you borrowed from, are storing for, or hold in trust for someone.

- ☐ No
- ☐ Yes. Fill in the details.

	Where is the property?	Describe the property	Value
Owner's Name			$________
Number Street	Number Street		
City State ZIP Code	City State ZIP Code		

Part 10: Give Details About Environmental Information

For the purpose of Part 10, the following definitions apply:

- *Environmental law* means any federal, state, or local statute or regulation concerning pollution, contamination, releases of hazardous or toxic substances, wastes, or material into the air, land, soil, surface water, groundwater, or other medium, including statutes or regulations controlling the cleanup of these substances, wastes, or material.
- *Site* means any location, facility, or property as defined under any environmental law, whether you now own, operate, or utilize it or used to own, operate, or utilize it, including disposal sites.
- *Hazardous material* means anything an environmental law defines as a hazardous waste, hazardous substance, toxic substance, hazardous material, pollutant, contaminant, or similar term.

Report all notices, releases, and proceedings that you know about, regardless of when they occurred.

24. Has any governmental unit notified you that you may be liable or potentially liable under or in violation of an environmental law?

- ☐ No
- ☐ Yes. Fill in the details.

	Governmental unit	Environmental law, if you know it	Date of notice
Name of site	Governmental unit		________
Number Street	Number Street		
	City State ZIP Code		
City State ZIP Code			

Debtor 1 ______________________________ Case number *(if known)*______________________
First Name Middle Name Last Name

25. Have you notified any governmental unit of any release of hazardous material?

- ❑ **No**
- ❑ **Yes. Fill in the details.**

	Governmental unit	Environmental law, if you know it	Date of notice
Name of site	Governmental unit		______
Number Street	Number Street		
	City State ZIP Code		
City State ZIP Code			

26. Have you been a party in any judicial or administrative proceeding under any environmental law? Include settlements and orders.

- ❑ **No**
- ❑ **Yes. Fill in the details.**

	Court or agency	Nature of the case	Status of the case
Case title______	Court Name		❑ Pending
	Number Street		❑ On appeal
Case number	City State ZIP Code		❑ Concluded

Part 11: Give Details About Your Business or Connections to Any Business

27. Within 4 years before you filed for bankruptcy, did you own a business or have any of the following connections to any business?

- ❑ **A sole proprietor or self-employed in a trade, profession, or other activity, either full-time or part-time**
- ❑ **A member of a limited liability company (LLC) or limited liability partnership (LLP)**
- ❑ **A partner in a partnership**
- ❑ **An officer, director, or managing executive of a corporation**
- ❑ **An owner of at least 5% of the voting or equity securities of a corporation**

- ❑ **No. None of the above applies. Go to Part 12.**
- ❑ **Yes. Check all that apply above and fill in the details below for each business.**

	Describe the nature of the business	Employer Identification number Do not include Social Security number or ITIN.
Business Name		EIN: __ __ - __ __ __ __ __ __ __
Number Street	Name of accountant or bookkeeper	Dates business existed
		From ______ To ______
City State ZIP Code		

	Describe the nature of the business	Employer Identification number Do not include Social Security number or ITIN.
Business Name		EIN: __ __ - __ __ __ __ __ __ __
Number Street	Name of accountant or bookkeeper	Dates business existed
		From ______ To ______
City State ZIP Code		

Debtor 1 ______________________________ Case number (if known)______________________
First Name Middle Name Last Name

______________________ Business Name	Describe the nature of the business	Employer Identification number Do not include Social Security number or ITIN.
______________________ Number Street		EIN: __ __ – __ __ __ __ __ __ __
______________________	Name of accountant or bookkeeper	Dates business existed
______________________ City State ZIP Code		From ______ To ______

28. **Within 2 years before you filed for bankruptcy, did you give a financial statement to anyone about your business? Include all financial institutions, creditors, or other parties.**

- ❑ **No**
- ❑ **Yes. Fill in the details below.**

	Date issued
______________________ Name	________ MM / DD / YYYY
______________________ Number Street	
______________________	
______________________ City State ZIP Code	

Part 12: Sign Below

I have read the answers on this *Statement of Financial Affairs* and any attachments, and I declare under penalty of perjury that the answers are true and correct. I understand that making a false statement, concealing property, or obtaining money or property by fraud in connection with a bankruptcy case can result in fines up to $250,000, or imprisonment for up to 20 years, or both. 18 U.S.C. §§ 152, 1341, 1519, and 3571.

✘ ______________________________ ✘ ______________________________
Signature of Debtor 1 Signature of Debtor 2

Date ____________ Date ____________

Did you attach additional pages to *Your Statement of Financial Affairs for Individuals Filing for Bankruptcy* (Official Form 107)?

- ❑ No
- ❑ Yes

Did you pay or agree to pay someone who is not an attorney to help you fill out bankruptcy forms?

- ❑ No
- ❑ Yes. Name of person______________________________ Attach the *Bankruptcy Petition Preparer's Notice, Declaration, and Signature* (Official Form 119).

Fill in this information to identify your case:

Debtor 1 ______________________________
First Name Middle Name Last Name

Debtor 2 ______________________________
(Spouse, if filing) First Name Middle Name Last Name

United States Bankruptcy Court for the: __________ District of __________

Case number ______________________________
(If known)

❑ Check if this is an amended filing

Official Form 108

Statement of Intention for Individuals Filing Under Chapter 7

12/15

If you are an individual filing under chapter 7, you must fill out this form if:

- **creditors have claims secured by your property, or**
- **you have leased personal property and the lease has not expired.**

You must file this form with the court within 30 days after you file your bankruptcy petition or by the date set for the meeting of creditors, whichever is earlier, unless the court extends the time for cause. You must also send copies to the creditors and lessors you list on the form.

If two married people are filing together in a joint case, both are equally responsible for supplying correct information. Both debtors must sign and date the form.

Be as complete and accurate as possible. If more space is needed, attach a separate sheet to this form. On the top of any additional pages, write your name and case number (if known).

Part 1: List Your Creditors Who Have Secured Claims

1. **For any creditors that you listed in Part 1 of *Schedule D: Creditors Who Have Claims Secured by Property* (Official Form 106D), fill in the information below.**

Identify the creditor and the property that is collateral	What do you intend to do with the property that secures a debt?	Did you claim the property as exempt on Schedule C?
Creditor's name: Description of property securing debt:	❑ Surrender the property. ❑ Retain the property and redeem it. ❑ Retain the property and enter into a *Reaffirmation Agreement.* ❑ Retain the property and [explain]: __________	❑ No ❑ Yes
Creditor's name: Description of property securing debt:	❑ Surrender the property. ❑ Retain the property and redeem it. ❑ Retain the property and enter into a *Reaffirmation Agreement.* ❑ Retain the property and [explain]: __________	❑ No ❑ Yes
Creditor's name: Description of property securing debt:	❑ Surrender the property. ❑ Retain the property and redeem it. ❑ Retain the property and enter into a *Reaffirmation Agreement.* ❑ Retain the property and [explain]: __________	❑ No ❑ Yes
Creditor's name: Description of property securing debt:	❑ Surrender the property. ❑ Retain the property and redeem it. ❑ Retain the property and enter into a *Reaffirmation Agreement.* ❑ Retain the property and [explain]: __________	❑ No ❑ Yes

Official Form 108 **Statement of Intention for Individuals Filing Under Chapter 7** page 1

Debtor 1 ______________________________ Case number (If known)______________________
First Name Middle Name Last Name

Part 2: List Your Unexpired Personal Property Leases

For any unexpired personal property lease that you listed in *Schedule G: Executory Contracts and Unexpired Leases* (Official Form 106G), fill in the information below. Do not list real estate leases. *Unexpired leases* are leases that are still in effect; the lease period has not yet ended. You may assume an unexpired personal property lease if the trustee does not assume it. 11 U.S.C. § 365(p)(2).

Describe your unexpired personal property leases	Will the lease be assumed?
Lessor's name: Description of leased property:	❑ No ❑ Yes
Lessor's name: Description of leased property:	❑ No ❑ Yes
Lessor's name: Description of leased property:	❑ No ❑ Yes
Lessor's name: Description of leased property:	❑ No ❑ Yes
Lessor's name: Description of leased property:	❑ No ❑ Yes
Lessor's name: Description of leased property:	❑ No ❑ Yes
Lessor's name: Description of leased property:	❑ No ❑ Yes

Part 3: Sign Below

Under penalty of perjury, I declare that I have indicated my intention about any property of my estate that secures a debt and any personal property that is subject to an unexpired lease.

✗ ______________________________ Signature of Debtor 1

✗ ______________________________ Signature of Debtor 2

Date ______________ MM / DD / YYYY

Date ______________ MM / DD / YYYY

Fill in this information to identify your case:

United States Bankruptcy Court for the:

__________ District of __________

Case number *(If known)*: ____________________

Official Form 121

Statement About Your Social Security Numbers

12/15

Use this form to tell the court about any Social Security or federal Individual Taxpayer Identification numbers you have used. Do not file this form as part of the public case file. This form must be submitted separately and must not be included in the court's public electronic records. Please consult local court procedures for submission requirements.

To protect your privacy, the court will not make this form available to the public. You should not include a full Social Security Number or Individual Taxpayer Number on any other document filed with the court. The court will make only the last four digits of your numbers known to the public. However, the full numbers will be available to your creditors, the U.S. Trustee or bankruptcy administrator, and the trustee assigned to your case.

Making a false statement, concealing property, or obtaining money or property by fraud in connection with a bankruptcy case can result in fines up to $250,000, or imprisonment for up to 20 years, or both. 18 U.S.C. §§ 152, 1341, 1519, and 3571.

Part 1: Tell the Court About Yourself and Your spouse if Your Spouse is Filing With You

	For Debtor 1:	For Debtor 2 (Only If Spouse Is Filing):
1. Your name	________________ First name	________________ First name
	________________ Middle name	________________ Middle name
	________________ Last name	________________ Last name

Part 2: Tell the Court About all of Your Social Security or Federal Individual Taxpayer Identification Numbers

2. All Social Security Numbers you have used	___ ___ ___ – ___ ___ – ___ ___ ___ ___ ___ ___ ___ – ___ ___ – ___ ___ ___ ___	___ ___ ___ – ___ ___ – ___ ___ ___ ___ ___ ___ ___ – ___ ___ – ___ ___ ___ ___
	☐ You do not have a Social Security number.	☐ You do not have a Social Security number.
3. All federal Individual Taxpayer Identification Numbers (ITIN) you have used	9 ___ ___ – ___ ___ – ___ ___ ___ ___ 9 ___ ___ – ___ ___ – ___ ___ ___ ___	9 ___ ___ – ___ ___ – ___ ___ ___ ___ 9 ___ ___ – ___ ___ – ___ ___ ___ ___
	☐ You do not have an ITIN.	☐ You do not have an ITIN.

Part 3: Sign Below

Under penalty of perjury, I declare that the information I have provided in this form is true and correct.	Under penalty of perjury, I declare that the information I have provided in this form is true and correct.
✗ ________________ Signature of Debtor 1	✗ ________________ Signature of Debtor 2
Date ________ MM / DD / YYYY	Date ________ MM / DD / YYYY

Fill in this information to identify your case:

Debtor 1 ______________________________
First Name Middle Name Last Name

Debtor 2 ______________________________
(Spouse, if filing) First Name Middle Name Last Name

United States Bankruptcy Court for the: __________ District of __________

Case number ______________________________
(If known)

Check one box only as directed in this form and in Form 122A-1Supp:

☐ 1. There is no presumption of abuse.

☐ 2. The calculation to determine if a presumption of abuse applies will be made under *Chapter 7 Means Test Calculation* (Official Form 122A–2).

☐ 3. The Means Test does not apply now because of qualified military service but it could apply later.

☐ Check if this is an amended filing

Official Form 122A–1

Chapter 7 Statement of Your Current Monthly Income

12/15

Be as complete and accurate as possible. If two married people are filing together, both are equally responsible for being accurate. If more space is needed, attach a separate sheet to this form. Include the line number to which the additional information applies. On the top of any additional pages, write your name and case number (if known). If you believe that you are exempted from a presumption of abuse because you do not have primarily consumer debts or because of qualifying military service, complete and file *Statement of Exemption from Presumption of Abuse Under § 707(b)(2)* (Official Form 122A-1Supp) with this form.

Part 1: Calculate Your Current Monthly Income

1. **What is your marital and filing status?** Check one only.

   ☐ **Not married.** Fill out Column A, lines 2-11.

   ☐ **Married and your spouse is filing with you.** Fill out both Columns A and B, lines 2-11.

   ☐ **Married and your spouse is NOT filing with you. You and your spouse are:**

   ☐ **Living in the same household and are not legally separated.** Fill out both Columns A and B, lines 2-11.

   ☐ **Living separately or are legally separated.** Fill out Column A, lines 2-11; do not fill out Column B. By checking this box, you declare under penalty of perjury that you and your spouse are legally separated under nonbankruptcy law that applies or that you and your spouse are living apart for reasons that do not include evading the Means Test requirements. 11 U.S.C. § 707(b)(7)(B).

Fill in the average monthly income that you received from all sources, derived during the 6 full months before you file this bankruptcy case. 11 U.S.C. § 101(10A). For example, if you are filing on September 15, the 6-month period would be March 1 through August 31. If the amount of your monthly income varied during the 6 months, add the income for all 6 months and divide the total by 6. Fill in the result. Do not include any income amount more than once. For example, if both spouses own the same rental property, put the income from that property in one column only. If you have nothing to report for any line, write $0 in the space.

	Debtor 1	Debtor 2		*Column A* Debtor 1	*Column B* Debtor 2 or non-filing spouse
2. **Your gross wages, salary, tips, bonuses, overtime, and commissions** (before all payroll deductions).				$________	$________
3. **Alimony and maintenance payments.** Do not include payments from a spouse if Column B is filled in.				$________	$________
4. **All amounts from any source which are regularly paid for household expenses of you or your dependents, including child support.** Include regular contributions from an unmarried partner, members of your household, your dependents, parents, and roommates. Include regular contributions from a spouse only if Column B is not filled in. Do not include payments you listed on line 3.				$________	$________
5. **Net income from operating a business, profession, or farm**	**Debtor 1**	**Debtor 2**			
Gross receipts (before all deductions)	$______	$______			
Ordinary and necessary operating expenses	– $______	– $______			
Net monthly income from a business, profession, or farm	$______	$______	Copy here→	$________	$________
6. **Net income from rental and other real property**	**Debtor 1**	**Debtor 2**			
Gross receipts (before all deductions)	$______	$______			
Ordinary and necessary operating expenses	– $______	– $______			
Net monthly income from rental or other real property	$______	$______	Copy here→	$________	$________
7. **Interest, dividends, and royalties**				$________	$________

Debtor 1 ______________________________ Case number (if known)______________________
First Name Middle Name Last Name

	Column A Debtor 1	Column B Debtor 2 or non-filing spouse
8. **Unemployment compensation** Do not enter the amount if you contend that the amount received was a benefit under the Social Security Act. Instead, list it here: ↓ For you .... $________ For your spouse.......... $________	$________	$________
9. **Pension or retirement income.** Do not include any amount received that was a benefit under the Social Security Act.	$________	$________
10. **Income from all other sources not listed above.** Specify the source and amount. Do not include any benefits received under the Social Security Act or payments received as a victim of a war crime, a crime against humanity, or international or domestic terrorism. If necessary, list other sources on a separate page and put the total below.		
________________________	$________	$________
________________________	$________	$________
Total amounts from separate pages, if any.	+ $________	+ $________
11. **Calculate your total current monthly income.** Add lines 2 through 10 for each column. Then add the total for Column A to the total for Column B.	$________ +	$________ = $________ Total current monthly income

Part 2: Determine Whether the Means Test Applies to You

12. **Calculate your current monthly income for the year.** Follow these steps:

12a. Copy your total current monthly income from line 11. .... **Copy line 11 here→** $________

Multiply by 12 (the number of months in a year). x 12

12b. The result is your annual income for this part of the form. 12b. $________

13. **Calculate the median family income that applies to you.** Follow these steps:

Fill in the state in which you live. [ ]

Fill in the number of people in your household. [ ]

Fill in the median family income for your state and size of household. .... 13. $________

To find a list of applicable median income amounts, go online using the link specified in the separate instructions for this form. This list may also be available at the bankruptcy clerk's office.

14. **How do the lines compare?**

14a. ☐ Line 12b is less than or equal to line 13. On the top of page 1, check box 1, *There is no presumption of abuse.* Go to Part 3.

14b. ☐ Line 12b is more than line 13. On the top of page 1, check box 2, *The presumption of abuse is determined by Form 122A-2.* Go to Part 3 and fill out Form 122A–2.

Part 3: Sign Below

By signing here, I declare under penalty of perjury that the information on this statement and in any attachments is true and correct.

✗ ______________________________ ✗ ______________________________
Signature of Debtor 1 Signature of Debtor 2

Date ____________ Date ____________
MM / DD / YYYY MM / DD / YYYY

If you checked line 14a, do NOT fill out or file Form 122A–2.

If you checked line 14b, fill out Form 122A–2 and file it with this form.

Fill in this information to identify your case:
Debtor 1 ____________ First Name / Middle Name / Last Name
Debtor 2 (Spouse, if filing) ____________ First Name / Middle Name / Last Name
United States Bankruptcy Court for the: ________ District of ________
Case number (If known) ____________

❑ Check if this is an amended filing

Official Form 122A–1Supp

Statement of Exemption from Presumption of Abuse Under § 707(b)(2) 12/15

File this supplement together with *Chapter 7 Statement of Your Current Monthly Income* (Official Form 122A-1), if you believe that you are exempted from a presumption of abuse. Be as complete and accurate as possible. If two married people are filing together, and any of the exclusions in this statement applies to only one of you, the other person should complete a separate Form 122A-1 if you believe that this is required by 11 U.S.C. § 707(b)(2)(C).

Part 1: Identify the Kind of Debts You Have

1. **Are your debts primarily consumer debts?** *Consumer debts* are defined in 11 U.S.C. § 101(8) as "incurred by an individual primarily for a personal, family, or household purpose." Make sure that your answer is consistent with the answer you gave at line 16 of the *Voluntary Petition for Individuals Filing for Bankruptcy* (Official Form 101).

   ❑ No. Go to Form 122A-1; on the top of page 1 of that form, check box 1, *There is no presumption of abuse*, and sign Part 3. Then submit this supplement with the signed Form 122A-1.

   ❑ Yes. Go to Part 2.

Part 2: Determine Whether Military Service Provisions Apply to You

2. **Are you a disabled veteran** (as defined in 38 U.S.C. § 3741(1))?

   ❑ No. Go to line 3.

   ❑ Yes. Did you incur debts mostly while you were on active duty or while you were performing a homeland defense activity? 10 U.S.C. § 101(d)(1); 32 U.S.C. § 901(1).

      ❑ No. Go to line 3.

      ❑ Yes. Go to Form 122A-1; on the top of page 1 of that form, check box 1, *There is no presumption of abuse*, and sign Part 3. Then submit this supplement with the signed Form 122A-1.

3. **Are you or have you been a Reservist or member of the National Guard?**

   ❑ No. Complete Form 122A-1. Do not submit this supplement.

   ❑ Yes. Were you called to active duty or did you perform a homeland defense activity? 10 U.S.C. § 101(d)(1); 32 U.S.C. § 901(1).

      ❑ No. Complete Form 122A-1. Do not submit this supplement.

      ❑ Yes. Check any one of the following categories that applies:

         ❑ **I was called to active duty after September 11, 2001**, for at least 90 days and remain on active duty.

         ❑ **I was called to active duty after September 11, 2001,** for at least 90 days and was released from active duty on ____________, which is fewer than 540 days before I file this bankruptcy case.

         ❑ **I am performing a homeland defense activity for at least 90 days.**

         ❑ **I performed a homeland defense activity for at least 90 days**, ending on ____________, which is fewer than 540 days before I file this bankruptcy case.

If you checked one of the categories to the left, go to Form 122A-1. On the top of page 1 of Form 122A-1, check box 3, *The Means Test does not apply now*, and sign Part 3. Then submit this supplement with the signed Form 122A-1. You are not required to fill out the rest of Official Form 122A-1 during the exclusion period. The *exclusion period* means the time you are on active duty or are performing a homeland defense activity, and for 540 days afterward. 11 U.S.C. § 707(b)(2)(D)(ii).

If your exclusion period ends before your case is closed, you may have to file an amended form later.

Fill in this information to identify your case:

Debtor 1 ______________________________
First Name Middle Name Last Name

Debtor 2 ______________________________
(Spouse, if filing) First Name Middle Name Last Name

United States Bankruptcy Court for the: __________ District of __________

Case number ______________________________
(If known)

Check the appropriate box as directed in lines 40 or 42:

According to the calculations required by this Statement:

❑ 1. There is no presumption of abuse.

❑ 2. There is a presumption of abuse.

❑ Check if this is an amended filing

Official Form 122A–2

Chapter 7 Means Test Calculation

04/16

To fill out this form, you will need your completed copy of *Chapter 7 Statement of Your Current Monthly Income* (Official Form 122A-1).

Be as complete and accurate as possible. If two married people are filing together, both are equally responsible for being accurate. If more space is needed, attach a separate sheet to this form. Include the line number to which the additional information applies. On the top of any additional pages, write your name and case number (if known).

Part 1: Determine Your Adjusted Income

1. **Copy your total current monthly income.** .... **Copy line 11 from Official Form 122A-1 here→** .... $________

2. **Did you fill out Column B in Part 1 of Form 122A–1?**
   - ❑ No. Fill in $0 for the total on line 3.
   - ❑ Yes. Is your spouse filing with you?
     - ❑ No. Go to line 3.
     - ❑ Yes. Fill in $0 for the total on line 3.

3. **Adjust your current monthly income by subtracting any part of your spouse's income not used to pay for the household expenses of you or your dependents.** Follow these steps:

   On line 11, Column B of Form 122A–1, was any amount of the income you reported for your spouse NOT regularly used for the household expenses of you or your dependents?

   - ❑ No. Fill in 0 for the total on line 3.
   - ❑ Yes. Fill in the information below:

State each purpose for which the income was used For example, the income is used to pay your spouse's tax debt or to support people other than you or your dependents	Fill in the amount you are subtracting from your spouse's income
______________________	$________
______________________	$________
______________________	+ $________
Total.	$________

Copy total here .... → − $________

4. **Adjust your current monthly income.** Subtract the total on line 3 from line 1. $________

Debtor 1 ______________________ First Name Middle Name Last Name   Case number (if known) ______________________

Part 2: Calculate Your Deductions from Your Income

The Internal Revenue Service (IRS) issues National and Local Standards for certain expense amounts. Use these amounts to answer the questions in lines 6-15. To find the IRS standards, go online using the link specified in the separate instructions for this form. This information may also be available at the bankruptcy clerk's office.

Deduct the expense amounts set out in lines 6-15 regardless of your actual expense. In later parts of the form, you will use some of your actual expenses if they are higher than the standards. Do not deduct any amounts that you subtracted from your spouse's income in line 3 and do not deduct any operating expenses that you subtracted from income in lines 5 and 6 of Form 122A–1.

If your expenses differ from month to month, enter the average expense.

Whenever this part of the form refers to *you*, it means both you and your spouse if Column B of Form 122A–1 is filled in.

5. **The number of people used in determining your deductions from income**

   Fill in the number of people who could be claimed as exemptions on your federal income tax return, plus the number of any additional dependents whom you support. This number may be different from the number of people in your household. [ ]

National Standards You must use the IRS National Standards to answer the questions in lines 6-7.

6. **Food, clothing, and other items:** Using the number of people you entered in line 5 and the IRS National Standards, fill in the dollar amount for food, clothing, and other items. $______

7. **Out-of-pocket health care allowance:** Using the number of people you entered in line 5 and the IRS National Standards, fill in the dollar amount for out-of-pocket health care. The number of people is split into two categories—people who are under 65 and people who are 65 or older—because older people have a higher IRS allowance for health care costs. If your actual expenses are higher than this IRS amount, you may deduct the additional amount on line 22.

People who are under 65 years of age

7a. Out-of-pocket health care allowance per person $________

7b. Number of people who are under 65 X ____

7c. **Subtotal.** Multiply line 7a by line 7b. $________ **Copy here➔** $________

People who are 65 years of age or older

7d. Out-of-pocket health care allowance per person $________

7e. Number of people who are 65 or older X ____

7f. **Subtotal.** Multiply line 7d by line 7e. $________ **Copy here➔** + $________

7g. **Total.** Add lines 7c and 7f. .... $________ **Copy total here➔** $________

Debtor 1 ______________________________ Case number *(if known)*______________
First Name Middle Name Last Name

Local Standards You must use the IRS Local Standards to answer the questions in lines 8-15.

Based on information from the IRS, the U.S. Trustee Program has divided the IRS Local Standard for housing for bankruptcy purposes into two parts:

- **Housing and utilities – Insurance and operating expenses**
- **Housing and utilities – Mortgage or rent expenses**

To answer the questions in lines 8-9, use the U.S. Trustee Program chart.

To find the chart, go online using the link specified in the separate instructions for this form.
This chart may also be available at the bankruptcy clerk's office.

8. **Housing and utilities – Insurance and operating expenses:** Using the number of people you entered in line 5, fill in the dollar amount listed for your county for insurance and operating expenses. .... $________

9. **Housing and utilities – Mortgage or rent expenses:**

9a. Using the number of people you entered in line 5, fill in the dollar amount listed for your county for mortgage or rent expenses.......... $________

9b. Total average monthly payment for all mortgages and other debts secured by your home.

To calculate the total average monthly payment, add all amounts that are contractually due to each secured creditor in the 60 months after you file for bankruptcy. Then divide by 60.

Name of the creditor	Average monthly payment
______________	$________
______________	$________
______________	+ $________

Total average monthly payment $________ Copy here➔ – $________ Repeat this amount on line 33a.

9c. Net mortgage or rent expense.
Subtract line 9b (*total average monthly payment*) from line 9a (*mortgage or rent expense*). If this amount is less than $0, enter $0.......... $________ Copy here➔ $________

10. **If you claim that the U.S. Trustee Program's division of the IRS Local Standard for housing is incorrect and affects the calculation of your monthly expenses, fill in any additional amount you claim.** $________

Explain why: ______________________________
____

11. **Local transportation expenses:** Check the number of vehicles for which you claim an ownership or operating expense.

- ☐ 0. Go to line 14.
- ☐ 1. Go to line 12.
- ☐ 2 or more. Go to line 12.

12. **Vehicle operation expense:** Using the IRS Local Standards and the number of vehicles for which you claim the operating expenses, fill in the *Operating Costs* that apply for your Census region or metropolitan statistical area. $________

William J. Patterson

Debtor 1 ______________________________ Case number (if known) ______________________________
First Name Middle Name Last Name

13. **Vehicle ownership or lease expense:** Using the IRS Local Standards, calculate the net ownership or lease expense for each vehicle below. You may not claim the expense if you do not make any loan or lease payments on the vehicle. In addition, you may not claim the expense for more than two vehicles.

Vehicle 1 **Describe Vehicle 1:** ______________________________

13a. Ownership or leasing costs using IRS Local Standard. .... $________

13b. Average monthly payment for all debts secured by Vehicle 1.
Do not include costs for leased vehicles.

To calculate the average monthly payment here and on line 13e, add all amounts that are contractually due to each secured creditor in the 60 months after you filed for bankruptcy. Then divide by 60.

Name of each creditor for Vehicle 1	**Average monthly payment**
________________	$________
________________	+ $________
Total average monthly payment	$________

Copy here → − $________ Repeat this amount on line 33b.

13c. Net Vehicle 1 ownership or lease expense
Subtract line 13b from line 13a. If this amount is less than $0, enter $0. .... $________ **Copy net Vehicle 1 expense here** → $________

Vehicle 2 **Describe Vehicle 2:** ______________________________

13d. Ownership or leasing costs using IRS Local Standard. .... $________

13e. Average monthly payment for all debts secured by Vehicle 2.
Do not include costs for leased vehicles.

Name of each creditor for Vehicle 2	**Average monthly payment**
________________	$________
________________	+ $________
Total average monthly payment	$________

Copy here → − $________ Repeat this amount on line 33c.

13f. Net Vehicle 2 ownership or lease expense
Subtract line 13e from 13d. If this amount is less than $0, enter $0. .... $________ **Copy net Vehicle 2 expense here** → $________

14. **Public transportation expense**: If you claimed 0 vehicles in line 11, using the IRS Local Standards, fill in the *Public Transportation* expense allowance regardless of whether you use public transportation. $________

15. **Additional public transportation expense:** If you claimed 1 or more vehicles in line 11 and if you claim that you may also deduct a public transportation expense, you may fill in what you believe is the appropriate expense, but you may not claim more than the IRS Local Standard for *Public Transportation*. $________

Debtor 1 ________________________ Case number *(if known)*________________________
First Name Middle Name Last Name

Other Necessary Expenses In addition to the expense deductions listed above, you are allowed your monthly expenses for the following IRS categories.

16. **Taxes:** The total monthly amount that you will actually owe for federal, state and local taxes, such as income taxes, self-employment taxes, Social Security taxes, and Medicare taxes. You may include the monthly amount withheld from your pay for these taxes. However, if you expect to receive a tax refund, you must divide the expected refund by 12 and subtract that number from the total monthly amount that is withheld to pay for taxes. $________
    Do not include real estate, sales, or use taxes.

17. **Involuntary deductions:** The total monthly payroll deductions that your job requires, such as retirement contributions, union dues, and uniform costs.
    Do not include amounts that are not required by your job, such as voluntary 401(k) contributions or payroll savings. $________

18. **Life insurance:** The total monthly premiums that you pay for your own term life insurance. If two married people are filing together, include payments that you make for your spouse's term life insurance. Do not include premiums for life insurance on your dependents, for a non-filing spouse's life insurance, or for any form of life insurance other than term. $________

19. **Court-ordered payments:** The total monthly amount that you pay as required by the order of a court or administrative agency, such as spousal or child support payments.
    Do not include payments on past due obligations for spousal or child support. You will list these obligations in line 35. $________

20. **Education:** The total monthly amount that you pay for education that is either required:
    - as a condition for your job, or
    - for your physically or mentally challenged dependent child if no public education is available for similar services. $________

21. **Childcare:** The total monthly amount that you pay for childcare, such as babysitting, daycare, nursery, and preschool.
    Do not include payments for any elementary or secondary school education. $________

22. **Additional health care expenses, excluding insurance costs:** The monthly amount that you pay for health care that is required for the health and welfare of you or your dependents and that is not reimbursed by insurance or paid by a health savings account. Include only the amount that is more than the total entered in line 7.
    Payments for health insurance or health savings accounts should be listed only in line 25. $________

23. **Optional telephones and telephone services:** The total monthly amount that you pay for telecommunication services for you and your dependents, such as pagers, call waiting, caller identification, special long distance, or business cell phone service, to the extent necessary for your health and welfare or that of your dependents or for the production of income, if it is not reimbursed by your employer. + $________
    Do not include payments for basic home telephone, internet and cell phone service. Do not include self-employment expenses, such as those reported on line 5 of Official Form 122A-1, or any amount you previously deducted.

24. **Add all of the expenses allowed under the IRS expense allowances.**
    Add lines 6 through 23. $________

William J. Patterson

Debtor 1 ______________________________ Case number (if known)______________________
First Name Middle Name Last Name

Additional Expense Deductions These are additional deductions allowed by the Means Test.
Note: Do not include any expense allowances listed in lines 6-24.

25. **Health insurance, disability insurance, and health savings account expenses.** The monthly expenses for health insurance, disability insurance, and health savings accounts that are reasonably necessary for yourself, your spouse, or your dependents.

Health insurance $__________

Disability insurance $__________

Health savings account + $__________

Total $__________ **Copy total here➔** .... $_______

Do you actually spend this total amount?

❑ No. How much do you actually spend? $__________
❑ Yes

26. **Continuing contributions to the care of household or family members.** The actual monthly expenses that you will continue to pay for the reasonable and necessary care and support of an elderly, chronically ill, or disabled member of your household or member of your immediate family who is unable to pay for such expenses. These expenses may include contributions to an account of a qualified ABLE program. 26 U.S.C. § 529A(b). $_______

27. **Protection against family violence.** The reasonably necessary monthly expenses that you incur to maintain the safety of you and your family under the Family Violence Prevention and Services Act or other federal laws that apply. $_______

By law, the court must keep the nature of these expenses confidential.

28. **Additional home energy costs.** Your home energy costs are included in your insurance and operating expenses on line 8.

If you believe that you have home energy costs that are more than the home energy costs included in expenses on line 8, then fill in the excess amount of home energy costs. $_______

You must give your case trustee documentation of your actual expenses, and you must show that the additional amount claimed is reasonable and necessary.

29. **Education expenses for dependent children who are younger than 18.** The monthly expenses (not more than $160.42* per child) that you pay for your dependent children who are younger than 18 years old to attend a private or public elementary or secondary school. $_______

You must give your case trustee documentation of your actual expenses, and you must explain why the amount claimed is reasonable and necessary and not already accounted for in lines 6-23.

* Subject to adjustment on 4/01/19, and every 3 years after that for cases begun on or after the date of adjustment.

30. **Additional food and clothing expense.** The monthly amount by which your actual food and clothing expenses are higher than the combined food and clothing allowances in the IRS National Standards. That amount cannot be more than 5% of the food and clothing allowances in the IRS National Standards. $_______

To find a chart showing the maximum additional allowance, go online using the link specified in the separate instructions for this form. This chart may also be available at the bankruptcy clerk's office.

You must show that the additional amount claimed is reasonable and necessary.

31. **Continuing charitable contributions.** The amount that you will continue to contribute in the form of cash or financial instruments to a religious or charitable organization. 26 U.S.C. § 170(c)(1)-(2). + $_______

32. **Add all of the additional expense deductions.** $_______
Add lines 25 through 31.

Debtor 1 ______________________________ Case number (if known) ______________
First Name Middle Name Last Name

Deductions for Debt Payment

33. **For debts that are secured by an interest in property that you own, including home mortgages, vehicle loans, and other secured debt, fill in lines 33a through 33e.**

To calculate the total average monthly payment, add all amounts that are contractually due to each secured creditor in the 60 months after you file for bankruptcy. Then divide by 60.

Average monthly payment

Mortgages on your home:

33a. Copy line 9b here .... → $______

Loans on your first two vehicles:

33b. Copy line 13b here. .... → $______

33c. Copy line 13e here. .... → $______

33d. List other secured debts:

Name of each creditor for other secured debt	Identify property that secures the debt	Does payment include taxes or insurance?	
______	______	❑ No ❑ Yes	$______
______	______	❑ No ❑ Yes	$______
______	______	❑ No ❑ Yes	+ $______

33e. Total average monthly payment. Add lines 33a through 33d. .... $______ Copy total here → $______

34. **Are any debts that you listed in line 33 secured by your primary residence, a vehicle, or other property necessary for your support or the support of your dependents?**

❑ No. Go to line 35.
❑ Yes. State any amount that you must pay to a creditor, in addition to the payments listed in line 33, to keep possession of your property (called the *cure amount*). Next, divide by 60 and fill in the information below.

Name of the creditor	Identify property that secures the debt	Total cure amount		Monthly cure amount
______	______	$______	÷ 60 =	$______
______	______	$______	÷ 60 =	$______
______	______	$______	÷ 60 =	+ $______
			Total	$______

Copy total here → $______

35. **Do you owe any priority claims such as a priority tax, child support, or alimony — that are past due as of the filing date of your bankruptcy case?** 11 U.S.C. § 507.

❑ No. Go to line 36.
❑ Yes. Fill in the total amount of all of these priority claims. Do not include current or ongoing priority claims, such as those you listed in line 19.

Total amount of all past-due priority claims .... $______ ÷ 60 = $______

Debtor 1 ______________________________ Case number (if known) ______________________
First Name Middle Name Last Name

36. **Are you eligible to file a case under Chapter 13?** 11 U.S.C. § 109(e).
For more information, go online using the link for *Bankruptcy Basics* specified in the separate instructions for this form. *Bankruptcy Basics* may also be available at the bankruptcy clerk's office.

- ☐ No. Go to line 37.
- ☐ Yes. Fill in the following information.

Projected monthly plan payment if you were filing under Chapter 13 $__________

Current multiplier for your district as stated on the list issued by the Administrative Office of the United States Courts (for districts in Alabama and North Carolina) or by the Executive Office for United States Trustees (for all other districts). x ______

To find a list of district multipliers that includes your district, go online using the link specified in the separate instructions for this form. This list may also be available at the bankruptcy clerk's office.

Average monthly administrative expense if you were filing under Chapter 13 $__________ **Copy total here➔** $__________

37. **Add all of the deductions for debt payment.**
Add lines 33e through 36. $__________

Total Deductions from Income

38. **Add all of the allowed deductions.**

Copy line 24, *All of the expenses allowed under IRS expense allowances* $__________

Copy line 32, *All of the additional expense deductions* $__________

Copy line 37, *All of the deductions for debt payment* + $__________

Total deductions $__________ **Copy total here** ➔ $__________

Part 3: Determine Whether There Is a Presumption of Abuse

39. **Calculate monthly disposable income for 60 months**

39a. Copy line 4, *adjusted current monthly income* $__________

39b. Copy line 38, *Total deductions* − $__________

39c. Monthly disposable income. 11 U.S.C. § 707(b)(2). Subtract line 39b from line 39a. $__________ **Copy here➔** $__________

For the next 60 months (5 years) x 60

39d. **Total.** Multiply line 39c by 60. $__________ **Copy here➔** $__________

40. **Find out whether there is a presumption of abuse.** Check the box that applies:

- ☐ **The line 39d is less than $7,700*.** On the top of page 1 of this form, check box 1, *There is no presumption of abuse*. Go to Part 5.
- ☐ **The line 39d is more than $12,850*.** On the top of page 1 of this form, check box 2, *There is a presumption of abuse*. You may fill out Part 4 if you claim special circumstances. Then go to Part 5.
- ☐ **The line 39d is at least $7,700*, but not more than $12,850*.** Go to line 41.

* Subject to adjustment on 4/01/19, and every 3 years after that for cases filed on or after the date of adjustment.

Debtor 1 ______________________ Case number (if known)______________________
First Name Middle Name Last Name

41. 41a. **Fill in the amount of your total nonpriority unsecured debt.** If you filled out *A Summary of Your Assets and Liabilities and Certain Statistical Information Schedules* (Official Form 106Sum), you may refer to line 3b on that form.......... $________

x .25

41b. **25% of your total nonpriority unsecured debt.** 11 U.S.C. § 707(b)(2)(A)(i)(I). Multiply line 41a by 0.25.......... $________ Copy here→ $________

42. **Determine whether the income you have left over after subtracting all allowed deductions is enough to pay 25% of your unsecured, nonpriority debt.**
Check the box that applies:

❑ **Line 39d is less than line 41b.** On the top of page 1 of this form, check box 1, *There is no presumption of abuse.* Go to Part 5.

❑ **Line 39d is equal to or more than line 41b.** On the top of page 1 of this form, check box 2, *There is a presumption of abuse.* You may fill out Part 4 if you claim special circumstances. Then go to Part 5.

Part 4: Give Details About Special Circumstances

43. **Do you have any special circumstances that justify additional expenses or adjustments of current monthly income for which there is no reasonable alternative?** 11 U.S.C. § 707(b)(2)(B).

❑ No. Go to Part 5.

❑ Yes. Fill in the following information. All figures should reflect your average monthly expense or income adjustment for each item. You may include expenses you listed in line 25.

You must give a detailed explanation of the special circumstances that make the expenses or income adjustments necessary and reasonable. You must also give your case trustee documentation of your actual expenses or income adjustments.

Give a detailed explanation of the special circumstances	Average monthly expense or income adjustment
________	$________
________	$________
________	$________
________	$________

Part 5: Sign Below

By signing here, I declare under penalty of perjury that the information on this statement and in any attachments is true and correct.

✗ ______________________ ✗ ______________________
Signature of Debtor 1 Signature of Debtor 2

Date __________ MM / DD / YYYY Date __________ MM / DD / YYYY

Fill in this information to identify the case:

Debtor 1 ______________________________
First Name Middle Name Last Name

Debtor 2 ______________________________
(Spouse, if filing) First Name Middle Name Last Name

United States Bankruptcy Court for the: __________ District of __________

Case number ______________________________
(If known)

Official Form 423

Certification About a Financial Management Course

12/15

If you are an individual, you must take an approved course about personal financial management if:

- **you filed for bankruptcy under chapter 7 or 13, or**
- **you filed for bankruptcy under chapter 11 and § 1141 (d)(3) applies.**

In a joint case, each debtor must take the course. 11 U.S.C. §§ 727(a)(11) and 1328(g).

After you finish the course, the provider will give you a certificate. The provider may notify the court that you have completed the course. If the provider does notify the court, you need not file this form. If the provider does not notify the court, then Debtor 1 and Debtor 2 must each file this form with the certificate number before your debts will be discharged.

- If you filed under chapter 7 and you need to file this form, file it within 60 days after the first date set for the meeting of creditors under § 341 of the Bankruptcy Code.
- If you filed under chapter 11 or 13 and you need to file this form, file it before you make the last payment that your plan requires or before you file a motion for a discharge under § 1141(d)(5)(B) or § 1328(b) of the Bankruptcy Code. Fed. R. Bankr. P. 1007(c).

In some cases, the court can waive the requirement to take the financial management course. To have the requirement waived, you must file a motion with the court and obtain a court order.

Part 1: Tell the Court About the Required Course

You must check one:

☐ **I completed an approved course in personal financial management:**

Date I took the course __________
MM / DD / YYYY

Name of approved provider ______________________________

Certificate number ______________________________

☐ **I am not required to complete a course in personal financial management because the court has granted my motion for a waiver of the requirement based on** *(check one)*:

☐ **Incapacity.** I have a mental illness or a mental deficiency that makes me incapable of realizing or making rational decisions about finances.

☐ **Disability.** My physical disability causes me to be unable to complete a course in personal financial management in person, by phone, or through the internet, even after I reasonably tried to do so.

☐ **Active duty.** I am currently on active military duty in a military combat zone.

☐ **Residence.** I live in a district in which the United States trustee (or bankruptcy administrator) has determined that the approved instructional courses cannot adequately meet my needs.

Part 2: Sign Here

I certify that the information I have provided is true and correct.

______________________________ Signature of debtor named on certificate

______________________________ Printed name of debtor

Date __________
MM / DD / YYYY

B2800 (Form 2800) (12/15)

United States Bankruptcy Court

_______________ District Of _________________

In re ____ Case No. ___________
Debtor
Chapter ___________

DISCLOSURE OF COMPENSATION OF BANKRUPTCY PETITION PREPARER

[Must be filed with the petition if a bankruptcy petition preparer prepares the petition. 11 U.S.C. § 110(h)(2).]

1. Under 11 U.S.C. § 110(h), I declare under penalty of perjury that I am not an attorney or employee of an attorney, that I prepared or caused to be prepared one or more documents for filing by the above-named debtor(s) in connection with this bankruptcy case, and that compensation paid to me within one year before the filing of the bankruptcy petition, or agreed to be paid to me, for services rendered on behalf of the debtor(s) in contemplation of or in connection with the bankruptcy case is as follows:

For document preparation services I have agreed to accept............................. $____________

Prior to the filing of this statement I have received.. $____________

Balance Due.. $____________

2. I have prepared or caused to be prepared the following documents (itemize):

and provided the following services (itemize):

3. The source of the compensation paid to me was:
Debtor Other (specify)

4. The source of compensation to be paid to me is:
Debtor Other (specify)

5. The foregoing is a complete statement of any agreement or arrangement for payment to me for preparation of the petition filed by the debtor(s) in this bankruptcy case.

6. To my knowledge no other person has prepared for compensation a document for filing in connection with this bankruptcy case except as listed below:

NAME SOCIAL SECURITY NUMBER

_________________________ _________________________ _______________
Signature Social Security number of bankruptcy petition preparer* Date

_________________________ ____
Printed name and title, if any, of Bankruptcy Petition Preparer Address

* If the bankruptcy petition preparer is not an individual, state the Social Security number of the officer, principal, responsible person or partner of the bankruptcy petition preparer. (Required by 11 U.S.C. § 110).

A bankruptcy petition preparer's failure to comply with the provisions of title 11 and the Federal Rules of Bankruptcy Procedure may result in fines or imprisonment or both. 11 U.S.C. § 110; 18 U.S.C. § 156.

Fill in this information to identify your case:

Debtor 1 ______________________________
First Name Middle Name Last Name

Debtor 2 ______________________________
(Spouse, if filing) First Name Middle Name Last Name

United States Bankruptcy Court for the: __________ District of __________

Case number ______________________________
(If known)

☐ Check if this is an amended filing

Official Form 106Dec

Declaration About an Individual Debtor's Schedules

12/15

If two married people are filing together, both are equally responsible for supplying correct information.

You must file this form whenever you file bankruptcy schedules or amended schedules. Making a false statement, concealing property, or obtaining money or property by fraud in connection with a bankruptcy case can result in fines up to $250,000, or imprisonment for up to 20 years, or both. 18 U.S.C. §§ 152, 1341, 1519, and 3571.

Sign Below

Did you pay or agree to pay someone who is NOT an attorney to help you fill out bankruptcy forms?

☐ No

☐ Yes. Name of person______________________________. Attach *Bankruptcy Petition Preparer's Notice, Declaration, and Signature* (Official Form 119).

Under penalty of perjury, I declare that I have read the summary and schedules filed with this declaration and that they are true and correct.

✘ ______________________________
Signature of Debtor 1

Date ______________
MM / DD / YYYY

✘ ______________________________
Signature of Debtor 2

Date ______________
MM / DD / YYYY

GLOSSARY

Adversary Proceeding – A lawsuit arising in or related to a bankruptcy case that is commenced by filing a complaint with the court. A nonexclusive list of adversary proceedings is set forth in Fed. R. Bankr. P. 7001.

Annuity – A contract for the periodic payment of money to you, either for, life or for a number of years.

Assume – An agreement to continue performing duties under a contract or lease.

Automatic Stay – An injunction that automatically stops lawsuits, foreclosures, garnishments, and all collection activity against the debtor the moment a bankruptcy petition is filed.

Bankruptcy – A legal procedure for dealing with debt problems of individuals and businesses; specifically, a case filed under one of the chapters of title 11 of the United States Code (the Bankruptcy Code).

Bankruptcy Administrator – An officer of the judiciary serving in the judicial districts of Alabama and North Carolina who, like the U.S. trustee, is responsible for supervising the administration of bankruptcy cases, estates, and trustees; monitoring plans and disclosure statements; monitoring creditors' committees; monitoring fee applications; and performing other statutory duties. Compare U.S. trustee.

Bankruptcy Code – The informal name for title 11 of the United States Code (11 U.S.C.§§ 101-1330), the federal bankruptcy law.

Bankruptcy Court – The bankruptcy judges in regular active service in each district; a unit of the district court.

Bankruptcy Estate – All legal or equitable interests of the debtor in property at the time of the bankruptcy filing. (The estate includes all property in which the debtor has an interest, even if it is owned or held by another person.)

Bankruptcy Judge – A judicial officer of the United States district court who is the court official with decision-making power over federal bankruptcy cases.

Bankruptcy Petition - The document filed by the debtor (in a voluntary case) or by creditors (in an involuntary case) by which opens the bankruptcy case. (There are official forms for bankruptcy petitions.)

Bankruptcy Petition Preparer – A person or business, other than a lawyer or someone who works for a lawyer, that charges a fee to prepare bankruptcy documents. Under your direction and control, the bankruptcy petition preparer generates bankruptcy forms for you to file by typing them. Because they are not attorneys, they cannot give legal advice or represent you in bankruptcy court. Also called typing services.

Business Debt – A debt that you incurred to obtain money for a business or investment or incurred through the operation of the business or investment.

Chapter 7 – The chapter of the Bankruptcy Code providing for "liquidation" (*i.e.*, the sale of a debtor's nonexempt property and the distribution of the proceeds to creditors).

Chapter 9 – The chapter of the Bankruptcy Code providing for reorganization of municipalities (which includes cities and towns, counties and school districts).

Chapter 11 – The chapter of the Bankruptcy Code providing (generally) for reorganization, usually involving a corporation or partnership. (A Chapter 11 debtor usually proposes a plan of reorganization to keep its business alive and pay creditors over time. People in business or individuals can also seek relief in Chapter 11.)

Chapter 12 – The chapter of the Bankruptcy Code providing for adjustment of debts of a "family farmer," or a "family fisherman" as those terms are defined in the Bankruptcy Code.

Chapter 13 – The chapter of the Bankruptcy Code providing for adjustment of debts of an individual with regular income. (Chapter 13 allows a debtor to keep property and pay debts over time, usually three to five years.)

Chapter 15 – The chapter of the Bankruptcy Code dealing with cases of cross-border insolvency.

Claim – A creditor's right to payment, even if contingent, disputed, unliquidated, or unmatured.

Codebtor – A person or entity that may also be responsible for paying a claim against the debtor.

Collateral – Specific property subject to a lien from which a creditor may be paid ahead of other creditors without liens on that property. This includes a mortgage, security interest, judgment lien, statutory lien, or other lien.

Community Property – A type of property ownership available in certain states for property owned by spouses and, in some instances, legal equivalents of spouses. Community property states and territories include Arizona, California, Idaho, Louisiana, Nevada, New Mexico, Puerto Rico, Texas, Washington, and Wisconsin.

Consumer Debt – A debt you incurred primarily for a personal, family, or household purpose. Personal as opposed to business needs.

Consumer Debtor – A debtor whose debts are primarily consumer debts.

Contested Matter – Those matters, other than objections to claims, that are disputed but are not within the definition of adversary proceeding contained in Rule 7001.

Contingent Claim – A debt you are not obligated to pay unless a particular event occurs after you file for bankruptcy. You owe a contingent claim, for example, if you cosigned someone else's loan. You may not have to pay unless that person later fails to repay the loan.

Creditor – One to whom the debtor owes money or who claims to be owed money by the debtor.

Credit Counseling – Generally refers to two events in individual bankruptcy cases: (1) the "individual or group briefing" from a nonprofit budget and credit counseling agency that individual debtors must attend prior to filing under any chapter of the Bankruptcy Code; and (2) the "instructional course in personal financial management" in chapters 7 and 13 that an individual debtor must complete before a discharge is entered. There are exceptions to both requirements for certain categories of debtors, exigent circumstances, or if the U.S. trustee or bankruptcy administrator has determined that there are insufficient approved credit counseling agencies available to provide the necessary counseling.

Creditor Matrix or Mailing Matrix – A list of names and addresses of all your creditors, formatted as a mailing list according to instructions from the bankruptcy court in which you file.

Creditor – A person or organization to whom you owe money or who claims that you owe it money.

Creditors' Meeting – See meeting of the creditors or 341 meeting.

Current Monthly Income – The average monthly income received by the debtor over the six calendar months before commencement of the bankruptcy case, including regular contributions to household expenses from nondebtors and income from the debtor's spouse if the petition is a joint petition, but not including social security income and certain other payments made because the debtor is a victim of certain crimes. 11 U.S.C. § 101(10A).

Current Value, Fair Market Value, or Value – The amount property is worth, which may be more or less than when you purchased the property. Absent specific instruction, the value should be the price that could be realized from a cash sale or liquidation without duress within a reasonable time. See the instructions for specific forms regarding whether the value requested is as of the date of filing of the petition, the date you complete the form, or some other date.

Debtor – A person who has filed a petition for relief under the Bankruptcy Code.

Debtor 1 – A debtor filing alone or one person in a married couple who is filing a bankruptcy case with a spouse. The same person retains this designation in all of the forms.

Debtor 2 – A second person in a married couple who is filing a bankruptcy case with a spouse.

Debtor Education – See credit counseling

Defendant – An individual (or business) against whom a lawsuit is filed.

Dependent – A person who is economically dependent on you regardless of whether the person can be claimed as a dependent on your federal tax return. However, Chapter 7 Means Test Calculation (Official Form 122A-2) and Chapter 13 Calculation of Your Disposable Income (Official Form 122C-2) use the term in a more limited way. See the instructions on those forms.

Discharge – A release of a debtor from personal liability for certain dischargeable debts set forth in the Bankruptcy Code. (A discharge releases a debtor from personal liability for certain debts known as dischargeable debts and prevents the creditors owed those debts from. taking any action against the debtor to collect the debts. The discharge also prohibits creditors from communicating with the debtor regarding the debt, including telephone calls, letters, and personal contact.) A discharge in bankruptcy relieves you after your bankruptcy case is over from having to pay debts that you owed before you filed your bankruptcy case. Most debts are covered by the discharge, but not all.

Dischargeable Debt – A debt for which the Bankruptcy Code allows the debtor's personal liability to be eliminated.

Disputed Claim – A debt you do not agree that you owe. For instance, your claim is disputed if a bill collector demands payment for a bill you believe you already fully paid.

Equity – The value of a debtor's interest in property that remains after liens and other creditors' interests are considered. (Example: If a house valued at $100,000 is subject to an $80,000 mortgage, there is $20,000 of equity.)

Eviction Judgment – A judgment for possession that your landlord has obtained in an eviction, unlawful detainer action, or similar proceeding.

Executory Contract or Lease – A contract between you and someone else in which both of you still have obligations to perform under the contract at the time you file for bankruptcy. (If a contract or lease is executory, a debtor may assume it or reject it.)

Exemptions, Exempt Property – Certain property owned by an individual debtor that the Bankruptcy Code or applicable state law permits the debtor to keep for use rather than surrender it for the payment of your debts, provided that you follow the correct procedure to claim the exemption. For example, in some states the debtor may be able to exempt all or a portion of the equity in the debtor's primary residence (homestead exemption), or some or all "tools of the trade" used by the debtor to make a living (*i.e.*, auto tools for an auto mechanic or dental tools for a dentist). The availability and amount of property the debtor may exempt depends on the state the debtor lives in.

Garnishment – A procedure by which a creditor can reach money of yours that is in the hands of a third party to satisfy a debt. Garnishments are sometimes used by creditors to obtain money from your wages or bank account.

Individual Debtor – A human being who is filing for bankruptcy either alone or with a spouse, whether or not the individual owns a business.

Insider (of Individual Debtor) – Any relative of the debtor or of a general partner of the debtor; partnership in which the debtor is a general partner; general partner of the debtor; or a corporation of which the debtor is a director, officer, or person in control.

Joint Case or Petition – A single case filed by a married couple together.

Judgment Lien – A lien that arises as a result of a Judgment against you.

Legal Equivalent of a Spouse – A person recognized by applicable nonfederal law as having a relationship with the debtor that grants legal rights and responsibilities equivalent, in whole or in part, to those granted to a spouse.

Legal or Equitable Interest – A broad term that includes all kinds of property interests in both tangible and intangible property, whether or not anyone else has an interest in that property.

Lien – The right to take and hold or sell the property of a debtor as security or payment for a debt or duty.

Liquidation – A sale of a debtor's property with the proceeds to be used for the benefit of creditors.

Liquidated Claim – A creditor's claim for a fixed amount of money.

Means Test – Section 707(b)(2) of the Bankruptcy Code applies a "means test" to determine whether an individual debtor's Chapter 7 filing is presumed to be an abuse of the Bankruptcy Code requiring dismissal or conversion of the case (generally to Chapter 13). Abuse is presumed if the debtor's aggregate current monthly income (see definition above) over 5 years, net of certain statutorily allowed expenses, is more than (i) $12,850, or (ii) 25% the debtor's nonpriority unsecured debt, as long as that amount is at least $7,700. The debtor may rebut a presumption of abuse only by a showing of special circumstances that justify additional expenses or adjustments of current monthly income.

Meeting of Creditors or 341 Meeting – The meeting of the creditors required by section 341 of the Bankruptcy Code at which the debtor is questioned under oath by creditors, a trustee, examiner, or the U.S. trustee about his/her financial affairs. Also called creditors' meeting.

Motion to Lift Automatic Stay – A request by a creditor to allow the creditor to take action against the debtor or the debtor's property that would otherwise be prohibited by the automatic stay.

Negotiable Instrument – A financial instrument that you can transfer to someone by signing or delivering it, including personal checks, cashiers' checks, promissory notes, and money orders.

No-Asset Case – A Chapter 7 case where there are no assets available to satisfy any portion of the creditors' unsecured claims.

Nondischargeable Debt – A debt that cannot be eliminated in bankruptcy. Examples include a home mortgage, debts for alimony or child support, certain taxes, debts for most government funded or guaranteed educational loans or benefit overpayments, debts arising from death or personal injury caused by driving while intoxicated or under the influence of drugs, and debts for restitution or a criminal fine included in a sentence on the debtor's conviction of a crime. Some debts, such as debts for money or property obtained by false pretenses and debts for fraud or defalcation while acting in a fiduciary capacity may be declared nondischargeable only if a creditor timely files and prevails in a nondischargeability action.

NonPriority Unsecured Claim – A debt that generally will be paid after priority unsecured claims are paid. The most common examples are credit card bills, medical bills, and educational loans.

Objection to Dischargeability – A trustee's or creditor's objection to the debtor being released from personal liability for certain dischargeable debts. Common reasons include allegations that the debt to be discharged was incurred by false pretenses or that debt arose because of the debtor's fraud while acting as a fiduciary.

Objection to Exemptions – A trustee's or creditor's objection to the debtor's attempt to claim certain property as exempt form liquidation by the trustee to creditors.

Party In Interest – A party who has standing to be heard by the court in a matter to be decided in the bankruptcy case. The debtor, the U.S. trustee or bankruptcy administrator, the case trustee and creditors are parties in interest for most matters.

Payment Advice – A statement such as a pay stub or earnings statement from your employer that shows all earnings and deductions form your pay.

Petition Preparer – A business not authorized to practice law that prepares bankruptcy petitions.

Plaintiff – A person or business that files a formal complaint with the court.

Postpetition Transfer – A transfer of the debtor's property made after the commencement of the case.

Prebankruptcy Planning – The arrangement (or rearrangement) of a debtor's property to allow the debtor to take maximum advantage of exemptions. (Prebankruptcy planning typically includes converting nonexempt assets into exempt assets.)

Preference or Preferential Debt Payment – A debt payment made to a creditor in the 90-day period before a debtor files bankruptcy (or within one year if the creditor was an insider) that gives the creditor more than the creditor would receive in the debtor's Chapter 7 case.

Presumption of Abuse – A rebuttable legal presumption that you have too much income after allowed expenses to be granted relief under Chapter 7. (Also see means test.)

Priority Unsecured Claims – The Bankruptcy Code's statutory ranking of unsecured claims that determines the order in which unsecured claims will be paid if there is not enough money to pay all unsecured claims in full. For example, under the Bankruptcy Code's priority scheme, money owed to the case trustee, income taxes, past due alimony and/or child support must be paid in full before any general unsecured debt (*i.e.,* trade debt or credit card debt) is paid.

Proof of Claim – A written statement and verifying documentation filed by a creditor that describes the reason the debtor owes the creditor money. (There is an official form for this purpose.)

Property You Own – All legal or equitable interests of the debtor in property as of the commencement of the case. Includes property you have purchased, even if you owe money on it, such as a home with a mortgage or an automobile with a lien.

Reaffirmation Agreement – An agreement by a Chapter 7 debtor to continue paying a dischargeable debt (such as an auto loan) after the bankruptcy, usually for the purpose of keeping collateral (*i.e.,* the car) that would otherwise be subject to repossession. For a reaffirmation agreement to be effective, there are many procedural and legal requirements that must be satisfied during the bankruptcy case.

Schedules – Detailed lists filed by the debtor along with (or shortly after filing) the petition showing the debtor's assets, liabilities, and other financial information. (There are official forms a debtor must use.)

Secured Creditor or Claim – A creditor holding a claim against the debtor who has the right to take and hold or sell certain property of the debtor in satisfaction of some or all of the claim. Some common examples of creditors who have secured claims are lenders from your car, your home, or your furniture.

Secured Debt – Debt backed by a mortgage, pledge of collateral, or other lien; debt for which the creditor has the right to pursue specific pledged property upon default. Examples include home mortgages, auto loans and tax liens.

Sole Proprietorship – A business you own as an individual that is not a separate legal entity such as a corporation, partnership, or LLC. Sole proprietors must use the bankruptcy forms that are numbered in the 100 series.

Statement of Financial Affairs – A series of questions the debtor must answer in writing concerning sources of income, transfer of property, lawsuits by creditors, etc. (There is an official form a debtor must use.)

Statement of Intention – A declaration made by a Chapter 7 concerning plans for dealing with consumer debts that are secured by property of the estate.

Substantive Consolidation – Putting the assets and liabilities of two or more related debtors into a single pool to pay creditors. (Courts are reluctant to allow substantive consolidation since the action must not only justify the benefit that one set of creditors receives, but also the harm that other creditors suffer as a result.)

Transfer – Any mode or means by which a debtor disposes of or parts with his/her property.

Trustee – The representative of the bankruptcy estate who exercises statutory powers, principally for the benefit of the unsecured creditors, under the general supervision of the court and the direct supervision of the U.S. trustee or bankruptcy administrator. The trustee is a private individual or corporation appointed in all Chapter 7, Chapter 12, and Chapter 13 cases and some chapter 11 cases. The trustee's responsibilities include reviewing the debtor's petition and schedules and bringing actions against creditors or the debtor to recover property of the bankruptcy estate. In Chapter 7, the trustee liquidates property of the estate, and makes distributions to creditors. Trustees in Chapter 12 and 13 have similar duties to a Chapter 7 trustee and the additional responsibilities of overseeing the debtor's plan, receiving payments from debtors, and disbursing plan payments to creditors.

Undersecured Claim – A debt secured by property that is worth less than the full amount of the debt.

Unexpired Lease – A lease that is in effect at the time you filed for bankruptcy.

Unliquidated Claim – A claim for which a specific value has not been determined. For instance, if you were involved in a car accident, the victim may have an unliquidated claim against you because the amount of damages has not yet been determined.

Unscheduled Debt – A debt that should have been listed by the debtor in the schedules filed with the court but was not. (Depending on the circumstances, an unscheduled debt mayor may not be discharged.)

Unsecured Claim – A claim or debt for which a creditor holds no special assurance of payment, such as a mortgage or lien; a debt for which credit was extended based solely upon the creditor's assessment of the debtor's future ability to pay.

You – A debtor filing alone or one person in married couple who is filing a bankruptcy case with a spouse.

ACKNOWLEDGEMENTS

First, I want to thank God, for always being with me every day, loving me unconditionally, mentoring, guiding and helping me each step of the way!

Many say that you do not know who your friends are until you are at your worst, and I had to learn the hard way – and learn I did. The people I mention below are those who were there for my family and me during one of the most difficult and trying times of my life. These are both old and new friends who went out of their way to help us emotionally, socially, and financially, never asking for anything in return. They are true friends indeed.

For my writing projects I received indispensable help from Thomas J, who volunteered his time and never asked for anything in return. He helped clarify my thoughts, translated my scribble, and edited my poor grammar and punctuation. He has also been a very dear friend and mentor in my life. Thank you for the encouragement, for believing in me, and for your constant inspiration throughout this particular project.

Thank you Greg S, for your unrelenting help and assistance in gathering all the research and necessary forms required to make this happen. You have been a blessing in my life in too many ways to list here, especially taking time out of your life to help with many varied tasks. You showed kindness, love, and compassion, as Jesus does. I look forward to sharing many more years of friendship with you.

Thank you, Tom M, for our continued friendship, for believing in me and showing me how people deserve a second chance. You and your family's love have been unconditional: from your helping my children receive gifts, to your invaluable gift of continued friendship. All that you have done is more than I could ever repay you.

Thank you Mitch F, for all the many errands you helped me with. Your upbeat, loving, and humorous letters have helped me travel this journey with a smile, knowing that you truly continue to love me as a human being.

Thank you, Pat G, for your continued friendship and support. You were willing to do what many would not at my pretrial hearing. You looked past my wrong behavior and saw a friend who was hurting and in need. I will always appreciate your compassion and your willingness to help.

Thank you, Larry H, for your continued friendship and support. For believing in me, that I would get through this and come out a better person than I was when I arrived. Your visits were a welcomed surprise, and you have no idea the comfort they provided to help me carry on. Thank you for your letters and those of support on my behalf.

Thank you, Jennifer, for your friendship and unrelenting love. Your continued encouragement and your belief in me have helped make the days and years shorter.

Thank you little brother for your lifelong love. You have always been there to help me however needed. You have never stopped believing in me. No matter how many mistakes I have made in the past, you continue to see past them all. I could not ask for a more loving brother.

Thank you, mom. Where do I start? There is not enough room here to give you the credit due. Your love has been that of a mother, truly unconditional. No matter how hurt your heart was by my past actions your love never faltered. You have been a constant support, helping me in too many ways to count, especially for the sacrifices you made in bringing my sons to visit me as well as all the financial support you provided. Thank you for believing in me, and I pray that all the changes I have made in my life will help you to fully heal in time.

To my former wife and the mother of my children: You gave me two of the greatest gifts a man could ever ask for – our sons. As a result of my past actions you endured pain a woman should never have to endure. And after all that you continued to support my relationship with our children. You have experienced the collateral consequences of our criminal justice system, and I regret every day that I was the cause of your having to live through it. I am in your debt forever. In addition, I would like to thank my son's step-father for providing a safe and secure home for our children.

To my children: You have been two of my best friends, a rock to support me throughout this very difficult time. You both are precious souls whose love has never wavered. I cannot be more proud of the young men you have become – honorable, strong, and courageous. You both truly are my inspiration for living. You both have suffered dearly as a result of my past decisions, but you are my greatest source of strength and motivation to do things better moving forward. Your love and support have inspired me to endure through my self-transformation.

There are many more loved ones to mention and thank. You know who you are, and I look forward to our continued communion as family and friends. Know that I am grateful to each and every one of you for the innumerable ways you have supported me throughout my incarceration.

And last but not least, I want to thank my friends at Freebird Publishers for accepting and supporting my work and their efforts in helping me to become a productive member of society again.

Sincerely,

William John Patterson

William John. Patterson

ABOUT THE AUTHOR

William J. Patterson is a lifetime resident of Tennessee. He enjoys the great outdoors and exploring new adventures with his sons, family members and friends. As evident in his recent publication of his book, Chapter 7 Bankruptcy: Seven Steps to Financial Freedom, Mr. Patterson dedicates his energy to new business ventures focused on providing goods and services for the benefit of others. Besides exploring his newest book idea, he's invested with several advocacy groups that assist inmates and families in their efforts toward a successful return to society.

Rate Us & Win!

We do monthly drawings for a FREE copy of one of our publications. Just have your loved one rate us on Amazon and then send us a quick e-mail with your name, inmate number, and institution address and you could win a FREE book.*

FREEBIRD PUBLISHERS
Box 541
North Dighton, MA 02764

www.freebirdpublishers.com
Diane@FreebirdPublishers.com

FREEBIRD PUBLISHERS

Thanks for your interest in Freebird Publishers!

We value our customers and would love to hear from you! Reviews are an important part in bringing you quality publications. We love hearing from our readers-rather it's good or bad (though we strive for the best)!

If you could take the time to review/rate any publication you've purchased with Freebird Publishers we would appreciate it!

If your loved one uses Amazon, have them post your review on the books you've read. This will help us tremendously, in providing future publications that are even more useful to our readers and growing our business.

Amazon works off of a 5 star rating system. When having your loved one rate us be sure to give them your chosen star number as well as a written review. Though written reviews aren't required, we truly appreciate hearing from you.

Sample Review Received on Inmate Shopper

★★★★★ **Everything a prisoner needs is available in this book.**
June 7, 2018
Format: Paperback

A necessary reference book for anyone in prison today. This book has everything an inmate needs to keep in touch with the outside world on their own from inside their prison cell. Inmate Shopper's business directory provides complete contact information on hundreds of resources for inmate services and rates the companies listed too! The book has even more to offer, contains numerous sections that have everything from educational, criminal justice, reentry, LGBT, entertainment, sports schedules and more. The best thing is each issue has all new content and updates to keep the inmate informed on todays changes. We recommend everybody that knows anyone in prison to send them a copy, they will thank you.

* No purchase neccessary. Reviews are not required for drawing entry. Void where prohibited. Contest date runs July 1 - December 31, 2018.

3 Book Series

NEW BOOKS PUBLISHED EVERY MONTH
SPECIALIZING IN PRISONER PUBLICATIONS
WWW.FREEBIRDPUBLISHERS.COM
FULL COLOR 52-PG CATALOG SEND $2 OR 6 STAMPS
BOX 541, N. DIGHTON, MA 02764
TEXT/PHONE 774-406-8682

PRISON LIVING MAGAZINE

FREE STUFF 4 YOU

Americas Only Up To Date MAGAZINE With Over 125 Contacts For Free Stuff 4 Inmates

Money is hard to come by in prison, let these Organizations and Businesses send you what you need for FREE!
This resource of FREE stuff pays for itself the very first time you use it. View it for FREE on our website. *Prisonlivingmagazine.com*

SAVE HUNDREDS OF DOLLARS RIGHT NOW!!!

SAVE

- FREE * Legal Research and Attorneys
- FREE * Case Law and Law Books
- FREE * Photos of Girls or Men
- FREE * Pen Pals and Pen Pal Websites
- FREE * Books * 26 Addresses
- FREE * Newsletters- Something for all
- FREE * Magazines - Where and how to get them
- FREE * Reentry Assistance - Housing and More
- FREE * Scholarships for your child
- FREE * Education, GED, College, Seminary
- FREE * Audio Books
- FREE * Christian Musics CD's
- FREE * Motivational Lectures
- FREE * Spiritual Talks
- FREE * Cell Phone for re-entry. (not while incarcerated)

FREE CATALOGS

Print Edition $14.98

ORDER TODAY—YOUR ORDER SHIPS WITHIN 24 HOURS OF BEING RECEIVED.

YOUR ORDER SHIPS THE NEXT DAY!!!!!!!!

Prison Living
Special Edition Magazine
2019 FREE STUFF FOR INMATES

Our new Magazine is a well researched, up to date, serious, professional publication for prisoners who are serious about improving their lives and saving money while in prison. This is absolutely the best $15.00 investment you'll find anywhere.

NO ORDER FORM NEEDED

Write clearly on paper, your complete name and mailing information and what you are ordering. Include payment $14.98 each payable to Girls and Mags.

GIRLS AND MAGS

BOX 319

REHOBOTH, MA 02769

Please allow 4 weeks for delivery before writing in about your order.

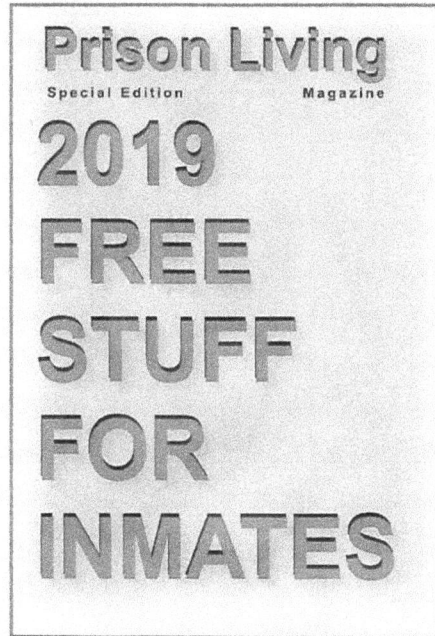

www.ingramcontent.com/pod-product-compliance
Lightning Source LLC
Chambersburg PA
CBHW080531220326
41599CB00032B/6269

* 9 7 8 0 9 9 8 0 3 6 1 8 2 *